THE WORLD THROUGH A MONOCLE

THE WORLD THROUGH A MONOCLE

The New Yorker at Midcentury

Mary F. Corey

HARVARD UNIVERSITY PRESS   Cambridge, Massachusetts / London, England

Second printing, 1999

Library of Congress Cataloging-in-Publication Data
Corey, Mary F.
  The world through a monocle : The New Yorker at midcentury / Mary
  F. Corey
    p. cm.
  Includes index.
  ISBN 0-674-96193-5 (alk. paper)
  1. New Yorker (New York, N.Y. : 1925)—History. 2. Popular
culture—United States—History—20th century. 3. United States—
Social life and customs—1945–1970. I. Title.
PN4900.N35C67 1999
051—dc21   98-41167
              CIP

FOR GEORGE AND FRANCES COREY, AND FOR MOLLY

CONTENTS

Preface: First Things ix

1 The Lay of the Land 1

2 Beyond the Manhattan Skyline 18

3 Red Hunting and the *New Yorker* Village 40

4 Slouching toward Anti-Communism 58

5 *The New Yorker* in Black and White 77

6 The Romance of the Other 101

7 Managing with Servants 124

8 The War between Men and Women 149

9 Goods and Goodness 181

Conclusion: Fault Lines 205

Notes 215

Acknowledgments 243

Index 247

PREFACE: FIRST THINGS

A very black-skinned African-American maid stands at the sink in the spacious kitchen of a prewar Manhattan apartment, gazing wistfully into space as she rinses a silver platter. Behind her lurks a small golden-haired girl wearing a ghost costume fashioned from a sheet. In one hand the child carries a glowing jack-o-lantern, in the other, a pair of white gloves. Tiny saddle shoes peep from beneath the sheet. The room is shadowy and the maid's eyes, her apron, her shoes, and the child's sheet and skeleton mask seem to glow. Soon the frozen scene will explode, when the child shouts "BOO!" and the housekeeper screams, her eyes widening with terror as the silver tray slips from her hands onto the checkerboard linoleum floor.

This Halloween tableau, suspended somewhere between domestic comedy and minstrel farce, is the cover (by Edna Eicke) of the October 28, 1950, *New Yorker* magazine. To step into the corner of the postwar world in which the black maid and her ghostly charge are easily recognizable players in a familiar household scenario is to enter a very particular time and place in midcentury American culture. Like a diorama in a natural history museum, this *New Yorker* cover is a perfect showcase in which the hallmarks of the period have been miniaturized and frozen in time.

Although *The New Yorker* has appeared without interruption from its first issue in 1925 to the present, the late forties and the fifties were certainly its greatest period of cultural potency. In the years following World War Two, the magazine was widely read and widely talked about and came to have serious social cachet. Writing of its postwar preeminence in *The Saturday Review of Literature* of January 30, 1954, Joseph Wood Krutch said that *The New Yorker* had "come to dominate a large group of devoted readers who took their every cue from its pages." These loyalists, he explained, recognized "one another as 'my kind' by exchanging recollections of this cartoon or that paragraph." "In fact," Krutch lamented, "certain groups have come to communicate almost exclusively in references to the sacred writings."

In the postwar years, *The New Yorker* meant something to its readers. It offered them both a mirror and a map, instructing them and confirming for them things they already suspected about their world. In particular, the magazine unapologetically offered readers a mix of overlapping, contrasting, even contradictory reflections of a world in flux. For a brief span of time, *The New Yorker,* its readers, and the historical moment joined in a harmony that resonated in the worlds of journalism, culture, and consumption.

By 1946 the magazine claimed close to a quarter of a million subscribers (second in the glossy weekly market only to *Time* and *Newsweek*) and enjoyed skyrocketing advertising revenues. Among its contributors were important writers such as Dwight Macdonald, James Agee, Clement Greenberg, John Cheever, Lillian Ross, E. B. White, John O'Hara, Edmund Wilson, A. J. Liebling, John Hersey, Janet Flanner, Andy Logan, Rachel Carson, Hannah Arendt, Mary McCarthy, Alfred Kazin, Irwin Shaw, J. D. Salinger, St. Clair McKelway, and Lewis Mumford.

At least a portion of *The New Yorker*'s postwar power was derived from its association with Manhattan, which had become the most powerful urban center in the world. Moreover, an infusion of writers, artists, and scholars who had fled the rise of fascism in their homelands gave Manhattan a boost toward assuming the cultural leadership of the world.

How did *The New Yorker* reflect the central preoccupations of this global hub? What version of reality did it transmit to its readers, more of whom lived outside of Manhattan than within it? What kind of world lay inside the magazine with the portrait of the small trick-or-treater and the black domestic on its cover?

An examination of any single issue of the magazine reveals the way the postwar *New Yorker* served its readers by acknowledging both the ideal of a triumphant America united in affluent consensus, and the troubling dilemmas of a less-than-perfect democracy. The Halloween issue I have singled out, for example, offered a distinctive mixture of elements which appealed alternately to reader's aspiration to know about things and a desire to possess them. Here advertisements for elite consumer goods, a psychiatric cartoon, tips on serving "unpretentious white wines," an interview with Somerset Maugham, and a humorous "Talk of the Town" item about domestic help mingle amiably with the magazine's more substantial fare, which is clustered on its back pages: A. J. Liebling on the "military experts" who are reporting on the Korean War, Joseph Wechsberg's "Letter From Vienna," and a review by Edmund Wilson of a book by Gilbert Seldes. The issue's last two pages are a virtual collage of the magazine's fixations: nestled between columns of advertisements for products as diverse as a Parisian "umbrella pin," Dash dog food, and the Broadmoor Hotel, are thumbnail reviews of a biography (*The Young Shelley*) and a book about the Lascaux Cave paintings. On the facing page is a two-column advertisement for the Foster Parents Plan for War Children, Inc., featuring a blurry black-and-white photograph of a small hunched girl in rags. The caption reads: "and our bones ache."

By combining these disparate elements, the magazine was able to transmit a version of the real world that incorporated some of that world's more troubling features. Advertisements for cigarettes or whiskey or luxury liners were not seen as inimical to serious articles concerning African-American heroin addicts, unwed mothers, or the bombing of the Bikini Atoll. This curious juxtaposition helps to place the magazine in the broader context of postwar liberalism, which, in this period, consisted of two principal strains: an absolute faith in the necessity of continued economic growth and, as Walter Lippmann put it in *The National Purpose,* an ongoing obligation to use this growth "wisely and prudently for public and immaterial ends." A corollary of this commitment to use affluence to benefit the whole society was the optimistic notion that social evils could be eliminated by the steady advance of reason and goodwill.

The New Yorker served its postwar audience alternately as a shopping guide, an atlas, and a Bible. What I have tried to reclaim are the precepts of its gospel, the substance of its chapter and verse. Over time the magazine developed a social contract with its loyal readers. For their part, readers would imbibe all or some of the magazine's contents on a fairly consistent basis. They might clip a cartoon, purchase a product advertised in its pages, put the magazine in their professional waiting rooms, share it with neighbors, or discuss its contents with students and peers. In exchange for this loyalty, the magazine promised to furnish them with a locale in which they could satisfy two sets of feelings, often in conflict with each other: the desire for comfort and the consciousness of national and global ills. In this peaceable *New Yorker* kingdom the lion of elite consumption could lie down beside the lamb of geopolitical awareness. This was a social setting in which the maintenance of household help, the trifling discontents of suburban life, the problem of social injustice, the uses of psychiatry, blue Persian-lamb car-coats, a knowledge of international affairs, Tiffany pearls, a concern about war orphans, and the proper wine to serve with scrod were consonant commonplaces of adult civilized life. Because *The New Yorker* was so effective in presenting its version of the world to its audience as *the world,* and because its version of reality was incorporated into the common moral grammar of postwar haut-bourgeois culture, the highly stylized nature of this presentation was often obscured.

I grew up in a facsimile of the culture represented in *The New Yorker.* My parents' presence in my early childhood was largely eclipsed by an African-American housekeeper whom I called (without prompting) my "black mommy." In what is perhaps my most vivid memory of childhood, I recall returning from school one day to find both of my parents seated miserably at the table in our kitchen. The fact that they were at home in the midafternoon baffled me. Usually, my mother worked long hours as a retail executive, and my father toiled away as a screen writer at Columbia Pictures. (My father, I learned later, had been fired that day because he had been blacklisted, and my mother had rushed home from her office to console him.) I remember that I was happy to find them at home because I had learned a new, puzzling word at school. "What's a nigger?" I wanted to know. Their gloom only seemed to deepen, and, without exchanging a word, my doting and permissive parents sprinkled Ivory Flakes on a toothbrush and washed out my mouth with soap, while Katherine Childers, "my black mommy," stood in the shadows watching the scene in troubled silence.

I have been the little girl in the Halloween costume waiting in the kitchen doorway to surprise the black woman who was the sovereign of my days. I have been sent to fervent summer camps in Vermont where the children of the rich and near-rich sang "You can get good milk from a brown cow." I had Capezio shoes, a progressive education, a pearl necklace, and a midget clown entertainer at my birthday parties. My own curiosity about the small but potent piece of postwar America embodied in *The New Yorker* comes very simply from the fact that I am of it and have, for much of my life, been blind to it, because it is my own.

As John Updike has explained (in *The Complete Book of Covers from The New Yorker, 1925–1989*), in the years following World War II the territory staked out on these covers had "a geography of its own." This peculiar locale was "Gotham, its cozy brownstone rows and vaporous gray towers . . . its galaxy of night lights and infinitude of furnished apartments." By the 1960s that visionary Gotham had lost its transparency and its universality, a loss that is strikingly elucidated when one examines the magazine's 1960s covers, which reveal the impossibility of assuming either a shared geography or a shared sense of who might inhabit such a place. In the 1960s and the 1970s, people had disappeared almost entirely from the magazine's covers, which can be studied in vain for any reflection of the social history of the period.

For a time after World War II, however, there was a recognizable *New Yorker* reader, habitat, and geography of the mind. What I hope to do here is to capture this evanescent moment of history, this peculiar fragment of postwar American social life, for which *The New Yorker* was a road map.

THE WORLD THROUGH A MONOCLE

THE LAY OF THE LAND

Eustace Tilley, *The New Yorker*'s dandified mascot who has appeared on each anniversary issue since 1925, became a woman on the cover of the magazine's 1996 anniversary issue. This provoked much spirited debate: applause from those who felt the acknowledgment of female readership was long overdue, and nervous hand-wringing from those *New Yorker* subscribers who regard any alterations in the magazine's format as proof of moral and cultural decline. The fact that this minor piece of gender-bending elicited so much comment—the effete Tilley had always teetered at the cusp of masculinity anyway—suggests both *The New Yorker*'s cultural sway and the intimacy of the relationship between the magazine and its readers. The degree to which readers identify with *The New Yorker* world view and share its assumptions is arguably without precedent in the American magazine market. This identification was particularly marked in the years immediately following World War Two.

The strong connection between *The New Yorker* and its readers during that period had its roots in the exceptional increase in the number of educated, middle-class liberals in the postwar years. For this distinctive cohort of Americans, newly empowered by unprecedented affluence, *The New Yorker* possessed an almost magical authority. The magazine lay claim to being the voice of an intellectual community—a kind of *New Yorker* village—in which readers' most compelling urges—to know about and possess elite goods and services and to be citizens of a truly progressive society—could coexist peacefully. For many readers, the magazine's appeal was that it furnished them with an apparently seamless version of the world of consumption and social engagement they wished to inhabit. The particulars of the magazine's evolution into so apt a mirror of the yearnings of its readership can be found in its origins, in the character of its founder and first editor, and ultimately in the history of the postwar period itself.

Harold Ross, who created *The New Yorker* in 1925 and remained its editor-in-chief until his death in 1951, was born in Aspen, Colorado, before the turn of the century. The son of a silver miner and a prim schoolmistress, Ross was often depicted during his lifetime as a raw-boned nineteenth-century throwback—the sort of rural rube whose idea of a great time was "to sit in a hotel dining room and toss spitballs and lit matches at the other guests." William Shawn, who became the magazine's editor after Ross's death in 1951, said that his predecessor had purposely "presented himself to the world as a . . . primitive, somewhat comic figure." In photographs, the former tramp reporter—known in his youth as Hobo Ross—posed as the quintessential nineteenth-century galoot. In spite of his yellow high-button shoes, his stiff hair that stood straight on end (a coiffure that he claimed was the result of a frightening childhood stagecoach accident), and his oafish manner, Ross created a distinctly modern magazine that altered the style and content of contemporary American fiction, perfected a new form of literary journalism, established new standards for humor and comic art, and shaped numerous social and cultural agendas.[1]

The two decades surrounding the turn of the century were a glorious time for American magazines. Because of the rise of national markets (and thus potential ad revenues), highly favorable postage rates, and advances in printing and papermaking techniques, there were, by 1885, over three thousand magazines being published in the United States. The older general-interest quality periodicals, such as *The Nation, Harper's,* and *Atlantic Monthly,* which have endured in much their original format to this day, were linked to genteel New England literary elites and were financed by subscriptions rather than advertising. The editors of such journals saw themselves as professional choosers, performing a service for their social peers by providing them with a select array of literary wares. The essential credential of these professional selectors was their good "taste," which was assumed to correspond, at least roughly, with that of their audience. While these editors often saw themselves as the custodians of the old public intellectual culture and felt that it was their job to raise the standards of their readers, they also assumed a certain collegiality with their genteel audience.

This period also saw the ascension of the behemoth "cheap" magazines such as *Collier's, Saturday Evening Post,* the *Ladies Home Journal* and *Munsey's.* These magazines were not aimed at the "gentle reader" of Gilded Age periodicals but rather at a more provincial audience—those whom H. L. Mencken described as the sort who "stashed their magazines behind the egg stove along with the Sears-Roebuck catalogue and advertisements for horse liniment."[2]

In these new mass-market magazines, financed by advertising rather than subscription, muckrakers, financial advisers, personality development experts, and home economists addressed their audience in a peppy, hortatory style that was a far cry from the collegial way nineteenth-century editors addressed their readers. While earlier gentlemen editors had made literary choices for readers who shared their tastes, the new magazines engaged in a kind of anticipatory production which was market-driven. Twentieth-century editors depended on readers' responses to assess content and plan future issues. Advertisers shaped their campaigns in accordance with customer response. Publishers of magazines found a way to minimize the risk entailed in such ventures by rendering the whole enterprise more predictable at both ends. There was a certain irony in this: while contributors to these periodicals patronized readers, advising them in the voice of lofty expertise, editors frankly yoked their magazines to the market and waited for the reader/driver to crack the whip.

During most of the nineteenth century, advertising, which consisted largely of closely printed lines of virtually unreadable type, was thought to be an entirely local function. As markets became national, advertising came of age and began to incorporate pictures, jingles, and catch phrases. The line between advertising and editorial content grew increasingly obscure. In the popular general-interest magazines, advertising *became* content. These magazines became topical versions of Sears and Roebuck "Wish Books," concomitantly marketing a catalogue of information, advice, and goods to a national audience. Edward Bok, the innovative founder of the *Saturday Evening Post,* perhaps the archetype of these magazines (and the magazine Ross's mother wished he had worked for), introduced the now pandemic practice of "tailing" or "adstripping," in which featured stories continued in the back pages in narrow streams which ran through double columns of advertising. This maneuver drew readers' attention to the promotions of advertisers who could not afford the premiums charged for ads in the front pages.[3]

Although the new "cheap" magazines were produced by huge metropolitan corporations and were a part of the larger urbanization and commercialization of American culture that took place between 1880 and World War One, they displayed a peculiar allegiance to an earlier agrarian ideal. They neither exalted metropolitan life, nor were they "modern." Crammed with dress patterns for home sewing machines and success stories saturated with Jeffersonian idealism, magazines like the *Saturday Evening Post* and *Collier's* consciously replicated the ambiance of small-town America and promulgated the "traditional home-spun values, of pluck and luck."[4]

The affluence that came in the wake of World War I gave rise to a huge, new, geographically and economically mobile segment of urban population with roots in provincial America. As these "new people" deserted the small island communities of their births and moved to the city, they effectively stepped out of their own histories. This repudiation of the past created a biographical vacuum. Identity was up for grabs. Cut loose from the traditional ties of family and place, separated from farms and shops and face-to-face communications of small-town America, these men and women acquired distinction by the company they kept and the commodities they accumulated. The appeal of the world of goods for those who had voluntarily extricated themselves from the familiar chains of personal history was its capacity to confer identity. Commodities became ways of telegraphing who one was, offering familiar landmarks through which people could situate themselves in a very uncertain world.[5]

The New Yorker, which first appeared in 1925, rode the wave of these transformations in America at large and in the magazine market in particular. The magazine was at once a late-blooming counterpart of the genteel journals of the Gilded Age and an upscale version of the twentieth-century "cheap" magazine. But while it borrowed elements from its predecessors, it was aimed directly at urbanites, many of whom were novice metropolitans who yearned for a map to guide them along the mysterious byways of city life. *The New Yorker,* built over a fault line between the realm of genteel intellectual curiosity and the glittering world of consumer goods, spoke directly to this new class of cosmopolitans.

The idea of fusing the companionate tone of a journal addressed to a gentle reader with the kind of advertising-driven magazine that dominated the periodical market after World War One, was not a slick scheme for selling expensive goods but was rather the product of contradictory decisions, history, and happenstance. While part of *The New Yorker*'s allure was that it claimed to be pitched at what Ross called "the snob appeal market," this assertion was more of a mannerism than a reality. Although Ross had, on a number of occasions, hired staff members on the basis of their connections to upper-class New York society, neither he nor any of the editors responsible for substantively shaping the magazine had genuine links to this world. *The New Yorker,* theoretically aimed at an elite, was produced by a community of editors and writers, many of whom came to New York from middle-class families in provincial America. As George Douglas has explained in his history of *The Smart Magazines, The New Yorker* was created to reach a sizeable audience. It could not, therefore, really build its readership exclusively from the social elite because "there were simply not enough rich people to make a magazine profitable." Thus Ross had to make his pitch to middle-class readers with upper-class aspirations, or to those who "believed themselves witty and clever (a group that is never in short supply)."[6]

The convergence of diverse elements—a new class of avid cosmopolitan readers, new techniques in advertising, and the ascendance of Manhattan as the first modern American city—produced a brilliant hybrid, a nineteenth-century magazine tethered to the particulars of an urban twentieth-century market. The magazine's curious blend of old and new, which fared so well after World War I, flourished in the period following World War II, becoming an unprecedented success in the history of weekly magazines.

World War II and its aftermath saw a huge increase in the circulations of the important general interest magazines such as *Harper's, Atlantic Monthly, Newsweek,* and *Time.* Between 1939 and 1949, *The New Yorker's* subscription base more than doubled. Much of this growth can be attributed to an expanding circle of intelligent, ambitious, upwardly mobile men and women professionals—"people who manipulated symbols rather than made things, whose stock in trade consisted of their organizational, technical, conceptual or verbal skills." This new urban group of second- and third-generation Americans (particularly from Jewish families) that coalesced in the late forties and fifties displayed a striking number of similarities to the new class that had been emerging nationwide when the magazine was created in the 1920s. Both groups were intent on escaping the constraints of their birth by recreating themselves. For the post-World War One generation, that often meant migration to the city from small towns in the West, the Midwest, and the South. For the post-World War Two generation, the escape was often from the limitations of social class or ethnicity, and the geographical journey may have been as brief as a trip across the bridge from Brooklyn into midtown Manhattan.

The line between those whose social standing was inherited and those whose influence depended upon their achievements had begun to blur during the Jazz Age and became virtually invisible in the period after World War Two. The inner circles of power such as academia and government were increasingly open to second-generation immigrants and people moving out of lower-middle-class backgrounds. The broader distribution of postwar affluence, combined with the international power of the dollar, gave the members of this new affluent middle class unprecedented economic clout. They could travel in Europe, buy imported goods, and purchase houses in upscale suburbs. What to wear, what to see, and what to read in order to become members in good standing of an aristocracy of mind and manners were certainly burning questions for those moving upward in the kaleidoscope of postwar urban society.

In the postwar years, America's global ascendancy, fast economic growth, and increased social mobility conspired to create a landscape in which optimism seemed to be destiny. Concurrently, many Americans worried about the moral flabbiness engendered by affluence and feared the possibility of nuclear extinction. The ongoing tension between the delights of postwar riches and the grave issues of the times contributed to the postwar *New Yorker*'s enormous cultural power.

For white middle-class Americans the astonishing economic growth that began in the mid-1940s and continued unabated into the 1960s began to seem like a permanent part of the future. The fact that the United States was an island of prosperity in a sea of economic hardship (the rest of the postwar world) bolstered notions of American exceptionalism and offered proof that the once chimerical American dream was now a fait accompli. At the heart of this belief in the fluidity of the social order was the certainty that it was possible through hard work and perseverance to transcend the circumstances of one's birth. The optimism, it seemed, had been warranted. By the late forties many Americans earned more, ate more, played more, lived longer, and owned more things than their parents could have imagined possible.

At the dawn of the atomic age, the American cornucopia was bursting with a vast array of futuristic goods: frozen foods, plastic toys, styrofoam coolers, vinyl flooring, automatic transmissions, garbage disposals, long-playing records, Polaroid cameras, and, of course, television. Not only were such fantastic goods available, but consumers purchased them with record-breaking enthusiasm. Between 1939 and 1948 clothing sales tripled, furniture and jewelry sales quadrupled, and liquor and household appliance sales increased five-fold. In 1949 alone over 5 million Americans bought new cars. Everyday life was suddenly filled with an array of merchandise that resembled the dreamy products of science fiction.[7]

In the midst of this harvest of plenty, Americans were pursuing domestic happiness in record numbers. The Depression and the war had delayed or destroyed many families' hopes of domestic tranquility. When the war ended, entrepreneurs grew rich marketing the single-family suburban home as the material fulfillment of the democratic ideal. In 1944 construction began on 114,000 single family suburban homes. Close to two million such homes were built in 1950 alone. In 1946 over two million Americans married, and divorce rates declined. The birth rate skyrocketed, especially among educated upper-middle-class white women. Nearly four million babies were born each year between 1947 and 1952, and more than four million each year thereafter, until the birth rate began its decline in 1964. While affluence encouraged the baby boom, the baby boom in turn generated more prosperity. Sales of Hopalong Cassidy costumes, toy atomic missiles, diapers, washer/dryers, maternity fashions, and new homes soared, followed by an explosion in secondary school construction. Many Americans, it seemed, regarded a safe and satisfying family life as a kind of miracle vaccine which offered them immunity from the contagions of war, Depression, Communism, human misery itself.[8]

Although large numbers of Americans hailed the bounties of postwar life, many journalists, novelists, and cultural critics expressed a sense that something had gone wrong. Sidestepping more serious dilemmas facing American society, these dissenters from the cheery orthodoxy of postwar consensus fastened upon the tackiness of consumer goods and suburban life as a sign of what was wrong with America. Terms like "slurb" and "sloburb" and books with titles like *The Split Level Trap* and *The Suburban Sadness* indicted the shoddy values and lackluster social organization of the new bedroom communities. These critiques of the suburbs as sterile and shapeless had the effect of reanimating the idea of the city as a mecca of art and intellect, a reversal that helped to increase *The New Yorker*'s cultural authority. For at the same time that New York had grown exponentially in cultural power, many of its middle- and upper-middle-class denizens were fleeing to the suburbs. Postwar housing developments, however, remained largely dependent upon urban centers for most of their commercial and cultural life. For educated middle- and upper-middle-class exurbanites, particularly former New Yorkers, the city they had abandoned held them in thrall. It became a memory and an aspiration—a bustling sanctuary of art, commerce, and cosmopolitanism. Although many people slept, ate, gardened, and sent their children to school in small semi-rural communities, the city governed much of their political, cultural, and economic life.[9]

Manhattan dominated far more than the cultural lives of its former inhabitants. European political, economic, and cultural hegemony had been shattered by the war, and many writers, artists, and scholars had fled the rise of fascism in their homelands and immigrated to New York City. By the war's end the burden of international cultural leadership had shifted to rest upon Manhattan's powerful shoulders. As the futuristic United Nations building was taking shape along East River Drive, it seemed that every eye on the planet faced toward New York City, which now sat at the hub of world politics, economics, and culture.[10]

This *idea* of Manhattan as the center of the universe amongst those who had left it, those who had immigrated to it, and those who aspired to it certainly added urgency to the phenomenal cultural and commercial sway of *The New Yorker* enterprise. According to a 1946 *New Yorker* marketing pamphlet, the magazine's subscribers were apt to be "at least all of the following: Intelligent, well-educated, discriminating, well-informed, unprejudiced, public-spirited, metropolitan-minded, broad-visioned and quietly liberal." While *The New Yorker* was certainly aimed at upscale urban readers who were "quietly liberal," and the marketing department successfully convinced advertising agencies that the magazine was "the national weekly of the leadership market" read by affluent urban consumers of elite goods, the actual social and economic profile of its readership was far more ambiguous and reflected the rapidly changing profile of what it meant to be middle-class in postwar America.[11]

The New Yorker generated a number of marketing surveys in this period, to try to understand what it called "The Character of Readers." Using an elaborate system administered by a national credit bureau, which combined mailed questionnaires, personal interviews, and indirect information provided by credit agencies, these surveys tell us a great deal about some specifics, such as how many readers ate at Schrafft's or Luchow's when they visited New York, but reveal little or nothing about other aspects. Race, for example, was never mentioned in any of these reader polls, although it is safe to say that the readership was so overwhelmingly white that this category would have been superfluous. These studies also impart very little information about the extent to which the magazine's contents were embraced—that is, how much of it was actually read, and of that, how much was absorbed into readers' lives. Likewise, this data tells us nothing of newsstand sales, or of those readers, perhaps more mobile, more bohemian, or more broke, who bought the magazine when they could or when it contained something that particularly interested them. Still, the results of these marketing reports offer us a shadowy profile of the households into which the magazine alit each week.

"It is quite possible," Dwight Macdonald wrote, "that most readers of *The New Yorker,* like most movie-goers, are comparatively humble folk who are willing to pay a small admission fee for a peep into the *haut monde.*" Perhaps, he added, subscribers' "center of gravity" was actually closer "to Lexington Avenue than to Park Avenue. In this country of all countries, the class war is complicated by the persistence of the old American custom of keeping up with the Joneses." Macdonald may well have been right, for what the magazine's marketing data suggests is that while many readers were affluent Manhattanites, there were also many who were neither wealthy nor metropolitan. These subscribers were often housewives isolated in bedroom communities, clerical or technical workers living in small towns, or foreign corporate offices. For these readers *The New Yorker* often came to represent a city of memory or imagination, a connection to an intellectual community that appeared reliably in their mailboxes week after week.[12]

In 1949 the age of the average *New Yorker* subscriber was somewhere between 35 and 44. Most were married, most had attended college, and over half had attended college for four years or more. Among the magazine's female subscribers, 73% had gone to college for at least a year, although only about half of them had finished or gone on to graduate school. Well over half of all the subscribers owned their own houses or apartments, 90% of which were valued somewhere between $10,000 and $75,000, hefty sums in the postwar economy. Three quarters of the magazine's subscribers had an annual family income of over $5,000 a year, at a time when the national average family income hovered around $1,900. Nearly half of subscribers were employed in "business and industry" (which included publishing and communications). Twenty-one percent were owners, partners, managers, or major executives (sales managers, advertising managers, department heads, etc.); 5% were employed in some kind of technical capacity. In 1949, 26% of all subscribers—the largest single occupational category—were listed as "housewives," and by 1959 more than 50% of regular readers came under this category. Nine percent of subscribers were educators (college presidents, teachers, librarians and headmasters); 3% were students; 5%

were retired and living on "private income"; and 2% were unemployed. Fewer clergymen subscribed than farmers, and close to 6% of those polled described themselves as clerical workers and secretaries. So while many subscribers did indeed inhabit the upper echelons of business and professional life, 13% of those who subscribed had not attended college at all, and 25% of subscribers had family incomes of less than $5,000 per year.[13]

The geography of the postwar *New Yorker* audience is also revealing. In 1925, when the magazine was founded, virtually all of its readers lived in New York City. The readership quickly grew more geographically diverse. By 1929 over half of subscribers lived outside New York State. By the end of the forties, 10% of the magazine's readers resided in foreign countries, 13% lived on the West Coast, 11% in the South, and 15% in Ohio, Wisconsin, Illinois, Michigan, and Indiana. Twenty percent lived in small communities with populations of less than ten thousand.[14]

Subscribers were extremely loyal to the magazine. Close to 70% had subscribed for over ten years. These loyal readers were people who were likely to hold passports, drink alcohol, own binoculars, enjoy gardening, smoke cigarettes, and, if they lived outside of Manhattan, visit the city. Between 1954 and 1959, 78% of *New Yorker* readers who did not live in New York City made cultural pilgrimages there, to visit the Museum of Modern Art, go to the theater, attend the opera or a concert.[15]

Reader surveys certainly suggest that the postwar *New Yorker* counted more "humble folk" amongst its readers than it ever had before. Some of these new readers had first been introduced to the magazine by the "pony" edition which was sent to the troops during the war. Another important contributor to the magazine's widening appeal was the genuine democratization of higher education which took place as a direct result of the G.I. Bill passed in 1944. Between 1949 and 1950 almost half a million Americans received university degrees, more than twice as many as in 1940. The widening base of higher education had a decisive impact on the postwar reading culture, and specifically affected the character of the typical *New Yorker* reader.[16]

The increased accessibility of a university education brought with it other privileges, opportunities, and anxieties. The doors of government, cultural life, and academia also opened wider, admitting into the corridors of power ambitious immigrants, second- and third-generation Americans (in particular those of Jewish origin), and people shedding the constraints of their upbringing. Many members of this new, more democratic cultural aristocracy were people who had recently climbed the upper echelons of a middle class that now had the means to emulate the very rich. Often the members of this new gentry used taste as a way to express their social superiority over the rest of the middle class from which they had so recently graduated. The criteria for membership into this uneasy elite were discrimination, style, and celebrity, commodities more accessible than high birth or great wealth, but also more insecure. This precariousness of social position produced a new kind of literary consumer for whom reading was a form of currency—a protection against being "outbrowed."[17]

Out of the loose coalition of professors, critics, artists, and journalists who led the cultural elite, a new power base emerged. Intellect and culture were conceded to confer a kind of power. Corporate executives attended seminars in the Great Books, upper-middle-class suburban housewives joined literary societies and perused *The New Yorker*, civic leaders raised public funds to build museums and cultural centers. The Aspen Institute, founded in 1949, perhaps epitomized the new corporate intellectual life. Here, in a consortium that C. Wright Mills once described as "Brains, Inc.," powerful entrepreneurial capitalists joined with intellectuals and leaders of the art world to ponder the responsibility of American experts to provide leadership for the Atlantic community.[18]

It is within this context that the postwar *New Yorker* and its readers constructed their global intellectual village. The act of reading the magazine in Los Altos, California; Evanston, Wyoming; a Park Avenue apartment; or a remote Government District Office in Djakarta was a form of participation in a civilized subculture separated by taste and affinity from the presumed vulgarities of the mass culture which surrounded it.[19]

The New Yorker provided readers with a substitute urban space and a vocabulary with which they could structure their desires. Readers could press their noses up against this journalistic shop window and select whatever they liked from a glittering array of goods and meanings, all of which promised to separate them from the cheesy hordes of mass consumers. In this way the magazine gave its readers the possibility of "imagining the transformation of the self by things, by others, and by places." It is to this phantom marketplace that many members of The New Yorker culture of letters repaired to shop for identity.[20]

Through the magazine readers could place themselves in a remembered or imagined New York City, contemplate the idea of a cosmopolitan future, or simply aspire to the goods pictured in its pages. In a "love letter" to the editors, a woman in Germany proclaimed that the New York of the magazine was "a fairy tale and a funny world at the same time." A secretary in Monroe, Michigan, wrote that the magazine was the only contact she had with the city she had left behind, and that it allowed her to feel that she had never left. A woman in Tucson who had been raised in Kentucky wrote admitting that her sole knowledge of New York City was based on a few visits, but that she received enormous pleasure from The New Yorker "not forgetting the advertisements," because the magazine "brought a touch of Eastern glamour and sophistication" into her "Western way of living."[21]

While the magazine certainly provided some readers with a symbolic city, others saw it as a bastion against the forces of cultural decline. Just as postwar critics decried the "shapelessness" and vacuity of American cultural life, so too did many of the magazine's subscribers—especially those who felt moved to take pen in hand and write to the magazine. These devotees saw The New Yorker as one of the last outposts of civilized society in a wasteland conspicuous for bad politics, bad architecture, and bad taste. They wrote elegiac letters to the magazine's editors to thank them for keeping civilization alive in the midst of chaos.[22]

"I don't know what civilization is," Hugh Gilchrist wrote the editors in the summer of 1954, "but it seems to be tied up with a complex of values which are neither inscrutable myths nor reflections of market quotations. *The New Yorker* comes close to those values." "In these troubled times," a reader wrote from Jackson, Michigan, "regular reading of *The New Yorker* is a valuable prophylaxis." The magazine was, in the words of one reader, "an expression of . . . 'man's humanity to man.'"

The power of *The New Yorker* to corroborate and to comfort was frequently invoked by those readers who were moved to communicate with its editors. Some felt a profound kinship with the magazine because it spoke for them, giving a public voice to their own private intelligences. It says "what I think and feel," a Washington D.C. woman wrote, "as I should like to have said it." "We're mature enough," a newspaper publisher wrote, "to recognize good sense when we see it in *The New Yorker*. It *has* to be good sense, because we agree with everything you say." In 1951 a woman wrote that for her the magazine had come to represent "intelligence, liberalism, sanity, tolerance and humaneness . . . After I have read my copy the world's confusion does not seem so unmanageable and hopeless . . . and I feel comforted." Many letter writers claimed that the magazine assuaged their fears about America. In spite of McCarthyism, our "terrifying policy in Asia," and the ascendance of "crooners . . . embalmers and promotion experts," *The New Yorker* reminded one reader from Australia that America was "after all the land of the Declaration of Independence, of Jefferson, Lincoln, the Gettysburg Address and of Marshall Aid."[23]

The authors of these letters were a diverse lot: a bird curator at a museum, a United Nations official, the editor of *The William and Mary Quarterly*, doctors, enlisted men, a British war bride, a feedstore employee, a member of the French legation in Beirut, President Truman's Press Secretary, and a former "chorus boy" become a "spieler" on a Miami Circle Line boat.[24]

At its most vigorous, subscriber devotion inspired concrete action. A reader in Wyoming wrote that the magazine arrived each week and was "as efficiently used up around here as the packing plants' claim for their pork. The covers go in an art scrap book, cartoons & quips clipped

& sent to a brother in Korea & the fiction & book reviews are passeled out among less fortunate acquaintances who have earned my good will." A Presbyterian minister in Michigan wrote that he kept a file of the magazine's cartoons "about clergymen, which to me is as good a source as the bible in maintaining perspective and humility in such a vocation."[25]

In what was perhaps the supreme expression of readers' sense of *The New Yorker* as a participatory endeavor, many subscribers submitted their own poems, short stories, "Newsbreak" items, and suggestions for "Talk of the Town" pieces. A professor of classics at the University of North Carolina suggested a "Profile"; a fellow in Norwalk, Ohio, submitted a poem about how to make a martini; an N.B.C. executive sent a short story; and an interior decorator submitted a cover idea.[26]

By the beginning of the 1950s readers of *The New Yorker* felt they were members of an intellectual community and used the magazine variously as a guide to tasteful consumption, a surrogate city, or an oasis of civilization. They could rely upon the magazine to give them the right information about night spots and polo teams, English movies and Italian Communism, French wine and Scotch whiskey, the Nuremberg trials, the bombing of the Bikini Atoll, nuclear reactors, dude ranches, *prêt-à-porter*, Tito's Party Congress, and Caribbean vacations. As *New Yorker* readers attempted to traverse the disorienting terrain of the postwar world, the magazine provided them with a road map in which the lakes were still green, the seas, blue, the highways marked in the usual fashion. Getting lost was still a distinct possibility, but at least it was not entirely uncharted territory. There was, after all, a map.

By following the guidelines encoded in the postwar *New Yorker*, it is possible to reconstruct *something* about the world of those who made it and those who believed in it. But it is risky to try to fabricate a sense of the values and attitudes of a potent historical subculture from cartoons, short stories, editorials and advertisements. The relationship between the magazine's readers and its text poses too many variables. If the postwar *New Yorker* is a mirror of its readership, it may, in fact, be a distorted fun-house mirror—a *Zerrspiegel*—its surfaces peculiarly designed to enhance certain images, distort others, and erase still others. It is not possible to determine whether the magazine was a reflection of subscribers' real circumstances or of their fantasies, or whether it was more of a mirror of the preoccupations of its editors and advertisers. The enormous success of the magazine in this period, however, offers compelling evidence that whether it was playing to readers' ambitions, illusions, or their material realities, it communicated something that its audience found profoundly satisfying.[27]

Because of its nonpartisanship, its lack of a monolithic editorial policy, and its peculiar mix of cartoons, fiction, advertising, serious journalism, and cultural criticism *The New Yorker* had an uncommon capacity to present overlapping and contradictory cultural ideas without apology. In its pages elitism coexisted with egalitarianism, conspicuous consumption commingled with anticommercialism, materialism with idealism, and sexism with gender equality. The question of how deeply these two components of sophistication conflicted with one another or complemented one another was, in fact, the dominant unconscious subtext of *The New Yorker* in this period. Both by appealing to and assuaging these longings, the magazine functioned as an organ of cultural absolution for an important sector of the postwar upper-middle class.

BEYOND THE MANHATTAN SKYLINE

Many *New Yorker* devotees faced distinct challenges in the postwar years that grew in weight over time. Chief among these was the need to attend diligently to issues of world relevance. While it was perhaps a simple enough matter to negotiate the slow-moving stream of civilized bourgeois social life by demonstrating a knowledge of wine and fashion, antiques and art, to navigate the white waters of the atomic age was a far more demanding task. The conviction, long one of the key tenets of American pragmatic liberalism, that enlightenment was in itself a form of social activism, made geopolitics a critical concern of postwar readers. The postwar world, which had lost the certainty that civilized nations would continue to honor some moral boundaries even in wartime, was a strange and volatile place, and it was difficult to get a purchase on it.

During World War II American liberals had needed to believe that the goals of the war were lucid and just and that the damage done by the Allies, especially the bombing of civilians, had been a necessity rather than an expression of unfocused violence. Some social critics, Dwight Macdonald for one, felt that the war had ultimately been an "irrational holocaust, with defenseless civilians as the main prey." Others raised serious questions about the morality of America's military strategies at the end of the war. While much of American society cheerfully examined photographs of mushroom clouds, drank atomic cocktails, and toasted the peace, and the Office of War Information sent out press releases full of millennial awe, *New Yorker* contributors helped readers to organize their jumbled emotions, in particular relief that the war was over coupled with the sense that although America had won the war, it had not escaped untarnished—it had "its own brutality to contemplate, its own amends to offer the world."[1]

The dovetailing of the end of World War II, the death of President Roosevelt, and the beginning of the atomic age created an unparalleled period of cultural flux in American life. American liberals had relied on Roosevelt's guidance and protection for more than a decade. With his death and the subsequent bombings of Hiroshima and Nagasaki that ended the war, journalists, politicians, and ordinary citizens struggled to understand the lay of the postwar land and to fit the atom into pre-existing patterns of thought. This was a time of intense, ardent discourse. Americans looked nervously to government, to scientific experts, and to journalists to forge a path for them through the uncharted nuclear field. How would the cultural consensus define atomic energy—as a means of destruction or as a benign agent of change? Was the bomb to be regarded as a weapon of triumph promising national security, or a technological curse that ought to be outlawed? It was hard to know what to think and even harder to know what to say. Members of the information elite thus took on a grave responsibility: to find a language with which to address the unbearable implications of the nuclear age.[2]

Anxiety about the bomb vied with optimism in America's postwar consciousness. A Gallup poll, taken one month after the bombing of Hiroshima, revealed that 69% of the respondents regarded the development of the bomb as "a good thing." A year later, however, the results of a Social Science Research Council poll were far more ambiguous. For example, a majority of the 600 people the Council polled felt that America's nuclear monopoly would soon end; 60% believed that the secret of the bomb was no longer a secret; and almost half of those questioned expressed a fear that a nuclear world war was highly likely within twenty-five years.[3]

American periodicals played a significant role both in forming and tabulating public opinion about the dawn of the atomic age. *Business Week* had a special Atomic Energy Department, as did *The Saturday Review*. In 1973, when Rob Paarlberg compiled a "fever chart" of America's early nuclear consciousness, he collected a list of over three hundred articles on the atomic bomb in major American periodicals in 1946 alone.[4]

The New Yorker's response to the bomb resembled that of other magazines in its scope and immediacy, but not in content. While five million readers of *Life* magazine studied full-page pictures of the mushroom-shaped clouds over Hiroshima and Nagasaki, accompanied by a text explaining cheerfully that Hiroshima had been "blown . . . off the face of the earth," and Nagasaki had been "disemboweled," and while the *Washington Post* was engaging in a debate about the possibility of developing a protective shield to defend us from attack, *The New Yorker*'s editorial voice at once argued mournfully for world federation as the only hope for a planet threatened by nuclear extinction and ridiculed the official language for the nuclear age. To be sure, *The New Yorker* was not the only magazine to express fear and loathing at the prospect of a nuclear age. Bruce Bliven, *The New Republic*'s editor, expressed a rather feeble wish that atomic power be used for good rather than evil, while T.R.B., that magazine's chief commentator on political affairs, scoffed:

"in a short week . . . man learned that he had at last found how to blow himself up." Dwight Macdonald, in his idiosyncratic one-man magazine, *Politics,* contended that it was absurd to imagine the bomb being used in a "good" cause and wrote that the bombings had placed "'us,' the defenders of civilization on a moral level with 'them,' the beasts of Maidanek." But while *The New Republic* had a subscription base of 41,000, and *Politics* was read by about 5,000 people, the postwar *New Yorker* was reaching close to half a million people each week.[5]

Like other Americans who were trusting various experts for direction, members of the cosmopolitan *New Yorker* tribe, feeling none too sure-footed on the rocky postwar terrain, huddled around the *New Yorker* village fire seeking guidance from its elders. The magazine's editors and contributors provided their readers with both direction and information—conveying the decentering news of neutrons and Bikini blasts, of Korea and HUAC and Socialist governments abroad, in a familiar package: *The New Yorker* looked just the way it had in 1930. Whether its familiarly formatted pages described the horrors of radiation, the hubris of the Bikini tests, or merely the alienation of upper-middle-class men returning from war to the banalities of civilian life, the magazine also displayed in the late forties and early fifties a consistent sense of the old and relatively carefree world of prewar cosmopolitan cafe society.

"Nobody feels funny now," Ross moaned when faced with the Second World War, an event that he was certain would destroy his magazine. He saw himself buried beneath mountains of "grim stuff." When Ross asked James Thurber's advice about handling this problem, Thurber suggested that he might try changing "the nature of the modern world and the grim course of the century." Instead of ruining the magazine, however, the war lifted it to another level, broadening its scope and lending a new urgency to its analysis of world affairs. Blending pathos with humor in its accounts, *The New Yorker* went to war.[6]

It was, in fact, the magazine's evolution during World War II—from a "chic comic weekly for East Coast sophisticates" into a powerful cultural agent—that allowed it to play a significant role in casting the terms of the debate about the shape of the postwar world. World War II altered the journal so profoundly that Thurber claimed the "Talk of the Town" should have changed its name to the "Talk of the World." A "pony" edition of the magazine was widely circulated amongst members of the armed forces, and according to E. B. White, "its fugitive little pages were studied by homesick men and women all over the uncivilized world." In spite of misgivings about publishing "grim stuff," Ross, once the editor of *Stars and Stripes,* saw the war as a "real *story*" and was ultimately willing to let *The New Yorker* tell it. He sent his reporters abroad to write firsthand accounts of poverty in Berlin; of the destruction of Santa Maria delle Grazie in Milan, and of the shelling of Saipan. By V.E. Day, descriptions of black markets, acres of rubble, and fuel shortages, along with images of starveling children in advertisements asking readers to become foster parents to war orphans, had become commonplaces in the magazine.[7]

By the end of the war it was clear that *The New Yorker* had become big and complex, and the world had become its beat. The magazine continued to publish ground breaking dispatches from around the globe, such as Janet Flanner's (a.k.a. Genet) "The Beautiful Spoils," about the plundering of European art by the Third Reich; Phillip Hamburger's dispatch from Argentina about Peron's harboring of Nazi war criminals; myriad reports from the Nuremberg war trials by Flanner, Rebecca West, and Andy Logan; and Kay Boyle's unsentimental short stories about occupied Germany. During this period Richard Rovere established his "Letter From Washington," while Joseph Wechsberg filed stories from Eastern Europe.

Harold Ross, who thought air travel so "unnatural that he never once set foot on a plane," was, not surprisingly, quite ill at ease with the exigencies of the atomic age. He did, however, make room in the magazine for contributors to confront the atomic era as they saw fit, and they wrote of it with unreserved consternation. As an editor, Ross was a curious mixture of permissiveness and rigidity. His elaborate belief system included assorted strict taboos: men shouldn't attend matinees, and the words "it," "and," and "but" should not be used at the beginning of an article. Yet he was quite flexible about important things. Above all he was dedicated to the proposition that a good editor allowed intelligent writers to write about what really concerned them in a comprehensible style and without interference. He also demonstrated an unflappable willingness to trust the judgment of the gifted people with whom he had surrounded himself. It was in part his trust in William Shawn, the magazine's "fact" editor, and the Whites (Katherine Angell and her husband, E. B. White), who often acted as the conscience of *The New Yorker*, which helped to broaden the magazine's horizons and lift it to its postwar level of distinction. "Ross," Shawn explained, "was no moral philosopher, and his social conscience was shaky, and he knew nothing whatever about politics, but he had a profound ethical sense when it came to journalism." Ross's journalistic broadmindedness helped to make the magazine a progressive forum, catering to a postwar audience that was hungry for knowledge of the world and often uncertain about what position to take on the issues.[8]

"The Atomic Age is scarcely a month old," E. B. White wrote in September 1945, "yet we feel as though we've been swimming in its dark, radioactive waters for centuries." White's warnings about the terrors of nationalism in a nuclear age rose above the clink of cocktail glasses gaily toasting the peace. A little more than a week after the bombing of Hiroshima, amidst advertisements for Charles of the Ritz leg make-up and Tiffany circle pins, "Notes and Comment" (the opening section of "Talk of the Town," the magazine's unsigned editorial segment which White had essentially invented) featured an elegiac piece by White in which he described himself, seated in the kitchen of his house in Maine, canning beans while listening to radio commentators discuss the Japanese surrender, and wondering "what it will mean to a soldier, having gone out to fight a war to preserve the world as he knew it, now to return to a world he never dreamt about, a world of atomic designs and portents."[9]

This rueful note was vintage White, "modest, sly, elliptical, allusive, prim, slightly countrified, wistful." It offered readers an analysis of the terrors of the postwar world couched in the nostalgic language of the rural kitchen. Two weeks before the first Christmas of the new peace,

"Notes and Comment" was entirely devoted to an Almanac which was "to be hung by the wood box in the kitchen" and would list a cheery calendar of important events that had promoted world government during the prior year. By the spring of 1946, White was growing increasingly certain that America was stalled between nationalism and internationalism, and that peace had become "a good in itself—the priceless vase upon the shaky table"; if it should "fall and shatter," the loss would destroy a lot of other "antique treasures—the freedom that has been gained painfully and violently, the culture, the civilization, the human rights."[10]

White, who had in the war years turned increasingly toward a fervent internationalism, was the contributor most synonymous with the postwar *New Yorker*'s editorial voice. Although Ross found White's one-world ideas naively optimistic, he admired his idealism, and, for a time, *The New Yorker* became a respectable soapbox for White, its own Cassandra, admonishing readers to take heed, for "The end of the world is near!" Like White, many liberal Americans were troubled about the shakiness of the peace, the prospect of nuclear annihilation, and the obvious disorder of the larger postwar world. However, in spite of this uneasiness and shortages of housing, beefsteak, and nylons, they were themselves unbombed, well fed, and untroubled by piles of rubble in their streets.[11]

For such people White was the ideal cicerone through the maze of postwar anxieties. He had a gift for putting huge changes into small, human packages. It was this gift for reducing the scale of vast problems through metaphor that enabled him to offer a bridge of words between the unthinkable and the thinkable, between the snug *New Yorker* village and the terrors of the larger world. In addition, he offered his readers the terms they could use to engage in an ongoing national debate about the perils of the world that they had inherited and had, at least indirectly, helped to create.

An examination of the "Notes and Comment" of August 18, 1945, less than two weeks after the dropping of the bombs, provides us with a sense of White's delicate touch in delivering cosmic horror in the gentle language of domestic reproach. There was a query about the possibility of outlawing science entirely, in which he pointed out that the "quest for a substitute for God" was over because a substitute had been found—"man himself stealing God's stuff." This was followed by a piece about a blind girl in Albuquerque, who had experienced "a strange brightness in the room" when an atom bomb was exploded one hundred and twenty miles away; and finally, a complaint addressed to statesmen that plans for the postwar political world were simply "not fantastic enough" because nuclear energy and foreign policy "cannot coexist on the planet." White then pleaded for a "universal structure" for world government, adding that the arrangements being made in San Francisco for the United Nations seemed trifling, like "the preparations some little girls might make for a lawn party as a thunderhead gathers just beyond the garden gate."[12]

White confronted a world in jeopardy by invoking a dreamy moral utopia. In the spirit of the folksy saying, "If wishes were horses then poor men would ride," White's postwar vision of the world—despite its obvious terrors—was a place in which poor men would ride: a geography steeped in the assumptions of liberal universalism, which claimed the fundamental unity and sameness of all mankind. Without apology, White as Everyman could begin a piece by saying: "The more a man thinks about it, the more clearly he sees . . ." Magically he dissolved geopolitical problems in universalist language. Writing of warfare, White explained that it was "now unpopular with the men who are engaged in it and with the people who are supporting it . . . And if a thing is unpopular, there is always the amusing possibility that it may not, then, be inevitable." In an early piece about the U.N. (for which he had passionate hopes), he suggested that the delegates immediately form an orchestra. "Eleanor Roosevelt could learn the triangle," he wrote, and one day a week all U.N. business would be "put aside and the public" could come to the General Assembly "to hear that rarest of sounds—the concord of nations." "Imagine a Gershwin morning . . . with an all-world symphony group playing ["Porgy and Bess"] music written by an American of Russian-Jewish extraction about Negroes whose ancestors had come from

Africa in slave ships!" From his own city on a hill, White invoked the credo of American exceptionalism and proclaimed the possibilities of Yankee decency, Thomas Jefferson, the Bill of Rights, liberty and justice for all. Thus despite his own sense of America's burden of guilt for unleashing the atom and continuing to use nuclear diplomacy, he employed the language of a universalized American democracy in which wishes were assumed to have transformative power. White invoked a magic village in which Eleanor Roosevelt could help resolve geopolitical problems by learning to "play the triangle." Although benign, White's metaphorical optimism opened up a small fissure in *The New Yorker*'s editorial logic that widened as the Cold War deepened.[13]

E. B. White was certainly not the only *New Yorker* contributor who regarded the postwar world with dread. The atomic explosions over Hiroshima and Nagasaki reverberated on almost every page of the magazine the first week after the bombings. "Fateful Night," an unsigned "Talk of the Town" entry, recounted the night in 1939 when John R. Dunning split the uranium atom at Columbia University. "Gags Away" offered a sampling of various bomb-"activated" jokes recounted by radio and nightclub "jokesperts," including the following bit of doggerel delivered at the Diamond Horseshoe nightclub by Bob Hall, known around town as "That Extemporaneous Chap":

> Atomic, Atomic, it had to be
> But just what it is is a mystery;
> For years they've heard it,
> Atom they knew
> Not until today
> Did they realize
> What it could do.

Noting that "Fred Allen, Jack Benny, Eddie Cantor, and Bob Hope were off the air—a great blessing to all," the anonymous "Talk" reporter offered a nod of approval to Milton Berle, who had telephoned to say that he had no bomb jokes and "considered it a poor subject for drollery."[14]

This same issue contained a long profile of William Laurence, the *New York Times* science reporter who had been chosen by the War Department to explain the bomb to Americans and familiarize them with the vocabulary surrounding it. In an interesting editorial choice, Karl Shapiro's mournful poem, "Homecoming," was printed alongside the Laurence "Profile"—set off only by small white borders.

"Homecoming" is about a ship coming back from the war, bearing returning soldiers—"green-skinned men in blue-lit holds." Much of the poem's descriptive force is derived from Shapiro's use of the language of nuclear destruction: a "smile that would light up all darkness"; an explosion so fierce that it could "shatter the tensions of the heaven and sea / To crush a hundred thousand skulls / And liberate in that high burst of love / The imprisoned souls of soldiers and of me."[15]

The juxtaposition of Shapiro's poem with the Laurence profile is notable because the poem explodes with the violence of the very language Laurence was trying to domesticate. For Shapiro that mother-tongue was the one that had delivered "Shame and all death on millions and on me"; it was not the benign lingo of scientific mastery.[16]

Most of the poetic offerings published in *The New Yorker* in the decade before the war had been high-doggerel celebrations of upper-middle-class social life. While the magazine continued to publish light humorous verse, much of its postwar poetry, notable for its gravitas, was suffused with the new atomic vocabulary. The grim locutions of atomic science imploded within familiar themes and forms, shattering old meanings. Poems now reflected a new and painful sense of evanescence, of the fragile nature of everything, even matter itself. Ernest Kroll's 1946 "In a Georgetown Garden" illuminated this transformation. While Kroll remained within prewar *New Yorker* poetic conventions, cleaving to the imagery of high-bourgeois domestic life, he disrupted the placid setting—a garden party—by infusing it with the knowledge of atomic destruction. The hostess speaks "sweetly of Atoms," and the guest seeing a "perfect rose," hesitates "to lean" against it, newly conscious of "its particles."[17]

As national newsreels and newsmagazines delighted in using a nuclear vernacular that invoked "cosmic power," "doomsday itself," "hell-fire," and "darkening heavens," *The New Yorker*'s Frank Sullivan explicitly ridiculed this hyperbolic vocabulary. In his comic piece "The Cliché Expert Testifies On the Atom," which was part of an ongoing "Cliché Expert" series, Sullivan twitted the stock images of the atomic age and demonstrated how these literary clichés limited the ways people thought and wrote about the atom. His piece illustrated the power of language to control ideology and effectively subverted the religious fervor with which many journalists were hailing the atom.

Mr. Arbuthnot, the Cliché Expert, explains that "usher" is the only verb that will do to describe the arrival of the atomic age, and that a pea is "the accepted vegetable" in explanations of how much U-235 it would "take to drive an automobile to the moon and back." "Harness and unleash" are two words everyone needed to learn if they "expect to talk about the atom or write about it either." When his questioner begs him to stop explaining the atom to him in "terms so simple a layman can understand," Mr. Arbuthnot obliges with a daffy free-associative soliloquy: "Then Einstein . . . equation . . . nucleus . . . electron . . . bombard . . . break down . . . impact . . . matter . . . military possibilities . . . isotopes . . . heavy water . . . New Mexico . . . mushroom shaped cloud . . . awesome sight."[18]

While the magazine often ridiculed the official language of the nuclear age, the larger part of its scorn was reserved for the idiocy of official nuclear policy. The inhumanity shown by the United States government in displacing a group of people from a remote tropical atoll in order to practice destruction there made the Bikini bomb tests a lightning rod for the magazine's flashes of outrage. The *New Yorker* contributors saw the tests as a portent of future nuclear horrors—a grim replication of Hiroshima in the name of scientific inquiry. This outrage was most often expressed in light ironic "casuals" exposing attempts by the government to turn destructive experiments into sportive media events. A "Fissionable-Press Note!" announced that the Navy had given press credentials to *Charm* magazine for the Bikini test. Another commentator suggested developing a pen that writes under water, because "There's some talk of a large wave being thrown up by the [Bikini] explosion, and the press may need unusual equipment." One item listed the gifts that the United States gave King Juda of Bikini for his "true contribution to the progress of mankind all over the world." Among them were "a pipe, a cigarette holder, some matches, some chocolate bars, and a complete set of photographs of the first atomic cloud over Bikini, taken as the old home caught hell."[19]

Some of the Bikini commentaries had the tone of doomsday prophecies. A spring 1946 item from "Notes and Comment" cited a letter from a physics professor at Yale, warning that "an atomic explosion in the Pacific might open up a hole in the floor of the sea . . . creating a chain of explosions which would transcend the imagination of most human beings." By and large *New Yorker* contributors saw the idea of an atomic future as something of an oxymoron. Thus Bikini, "the one time habitation of some queer ducks who failed to drop things on each other," became a harbinger of the extinction of mankind. "If one atomic bomb goes off, in real earnest," E. B. White wrote, "the rest of us will leave our Bikinis for fair—some in the heat of stars, some in the remains of human flesh in a ruined earth."[20]

Perhaps the magazine's most trenchant critique of the Bikini tests was Roger Angell's disturbing story, "Some Pigs in Sailor Suits." It is about three men—two businessmen and an Army colonel—who meet at their college club, drink highballs, and discuss the war damage in Japan. The blowhard colonel boasts that morale has never been so high and enthusiastically explains: "fire bombs were right for Japan. Those flimsy houses and slums were all built for us. They were what gave us our percentages." As the drinking progresses, George Swan, the story's narrator, becomes increasingly alarmed at the colonel's zeal for "this Big A Stuff." Swan points out that he had seen some pictures of the Bikini natives and "that *their* morale didn't seem all that high."

"Oh, hell," the colonel bellows, "you mean the gooks. Well, I wouldn't worry about them." As Swan gets drunker he confronts the colonel about the rumor that pigs and goats are going to be used as human proxies in the Bikini test. The colonel explains that the scientists need test victims and that pigs and goats are admirably suited to the job because "they're big like men. And pigs have skin like human's skin." He then adds brightly that some of the pigs will even be dressed up in flashproof clothing, "like Navy gunners."[21]

White and his colleagues often expressed concern about the way people simply accepted the bomb as an inevitability. Commenting on the human capacity to adjust to the probability of nuclear extinction, White wrote: "On Monday, man may be hysterical with doom, and on Tuesday you will find him opening the Doomsday Bar and Grill and settling down for another thousand years of terrifying queerness." During 1945 and 1946, the magazine frequently commented on the way commerce had cozied up to the atomic future: Hofritz's Fifth Avenue store "was clearing out its stock of perpetual calendars"; a new electronic rat trap had been invented that is "very right for the atomic age" because it "lures the rat not through his stupidity but through his intelligence"; and a garbage collector in Kew Gardens had painted "World Ashes Removal" on the side of his truck. The Golden Star Valet Service both "cleans and vaporizes clothes," and the Camille Luggage Shop had "just held an Atomic Clearance Sale."[22]

While the magazine's contributors attributed lay men and women's passive acceptance of an atomic future to a lack of awareness, they held scientists and bureaucrats accountable for the unleashing of the atom. By the postwar period, much of the larger society had developed an almost euphoric belief in the power of science. Politicians and mainstream journalists hailed atomic science for its potential to end war, poverty, and disease. Science did, however, have its detractors. Those who resisted its marvels saw science as something ominous, especially because it was in the hands of scatterbrained geniuses whose curiosity about arcane formulae had unleashed the contents of an atomic Pandora's box on an unsuspecting public.

The New Yorker helped its audience to find the appropriate position in the debate over the moral accountability of science, a question that resonated with readers' sense of their own social and moral responsibility as thinking Americans. While *New Yorker* contributors were generally not atomic science boosters, they did distinguish between science and its practitioners, who were often the very sort of liberal intellectuals who read the magazine. Where atomic science was concerned, the magazine hated the sin but not the sinner. In the editorial perspective science was its own agent, detached from the actions of particular scientists.[23]

Often scientists were depicted as clown-like crackpots, too wrapped up in theory to see the long-term ramifications of their work while developing the bomb, but who had come to their senses since Hiroshima. They were daft rather than sinister. In Geoffrey T. Hellman's "Reporter at Large" piece about Alexander Sachs—"the man who got President Roosevelt interested in atomic research"—the scientist was described as a "fifty-two year old with curls" who "looks so much like Ed Wynn" (a famous vaudeville comedian who became a reigning star of early television) "that when he was in Washington with the NRA his colleagues would tell visitors that Ed Wynn was working there." Sachs was further characterized as an absent-minded, long-winded obfuscator, who owned "forty second-hand briefcases" and had pockets full of memoranda which he unceremoniously scattered on the floor.[24]

One *New Yorker* writer's postwar beat was the atom and its absorption into American economic and cultural life. Daniel Lang often castigated atomic science and its long term consequences while simultaneously humanizing its practitioners. While E. B. White's meta-utterances about the dangers of nationalism in a nuclear age were issued from a metaphorical high ground, Lang's micro-examination of America's booming nuclear industry took place in the atomic lowlands, where he explored the implosion of the atom in the day-to-day lives of Americans. Lang mapped the eerie geography of the atomic age: technocrats split atoms in antiseptic communities, while Nevada cattle ranchers could not graze their cows on "launching days" at nearby test sites. He noted the phenomenon of the Las Vegas "dawn parties" in rooftop hotel piano bars, where patrons waited for the light shows provided by bomb tests in the Nevada desert. He wrote about the workaday lives of the men and women who earned their living in nuclear laboratories, and the "human booty" of the postwar period—the "haul" of German atomic scientists who had been recruited by the U.S. government—men who were "willing to work for anyone" as long as there was work. He described a laboratory in Long Island devoted to the peaceful atom, the struggles of the men appointed to consider the formation of an international Atomic Energy Commission, the fierce competition between rocket scientists and bomb scientists, and "the lovely, flourishing setting" in which atomic bombs were being manufactured at Los Alamos in the Sangre De Cristo Mountains of New Mexico.[25]

At the heart of Lang's work was the essential ambiguity of pure science: its claim to being value-free and its unintended consequences. As he saw it, neither science nor scientists were at fault. The problem was the way government commandeered scientific theory for its own purposes. Indeed, if there was a villain present, it was the government and its policy of financing the proliferation of nuclear facilities and trying to convince an untutored public that "atomic energy has an attractive side." A high-ranking Army officer told Lang: "[D]on't give that conscience angle a second thought . . . fissionable materials are good for either peace or war. It's like gasoline. You can pour it into a Sherman tank or a sightseeing bus." But the reporter was quick to remind readers of the "chilling fact" that almost all "fissionable materials were allocated for nuclear weapons."[26]

Although he wrote in the tragic trope characteristic of *The New Yorker*'s response to the atomic age, Lang's work was rooted in the deeply liberal idea that knowledge and consciousness were a kind of antidote to the anxiety engendered by the atom. In Lang's view, there was no hope of wishing the atomic toothpaste back into its tube. The atom had been split. A bomb had been dropped on Hiroshima. Scientists were working all across America to build bigger bombs and faster, more accurate rockets with which to deliver them. Regardless of the agonizing of David Lillienthal and the efforts of other members of the Atomic Energy Commission, atomic science had become big business in America. And despite the complexity and scale of the atomic problem, a conscientious citizenry had a responsibility to pay attention to it. If, in fact, the government was an unreliable narrator, as Lang suspected, then other sources of information had to be sought. Without gilding the atomic lily, Lang delivered the horrible possibilities of America's nuclear future to *New Yorker* readers and in this way denied the optimistic assessments of many statesmen and government publicists about the potential of the atom to be put to "good" uses.

Prefiguring the magazine's publication of "Hiroshima," Lang's "A Fine Moral Point" reports on an American scientific mission sent to make a spotcheck on Hiroshima thirty days after the blast. The War Department, sensitive to criticism of a lack of "humaneness" in American methods of warfare, wanted the mission to prove that only a "small percentage of the 178,000 casualties were the result of radioactivity." In Hiroshima, the members of the mission met Masao Tsuzuki, a professor of Radiology at the University of Tokyo, who in 1926 had written a thesis called "Deaths Induced by Severe X-Ray Radiation in Laboratory Animals." In that work Tsuzuki had described in detail the "hemorrhages, oozing of blood through the pores, and other disorders brought on by X-Ray radiation." After one of the mission's scientists had read the thesis and handed it back to him, Tsuzuki slapped him on the knee and exclaimed: "Ah, but the Americans—they are wonderful. It has remained for them to conduct the human experiment."

Just as Lang allowed Tsuzuki's bitter humor to speak for itself, he let the mission scientists' justifications of the experiment stand alone: "It was the magnitude of the damage that was appalling," one of the scientists explained. "I looked at the ruins of the castle, and I could see, here and there, a burned body or maybe a hearthstone or a dish. Most of us who hadn't dropped out of this atom project during the last two or three years had developed our own private justifications for staying with it. I know I had done so. They helped me in Hiroshima." At the end of the mission's trip, even as thirty people were dying each day of radiation injuries, the members were pleased at their findings, reporting in a "tone of quiet triumph that 'the bomb had burst at precisely the spot we wanted it to, high over Hiroshima . . . that was what we had all been wanting to know.'"[27]

In "The Atomic City," published just two months after the bombing of Hiroshima, Lang concerned himself with Oak Ridge, the army site where scientists manufactured plutonium and U-235 in order to "increase America's stockpile of atomic bombs, now that peace has come." Lang depicted the sterility of this futuristic village, with its "tradition" of secrecy and an architectural style that "might be called Early Alphabet Cemesto."[28]

By juxtaposing the antiseptic serenity of Oak Ridge with its destructive function, Lang offered a disturbing portent of the American future, in which scientists could go cheerfully about the business of developing instruments of destruction in sterile suburban edens. Lang's meticulous portraits of scientific communities always emphasized their creepy ordinariness, the way in which they seemed to blend easily into the postwar American landscape. He reminded his readers that while the "thriving new industry—factories producing radioactive fuels, piles, cooking fissionable materials, laboratories housing novel research equipment" were as "eerily silent and generally as well-behaved as a hosiery mill," they were in the business of creating weapons that could bring about the destruction of the planet.[29]

Lang's "Blackjack and Flashes" recorded the reactions of Nevadans to the installation of a continental proving-ground for nuclear weapons, only sixty-five miles northwest of Las Vegas. Taxpayers in this haven for "gamblers, divorcees, and elopers" were "getting at least a sketchy idea of the nature of the product they were helping to finance." The "unearthly hues" of atomic clouds were plainly visible in Las Vegas, and the bomb tests' shock waves had left cracks in hotel walls, had broken china, and had shattered the window displays of numerous merchants. But like E. B. White's man who is "hysterical with doom" on Monday and opens the Doomsday Bar and Grill on Tuesday, the Las Vegans in Lang's piece were quick to recognize the commercial potential of the monster in their midst. As soon as reports of the plan to build a proving ground began circulating, the Chamber of Commerce sent out publicity releases to allay anxiety about its possible effect on the tourist trade. "The angle" was to make people think that "the explosions wouldn't be anything more than a gag." "One showed a girl sporting an Atomic Hairdo . . .

Another heralded the Atomic Cocktail." A local haberdashery which had its windows shattered in a bomb blast, put a barrel full of the glass shards in front of their shop, bearing a sign: "ATOM BOMB SOUVENIRS— FREE!" The Governor of Nevada said he was pleased that what had once been a wasteland was now "blooming with atoms." People even began to celebrate the blasts in post-midnight drinking and singing revels at which locals and tourists mingled together to catch early glimpses of bomb tests.[30]

Describing the laughing-to-keep-from-crying quality of such parties, Ted Mossman, the piano player at the Sky Room, told Lang: "Standing room only. They were drinking like fish . . . Everyone wanted to sing. They requested all the old numbers . . . 'Bye, Bye, Blackbird,' 'Put Your Arms Around Me Honey.' They sang as if they were on the Queen Mary and it was going down—loud desperate voices . . . I improvised some boogie-woogie that I called 'The Atomic Bomb Bounce.'" The wife of a Las Vegas journalist described the dawn viewing of a bomb test to Lang: "When I could see again after the blinding, terrifying flash, I was looking at the sun. It was just coming up over the mountains. The sun, you know, isn't always kind to us here in the desert, but at that moment it seemed like an old friend."[31]

Lang's description of Las Vegans' peculiarly chipper response to the nuclear presence has a particular resonance because of common stereotypes about Las Vegas itself, a place understood by many Easterners and *New Yorker* readers to exemplify all that was crass and tasteless in mass consumer culture. "It's a wonderful town, all right!" a stickman at the Thunderbird opined. "Where else can a fellow gamble all day, get drunk, go to sleep, get up at four in the morning, and find plenty of company when he walks into the lobby?" And indeed, Lang seemed to be saying, what other town would embrace the bursts of light accompanying a bomb test as just another amusement, encouraging "more business than if we had television out here." Lang seemed to be suggesting that Las Vegas and the nuclear industry were a perfect match—twin auguries of the doom of a civilization that had allowed itself to be lulled into a stupor.

Lang's atomic pieces comprised a series that brightly illuminated the nuclear future —a future that was at once routine and nightmarish. He delivered the human, the benign, and the horrific dimensions of the new atomic presence in American life in a manner that was both comfortable and disturbing. In this way he gently guided *New Yorker* readers into the moral debate regarding the atom and its uses.

The cover of the August 31, 1946, *New Yorker,* with its hieroglyphic rendering of people participating in summer games, gave no hint that the entire issue was to be devoted to the publication of John Hersey's 30,000 word "Hiroshima," the "most famous magazine article ever published." Hersey's essay was a masterful piece of social realism—an account of what happened to six survivors before, during, and after the blast. Rendering in spare, unemotional prose the oral testimony of a German Jesuit priest, a seamstress, a Japanese minister, two doctors, and a ten-year-old boy, Hersey succeeded in transforming the way many Americans perceived the atom bomb. In opposition to the exotic and aesthetically pleasing image of the mushroom cloud, he showed the reality of the bomb's destructive impact upon ordinary human beings—people with whom readers could identify. By rendering the effects of the bomb in the language of human tragedy, Hersey managed to shift the terms of the national debate concerning nuclear weapons. "Once in a lifetime," a reviewer wrote, "you read a magazine article that makes you want to bounce up out of your easychair and go running around to your neighbors, thrusting the magazine under their noses and saying: 'Read this! Read it now!'" Newsstands were deluged with demands for the issue, which sold out immediately. Albert Einstein requested one thousand copies. When the piece was published as a book, it became a huge bestseller. The entire book was read aloud in four segments on the ABC radio network. The Book-of-the-Month Club distributed close to a million free copies to its members. Henry L. Stimson, the administration's Hiroshima "spin doctor," wrote his 1947 apologia, "The Decision to Drop the Bomb," in part as a response to Hersey's essay. Stimson explained with surprising candor that he was writing to "satisfy the doubts of that rather difficult class of the community which will have charge of the education of the next generation, namely educators and historians." Hersey's piece had done much to bolster these doubts.[32]

William Shawn's decision to commit an entire issue to "Hiroshima" represented the culmination of *The New Yorker*'s developing sense of social responsibility. Allowing the piece to explode long-standing *New Yorker* formulaic constraints greatly magnified its moral force. What television news did for Vietnam, Hersey's account did for atomic warfare. By delivering searing descriptions of how the bombing was experienced by six survivors to the doorsteps of *The New Yorker*'s readers (including presumably members of the "rather difficult class" Stimson had referred to), Hersey succeeded in raising the specter of American terrorism. Immediately after the bombings of Hiroshima and Nagasaki, whatever disquiet liberal intellectuals may have felt about them had been drowned out by the revelry surrounding the end of the war. "Hiroshima" at last gave a voice to their concerns—a voice that was heard all over America.

"Hiroshima" was not universally acclaimed. Without a doubt, some of the magazine's older, more conservative subscribers were perplexed by the magazine's decision to abandon its traditional format. Helen Hokinson, one of the magazine's foremost cartoonists, loved to repeat the comment of a woman acquaintance who said: "I've just read that long Hiroshima article from beginning to end, and I just wish you'd tell me what was funny about it?"[33]

The objections to Hersey's piece were not confined to the magazine's more traditional readers. The Left had long criticized *The New Yorker* for what Dwight Macdonald (who later wrote for the magazine) called its "Park Avenue attitude," and its "Jovian aloofness from the common struggle." Some critics on the left were particularly vexed by the fact that the magazine had run "Hiroshima" amidst the usual ads for imported spirits and Caribbean vacations. In a letter to the editors of *Politics* concerning the publication of Hersey's essay, Mary McCarthy maintained that *The New Yorker* had typically placed the bomb in the "familiar order" of journalistic "catastrophes—fires, floods, earthquakes" which had long provided reporters with "marvelous, and true-life narratives of incredible escapes." In these accounts, McCarthy claimed, immense disasters were always juxtaposed with "human-interest" stories, which made them small and manageable, on a par with Mrs. O'Leary and her cow. By interviewing survivors, Hersey had populated an unthinkable historical moment with "busy little Japanese Methodists," and by so doing had created "an insipid falsification of the truth of atomic warfare." To do justice to the enormity of the bombing, she insisted, Hersey would have "had to interview the dead," a job he would be incapable of doing because "Hell [was] not his sphere."

There is some truth in the charge that as *The New Yorker* published more and more serious journalism focused on global affairs, the coexistence of these pieces with advertisements for Mark Cross luggage and snug little inns in Bar Harbor looked increasingly peculiar. The Left saw this idiosyncracy as a mannerly plot designed to provide *New Yorker* readers with a cultural commodity more precious than a Tiffany diamond—the "suitable attitude" toward terrible geopolitical events. "Hiroshima," Mary McCarthy claimed, was not an indictment of the atomic bomb but rather an assimilation of it into the *New Yorker* world—"to Westchester County, to smoked turkey, and the Hotel Carlyle." While McCarthy's snarly comments are an example of critical overkill, they do touch upon a notable tension in the magazine's presentation of self.

The publication of "Hiroshima" and the fervor with which it was embraced by *New Yorker* readers illustrates some of the tensions of postwar cosmopolitanism. By providing a nonthreatening forum to express the anxiety felt by many Americans about the moral cost of the peace, the magazine performed a critical social function. "Hiroshima" both touched a nerve and acted as a balm. However passive the act of reading the essay may have been, it was experienced by many as a form of social activism. The *New Yorker* village seized upon the opportunity to acknowledge its collective feelings of guilt with alacrity. For socially conscious people of status and wealth, virtue was a precious commodity—a quality that made it easier to savor privilege. While the effects of the bombings could not be reversed, a public expurgation of guilt for them could cleanse the American soul. There is, therefore, no irony in the fact that this opportunity for self-absolution took place in a venue brimming with the bounties of postwar affluence.

While there was certainly no conscious attempt by *The New Yorker*'s editors to assuage readers' guilt or soft-pedal the awful possibilities of the postwar world, the magazine's unapologetic conflation of high commerce with high-mindedness did allow the perquisites of privilege to be presented as integral to the socially conscious civilized world. An advertisement for an Abercrombie & Fitch English wicker picnic basket was not presumed to appreciably interrupt the editorial text, nor was a dire subject assumed to spoil readers' enjoyment of luxury goods. By allowing for a symbiotic relationship between the possession of goods and the quality of goodness, the magazine was able to foreshorten the distance between social privilege and social consciousness.[34]

3

RED HUNTING IN THE *NEW YORKER* VILLAGE

During his long presidency, Franklin D. Roosevelt had provided liberals with a consistent source of intellectual and moral leadership. He had become for them a bulwark of confidence in a world of chaos. Because Roosevelt had been a father image for left-of-center Americans in "the Freudian rather than the Fourth-of-July sense," as Dwight Macdonald explained, his death created an emotional and intellectual vacuum. In their newly orphaned and disoriented condition, postwar American liberals faced a terrifying challenge in the form of the House Un-American Activities Committee's (HUAC) search for domestic subversives from among their ranks.[1]

In its vigorous responses to HUAC's hunt for domestic subversives, *The New Yorker* stepped into the ideological vacuum created by the death of the president and the decline of the Left and proved its mettle as a guide through the shifting values of the postwar political world. *The New Yorker*'s outspoken censure of McCarthyism illuminates a number of significant themes concerning its role in postwar American culture. First, the magazine's capacity to respond to this crisis as a monolithic intellectual community, depended on addressing (and trusting) an assumed readership that clearly shared the ethos of that community. Second, the form of the magazine's assaults on HUAC, in which *New Yorker* contributors seized the high ground of civic virtue as they depicted the anti-Communist right groveling about in an undemocratic slough of bad citizenship and worse grammar, suggests a great deal about this subculture's sense of itself as an entitled elite suited by taste and intellect to determine the course of government. There is, in fact, a peculiarly undemocratic undercurrent in *The New Yorker*'s incursions against the sort of people who constituted the anti-Communist right. In staking a claim to goodness here, the magazine situated itself credibly as a beacon of enlightenment in a dark age of suspicion, an era largely populated by boobs and cretins. The magazine's position concerning the postwar anti-Communist investigations, along with its timely publication of "Hiroshima," created a perception of *The New Yorker* as a progressive force and ally of victims of injustice, whether they were Japanese seamstresses or wrongly accused members of the State Department.

McCarthyism was more than a fringe phenomenon associated with an alcoholic junior senator from Wisconsin. It was a widely accepted political, social, and cultural crusade that penetrated the entire social order. Ordinary citizens were expected to enlist in the struggle; teachers, actors, and engineers had to take loyalty oaths or lose their jobs. Every aspect of American culture—literature, films, art, and television—"consistently hammered the theme of an enemy within, working to subvert the American Way of Life." Popular fiction celebrated violations of constitutional rights and democratic principle in the service of subjugating the Communist threat. Hollywood movies like "The Iron Curtain,"

"The Red Danube," "The Red Menace," "I Was a Communist for the FBI," and "Red Snow" depicted spies and Communist party functionaries as hardened thugs with a penchant for brutality, and justified informing on one's friends and family. Communism, it seemed, had become "more loathed than organized crime."[2]

After 1945 the antireformist forces increasingly dominated the political climate, as congressional conservatives in both the Republican and Democratic parties insisted that the Roosevelt and Truman administrations had been "soft" on Communism abroad and far too tolerant of disloyalty at home. These congressmen began a series of investigations of domestic subversion, designed in part to discredit the Truman administration. Most of these inquiries, initially targeting trade unions, New Deal agencies, and Hollywood, were carried out by the House Un-American Activities Committee, led by J. Parnell Thomas, a Republican from New Jersey.

Amidst fears that atomic warfare might vaporize the globe, the HUAC investigations and the spy trials threatened to vaporize specific citadels of elite, civilized, intellectual life. Although *The New Yorker* itself poked fun at Communists for being wrong-headed, this disdain lacked intensity. It was with profound conviction, however, that the magazine declared fervent anti-Communists to be hysterical, vulgar, paranoid, and ultimately un-American. Against them the tone of the magazine was both personal and passionate. This was not an obscure social problem happening to less fortunate others in some remote clime. Magisterial composure was not the order of the day.[3]

With the publication of her short story "The Groves of Academe" in *The New Yorker* in 1951, Mary McCarthy, who had often criticized the magazine for its tepid politics, now chose it as a forum for her attack on the failure of the academic community to stand up to HUAC. McCarthy's transformation from *New Yorker* critic to *New Yorker* contributor is emblematic both of the magazine's shift to the left during the loyalty purge, and the concurrent shift toward the middle of many left-wing intellectuals. In fact, during this period there were so many writers from the radical though anti-Stalinist *Partisan Review* working at *The New Yorker,* that

Midge Decter claimed the "*Partisan Review* was getting to be like a farm team" for the magazine.

Set on the campus of the fictive Jocelyn College, McCarthy's "The Groves of Academe" depicts the firing of a professor with leftist leanings in a "progressive community where the casserole and the cocktail and the disposable diaper reigned." The president of the college, who had once led a torch parade against loyalty oaths, has since removed his name from the Stockholm Peace Petition; in defense of this action he explains that many academics, including "a former Jocelyn physics student," have "been tried for atomic spying," and there has even "been a suicide among the former Students for Wallace." In "these times" of Alger Hiss and Joseph McCarthy, to appear at a peace rally is as risky for him as "playing strip poker on Sunday in a whore house."[4]

During the postwar anti-Communist investigations, *The New Yorker* brazenly played in a high-stakes game of journalistic "strip poker." The ascendance of HUAC's inquisition, piloted by men like Joseph McCarthy, Richard Nixon, and J. Parnell Thomas, constituted a terrifying "smart bomb" aimed directly at journalists, actors, directors, artists, professors, and liberal intellectuals in general. For members of the *New Yorker* community, this historical phenomenon was experienced as a series of personal assaults—a disturbing penetration into the sanctity of a privileged cultural enclave. Contributors' blatant expressions of personal identification with the victims of the investigations drew the magazine into the fray as an outspoken voice in a whispering world, offering its readers, many of whom felt genuinely vulnerable to attack, comfort and courage. Because of *The New Yorker,* a Washington D.C. woman wrote, there are many Americans who feel they "have a spokesman." It is encouraging, a reader wrote from New York City, "to see your intelligent counterattack against these modern hound dogs who would rewrite history in the image of their own contemptible philosophies."[5]

The sense among many of the magazine's contributors, editors, and readers of being under personal attack was not paranoia. During the late forties and early fifties, as an increasingly powerless Left feebly persevered in its traditional attacks on *The New Yorker* for fusing hard journalism with advertisements for upscale goods, the magazine took its share of licks from the Right as well. For whatever "the lukewarm rightist" Harold Ross's own politics were, he presided over a staff ranging from very moderate Democrats to members of the anti-Stalinist Left. His own editorial scruples were such that he would look at an incendiary item by a regular contributor, wince, and publish it anyway. Much to Ross's dismay, in some quarters *The New Yorker* was attacked as "pink" and even nicknamed *The New Worker*. Right-wing journalist and onetime Ross crony, Westbrook Pegler, vilified his old friend for allegedly promoting the work of fellow travelers. Even J. Edgar Hoover saw fit to harass Ross for various cartoons and casual items that poked fun at the F.B.I. Although the Bureau asserted that Ross had been "evasive" when questioned about "subversive" material he had published, they had no file on him. They did, however, keep copious dossiers on Dorothy Parker (a thousand pages), A. J. Liebling, E. B. White, Kay Boyle, Edmund Wilson, S. J. Perelman, John O'Hara, Irwin Shaw, and Richard Boyer. By 1951, Ross, who claimed to be the only Republican on *The New Yorker*'s staff, had died and was replaced by William Shawn, who was more political and more liberal than his predecessor.[6]

Certainly *The New Yorker* was not the only moderate liberal journal that stood up to the anti-Communists. The government's search for domestic Communists sent shock waves across the larger sector of liberal journalism. Month after month in "The Easy Chair," his editorial column in *Harper's*, Bernard DeVoto spoke out against the HUAC's investigations. "I like a country," he wrote in 1949, "where it's nobody's damned business what magazines anyone reads, what he thinks, whom he has cocktails with . . . We had that kind of country a little while ago, and I'm for getting it back." While DeVoto's remarks are of a piece with those of many liberal editors and writers in this period, the widely read *New Yorker*, a journal that was also deeply enmeshed in affluent consumer culture, had perhaps a greater capacity than the less popular magazines to give courage to terrified liberals under assault from postwar anti-Communism.[7]

With E. B. White leading the charge, *The New Yorker*'s contributors used moral and patriotic arguments in their attacks on the anti-Communist investigations. White, in particular, wrapped his grievances against the investigators in the flag, often citing their reckless violations of the Constitution, their attack upon what Hannah Arendt called "the right to have rights." "The Committee," White wrote in 1948, "destroys reputations in wholesale lots" by "implying guilt by association," a tactic that was "most certainly inconsistent with the spirit of the Bill of Rights." White saw the inquisitors' methods as a threat to America's democratic institutions and pointed out how the Committee used the methods of the totalitarianism it claimed to despise. What was to him especially disturbing was the "impatience with liberalism" implicit in the Committee's actions. Describing anti-Communism as "strong drink," White argued that HUAC's fight against tyranny had brought only the "tyrant fear"—a fear which has produced a "preoccupation with loyalty, the tightening of censorship, the control of thought by legislative committee, the readiness to impute guilt by association"—all themselves earmarks of totalitarianism.[8]

New Yorker contributors assumed the posture of watchdogs of liberty, snapping at those who threatened America's democratic institutions. One of the central conceits of the magazine's attacks on HUAC was that by questioning the patriotism of the kind of people who were part of the *New Yorker* community, the Committee was proving itself to be a highly dubious institution. One of the most "questionable things about the House Committee on un-American Activities," White wrote, "is its name." "The word 'un-American,' besides beginning with a small letter and gradually working up to a capital, is essentially a foolish, bad word, hardly worth the little hyphen it needs to hold it together." In this country, White argued, there is virtually nothing that can be called un-American. "'Un' means 'not,' and anything that happens within our borders is American." If un-American means "straightforward," then the Committee would have to "investigate the activities of every honorable man in the United States—a colossal, expensive, silly project, in our opinion."[9]

As politicians, Hollywood studio chieftains, and government agencies leapt onto the Red-menace bandwagon, *New Yorker* writers attacked these anti-Communist investigations vigorously while making it clear that they were not themselves Communists. In satirical essays, cartoons, casual pieces, and short stories, the magazine's contributors cast a jaundiced eye on both the media's frantic embrace of the investigations and the activities of the investigators themselves. Considering the prevailing climate of fear and suspicion, the magazine's offensives were both confrontational and courageous.

Like the Danish Christians who wore Stars of David on their sleeves to express solidarity with the Jews, *New Yorker* writers frequently flaunted their own "subversive" activities, and by so doing called into question their accusers' credibility. These writers had complete confidence in their own patriotism, and by identifying themselves with the accused, by claiming to be un-American themselves, they made of such un-Americanness a virtue. Often they saw the search for subversion as a culture war—an attack upon both their kind of people and their kind of prose. In its critiques of the people and institutions who participated in the purge, the magazine frequently invoked their crude populism, bad grammar, bad logic, and bad taste. This display of subversiveness stemmed from the contributors' firmly held notion that they and the larger *New Yorker* community, and not their vulgar attackers, were the model Americans. The tone of their discourse against the investigations was one of outraged privilege. If people of our ilk are objects of suspicion, they seemed to declare, no decent American is safe.

When Alger Hiss was accused of perjury, Walter Lippmann assured a fellow journalist: "I know Alger Hiss. He couldn't be guilty of treason." People like Dashiell Hammett, Dalton Trumbo, and Robert Oppenheimer, men who had gone to the best schools, toiled in the service of the New Deal, fought in World War II, and held prominent positions in government and the media, suddenly found themselves under suspicion. Hiss, as historian John P. Roche has explained, "wore no beard, spoke with no accent, moved casually in the best circles . . . [He] looked like the man down the block in Scarsdale or Evanston, the man in the office across the hall on Wall Street or State Street. If this man could be a spy, anybody could."[10]

The New Yorker ridiculed the Committee's transformation of innocent allegiances into evidence of Communist sympathies. In one 1947 Alan Dunn cartoon, two F.B.I. agents are seated at the desk of a superior. As one agent sifts through a massive file, the other reads a list to his boss: "Here's the record Chief. He's a member of the Sons of Democracy . . . the Guardians of the American Heritage . . . the Conference for the Furtherance of Constitutional Government . . . the Conference for the Observance of the Ten Commandments, and the Society for the Preservation of North American Wildlife. We think he's a Commie."[11]

A 1945 "Notes and Comment" (The New Yorker's editorial voice) described the case of an Oak Ridge employee who was under suspicion because he had carelessly left a copy of the New Masses in his office. Likewise, ever since The New Yorker "published a few complaints" about the mass firing of the Hollywood Ten, White wrote, the editorial offices had been deluged with "communications from blacklisted organizations." "Mostly," he explained, "the stuff just gets left around," although "we occasionally toss an old paisley shawl over the more incriminating items."

The tone of this "Note" is a far cry from the poignant and dreamy style of White's writings about the dawn of the nuclear age. Here anger, irony, and derision are fused in taunting challenge. The choice of the genteel image of a paisley shawl used to conceal "subversive" office clutter highlights the innocence of those accused and the absurdity of the Committee's charges. In this way White and other New Yorker writers consciously made themselves into potential targets for accusation and by so doing undercut the credibility of those who would accuse them.[12]

"A friend of ours," E. B. White wrote in a 1948 "Notes and Comment," "an odd cuss with no memory for details," has been thrown into a state of high anxiety by the Alger Hiss spy hearings. As the congressmen grill Hiss about his typewriter, his apartment number, people whom he may have let sleep on his couch—the minutiae of his life between 1934 and 1935—"our friend" Abbot finds himself "trying to reconstruct his own moth-eaten past," because "who knows when he's going to be called?" And White goes on to say that Abbot does recall being visited by various down-and-out acquaintances, "some of them with bizarre economic theories, some of them connected with newspapers," but he is pretty sure he didn't know anybody named Whittaker Chambers. However, he might have let Chambers sleep on his couch "under another name. (Times were bad.)" White was clearly identifying his friend (and himself) as potential casualties of the purge. Perhaps, White wrote, our friend is "needlessly worried, but we are certain he is typical: millions must be trying to put their dead lives together for presentation to the Committee . . . Those living-room couches in the early thirties . . . Brrrr, it gives you the shivers."[13]

Certainly among the "millions" who were sifting through their own histories for some inadvertent subversion were numerous *New Yorker* readers. In a letter to White, one reader wrote: "You have the support of many thousands who, while not being writers, are fighting side by side with you in other ways." Other readers responded to *The New Yorker*'s strong position on the anti-Communist investigations in letters that expressed both their gratitude for the magazine's forthrightness and their own fear of open expression.

A newspaper editor in Oakland wrote: "Your comments in recent months represent just about the sanest approach to real Americanism we have currently seen in print." "Your editorials," Margaret Countryman wrote from Minnesota, "cheer the dreary winter . . . With each newspaper account of McCarthy and his skullduggery I reread what Mr. White has written . . . (I'm still not afraid to sign my name)." Mrs. Kent Lighty wrote from New York City to say that she hoped *The New Yorker* would continue to be guided by "the essential American principles." Describing herself as a "charter reader" of the magazine, "safely middle-aged," Mrs. Lighty wrote that "the loss would be great, and perhaps irreparable, if *The New Yorker* stopped being American in the way it has led us to expect, or got over-cautious." That, she claimed, would "make militant defenders of the faith out of the meekest of us. P.S. The letter is not submitted for publication."[14]

The identification of *New Yorker* contributors with the victims of the anti-Communist purge produced a virtual subgenre in which authors comedically put themselves in the line of the committee's fire. Often, a contributor would describe some utterly innocent incident from his own past, which could, in the current climate of fear and distrust, easily place him under suspicion. Stylistically, the magazine's come-and-get-me counteroffensives against HUAC resembled nothing so much as a daring child sticking his tongue out at a big stupid bully, while in the protective presence of an older brother. There was a peculiarly conjoined sense in these pieces of a community that saw itself both maligned by boorish clods and rendered unassailable by virtue.

Perhaps the crowning example of this approach was "Afternoon of an American Boy," in which E. B. White, who had grown up in Mt. Vernon, New York, on the same block as J. Parnell Thomas (the Chair of the House Investigating Committee) recalled escorting Thomas's little sister, Eileen, with whom he was infatuated, to a tea dance at the Plaza Hotel. This was an excruciating experience for the fourteen-year-old White, who was extremely shy and did not know how to dance. He was, he explained, terrified of girls and had none of the "peculiar gifts" that girls seemed to look for in their male companions: the capacity to "dance, play football, to cut up a bit in public, to smoke, and to make small talk." The things he did excel at—riding his bicycle while sitting backward on the handlebars, writing poetry, and playing "selections from *Aida* on the piano"—were all, he wrote, very suspicious traits in a young fellow.

In the thirty years since that dreary, silent afternoon during which he led Eileen "onto the dance floor to execute two or three unspeakable rounds," he had often been plagued by guilt over the "mental and physical torture" he had forced her to endure. Now, in the light of her brother Parnell's investigation of writers, White recollects the incident with mock stark terror. He even imagines himself being questioned by Thomas:

Parnell: Have you ever written for the screen, Mr. White?
Me: No, Sir.

Parnell: Have you ever been, or are you now, a member of the
  Communist Party?
Me: No, Sir.

Parnell: Do you recall an afternoon . . . when you took my sister
  to the Plaza Hotel for tea under the grossly misleading and
  false pretext that you knew how to dance?

White wonders if the incident "stacks up as a sort of unintentional
un-American activity." Ultimately, he decides that the event was highly
American—just a boyish "journey into ineptitude, in that precious,
brief moment in life before love's pages, through constant reference"
become worn, and before "its narrative through sheer competence" has
lost something of its "first, wild sense of derring-do."[15]

The structure of "Afternoon of an American Boy," in which the
sweet detritus of a personal history was reconsidered in the harsh light
of anti-Communist paranoia, became a formula for the magazine's
assaults on the investigations. In "Noontime of an Advertising Man,"
for example, White recollected his friendship with Whittaker Chambers's father, Jay, whom he met when they were both unhappily employed at an adverting agency. White remembered the senior Chambers
as a sweet, middle-aged man, a talented artist who hated advertising.
The senior Chambers spent his spare time building tiny model houses
out of matchboxes, and often worked as an usher at the Metropolitan
Opera House during his lunch hour, a harmless truancy in which White
often joined him. Was this, White wondered, now to be viewed as a
"sort of innocent subversive activity?" It was not, White insisted, that he
wanted to "overthrow the world of advertising," but he did "long to slip
quietly away from it" for an hour or two, and he still felt enormous
gratitude to the elder Chambers "for those noontimes when he showed
me how it could be done."

Many other *New Yorker* writers followed White's lead and feigned
membership in the ranks of the inquests' victims. Albert Hubbell wrote
about an afternoon in 1937 when he was strolling around Columbus
Circle, happened to run into a group of Italian anti-Fascist anarchists,

and agreed to have his picture taken with them. C. H. Michaels described an incident in which some university professors, innocently involved in an amateur theatrical production, found themselves enmeshed in an alleged Communist plot. In "A Glass of Fashion," James Thurber, referring to this period as an "era of suspicion," concluded snidely that it was "a wise citizen who disproves any dark rumors and reports of his secret thoughts and actions before they can be twisted into charges of disloyalty by the alert and skillful minds now dedicated to that high minded and patriotic practice." It was for this reason that Thurber wished to dispel the vicious rumors that *Women's Wear Daily* was circulating about him, which suggested that he was "hand in glove (and a fetching arrangement it makes, too) with some of the most important figures in the fashion industry who lunch at the Algonquin." In his "Reflections on a Subversive Past," E. J. Kahn, Jr. described with comic alarm the intentions of HUAC to investigate the National Council of American-Soviet Friendship, revealing that such an inquiry would ultimately implicate "such alumni of the American armed forces as a certain White Russian of princely heritage, General Eisenhower, and me."[16]

In "The Greenwich Tea Party," Kahn identified himself with two victims of the anti-Communist purge, Larry Adler and Paul Draper, frankly describing the pair as "friends of mine." In a lengthy footnote to the piece, Kahn explained that his friends, one a dancer, the other a musician, were placed under investigation because they had performed at a Henry Wallace presidential rally. Although Kahn claimed to find the "political behavior of Wallace supporters nonsensical," he added that he has "a high regard for the right of an American to be as nonsensical as he damn pleases."[17]

The extent to which members of the *New Yorker* community identified with the investigation's victims was perhaps most powerfully expressed by Daniel Lang in his lengthy profile of William W. Remington, a Department of Commerce economist, who in 1948 was accused of being a Communist. Although Remington was eventually vindicated, given his back pay, and reinstated in the Commerce Department, Lang's nightmarish description of one man's season in Hell was a tale in which an upstanding citizen was reduced to poverty and despair by the malign force of the state. Remington's experience seemed to have a great deal in common with the horrific accounts of repressive totalitarian regimes which had become so popular in the American press.[18]

This was a cautionary tale, proof that at any time the inhumane apparatus of government inquisition could swoop down upon even a model citizen. According to Lang, the facts of Remington's biography, so reminiscent of Hiss's, suggested that he was just such an exemplary character. He was thirty-one-years old, "blond and blue-eyed," and "handsome enough to be a movie star." His manner was "intellectual, earnest, and reflective." His father was an insurance executive and his mother was an art teacher at a New York City school. He had put himself through Dartmouth and had been first in his class. During the Depression Remington had worked for the Tennessee Valley Authority and later was with the O.P.A. and the National Resources Planning Board. He had a Master's degree in Economics from Columbia, and had served as an ensign in the Navy during the war. Remington had met his accuser, Elizabeth Bentley (a self-confessed spy for the Soviet Union) under her assumed name, Helen Johnson, at his mother-in-law's house. His own politics were moderate. A friend of his, a psychologist for the Department of National Defense, testified on his behalf, describing Remington's politics as "the sober and middle-of-the-road kind that would be about as welcome to Communists" as "a case of measles to a nursery school."[19]

At the core of Lang's piece is a sense of a world turned on its head—a world in which bureaucratic and intellectual elites were unjustly expelled from the corridors of power and made into outsiders. Remington described this transformation poignantly. When his pay was suspended, he was forced to occupy one tiny room into which he crammed all of the furniture from his former home because he could not afford to store it. He lived on canned beans and bread. Remington described a moment of epiphany during this grim period in which he was waiting for a bus and a Negro acquaintance, whom he had known as a messenger at the

War Production Board, stopped and offered him a ride in his "beat-up jalopy." Remington recalled being confused by the offer because Washington was "a Southern town for Negroes. They don't often issue invitations to whites here." Both touched and depressed by the man's kindness, Remington understood that the offer was made only because the Negro "recognized" him as "a fellow out-cast."[20]

In the *New Yorker* village, the Communist-hunters were always the moral and intellectual inferiors of their prey. Ambitious vulgarians such as Richard Nixon and Joseph McCarthy were targets of the magazine's unbridled contempt. From a perspective of absolute intellectual superiority, *New Yorker* contributors assailed these middle-class opportunists for their disrespect of democracy, but the magazine's weapons of choice came from a profoundly undemocratic arsenal: the enemies were illogical, they used bad grammar, they couldn't spell or capitalize, and they displayed an unsavory hunger for power.

In a piece that directly tackled the small-mindedness and opportunism of the inquisitors, E. B. White argued that they posed a real threat to democracy, which he described as a "pesky" construct that "always hangs by a thread." The fragility of the democratic thread was especially troubling "to men of tidy habits and large affairs." They transformed activities that were once understood to be signs of civic virtue into proofs of subversion. No one who ever signed a peace treaty, or donated money to the Spanish Civil War or the Wobblies could feel entirely secure.[21]

Writing derisively of the Mundt-Nixon Bill, a proposed law demanding that Communist political organizations register with the Attorney General as officially subversive, E. B. White exclaimed: "To define Communism as wicked in a legal preamble and then ask Communists to report to the keeper of the wicked is like addressing an audience and saying 'All heels and jerks will now rise and give their names to the usher.'" Another dubious aspect of the Mundt-Nixon Bill, according to White, was Section 4, which would make illegal any act that had as its intention the "establishment in the United States of a totalitarian dictatorship under foreign control." White characterized this proposal as "frantic"—the equivalent of "making it illegal for babies to swallow buttons." The thing that most disturbed White about the bill was that it represented a genuine threat to the freedom of the press. Anyone "who writes a paragraph or two against the Mundt-Nixon Bill is engaging in the sort of activity the bill is designed to supervise."

The "Talk of the Town" enjoyed mocking the anti-Communist right. There was, for example, the story of an Atomic Energy Commission scientist who answered a summons to appear before HUAC, and was summarily exonerated by the Committee. He then received a government check reimbursing him for his travel expenses along with a note which read: "Inclosed [sic] please find check on United States Treasurer, payable to your order, being the amount due you from this office on account of Un-American Activities." Another item recounted the adventure of a British UNESCO agent who, upon his arrival at La Guardia airport, was asked by an immigration official if he "planned to engage in any un-American activities while here." A businessman recently "mustered into government service" requested a safe for top-secret documents. His request was denied, and he was informed that until he had "been proved loyal to the United States," he would simply have to keep his secret documents in an open file.[22]

Frank Sullivan's comic essay, "These Are the Trials That Try Men's Souls," satirized both the underlying idiocy and the confusing minutiae of the spy trials. Hilariously, Sullivan scrambled the mind-numbing details of the various trials: "Now, it was after J. Edgar Hoover and the F.B.I. called the Army unemployable that John Gates called United States Attorney John F. X. McGohey a kangaroo. No, he didn't call him a kangaroo. It was a court that Gates called a kangaroo."[23]

General witlessness was also the grounds upon which the magazine assailed Hollywood's responses to the HUAC investigations. Here the magazine's traditional disdain for all of Southern California and the movie people—the crass grasping at the vulgar—was fused with its contempt for the Committee. Lillian Ross, who had excoriated Hollywood in her book-length "Picture," published in the magazine in 1947, continued her attack on the moral vapidity of Tinsel Town in "Come in

Lassie," a piece that focused on the effect of the anti-Communist purge in a place where it was "possible to take an impregnable position on both sides of any controversy," and where party guests were "chosen from lists based on their weekly income brackets." According to Ross, Hollywood was also a community in which it was rumored that the F.B.I. was about "to take over casting operations at the studios," and having been a guest at the Roosevelt White House was "one of the few criteria for judging whether a person is or is not a Communist."[24]

Fear was running strong in movieland, Ross reported, especially since the Motion Picture Association of America had published and distributed its "Screen Guide for Americans," which put forward such tenets as: "'Don't Smear the Free Enterprise System,' 'Don't Deify the Common Man,' and 'Don't Glorify the Collective.'" Ross found that actors, writers, and directors were caving in under pressure from the Committee and capitulating to its restrictions on film content. She also noted that many actors had become fearful of portraying certain kinds of characters, "say, a legendary hero who stole from the rich to give to the poor, or an honest, crusading district attorney, or a lonely, poetic, antisocial gangster." One actor told Ross that he could no longer afford to have moviegoers think of him as a crusader. Heroism itself was seen as subversive in purge-conscious Hollywood. In fact, Ross wrote, the only movie star that is working steadily is Lassie, "a reddish-haired male collie, who is probably too mixed up emotionally over being called by a girl's name to worry about the box-office" or politics. An M-G-M executive told Ross that if it weren't for Lassie, his studio would be in serious financial trouble. "We like Lassie. We're sure of Lassie . . . Katherine Hepburn goes out and makes a speech for Henry Wallace. Bang! We're in trouble. Lassie doesn't make speeches. Not Lassie, thank God." Offering a pointed example of the way the Red Scare had influenced film content, the executive explained that Lassie's most current film had originally been about a country doctor who hated dogs, "but a part has been written for Lassie, the plot has been changed, and the picture is to be called 'Master of Lassie.'"[25]

Hollywood's inability to stand up to the Committee was the subject of a number of E. B. White's jeremiads. He chastised the film community for endorsing the loyalty check and admonished Hollywood to make up for its cowardice by offering America "a great picture," a film that was "conceived in faith and not seasoned to the taste of any man except the man who produces it." According to White, the public en-masse firing of the Hollywood Ten "set a precedent for the American purge" and caused "every pen, every typewriter" to reel under its blow. Citing Hollywood's lack of moral fibre and intellectual rigor, White argued that the movie industry handled the loyalty theme "the way it has handled most great themes," by essentially missing the point and "perverting its meaning." "What is loyalty?" White asked rhetorically, and then answered his own question, by citing the *dis*loyalty of Hollywood to artistic integrity. Turning the Committee's definition of loyalty on its head, White argued that "[i]f it is American to aim high and to respect one's own intelligence, then ninety-nine percent of Hollywood films are un-American." Certainly it was un-American, he said, to devalue the creative spirit in favor of "the accommodating spirit."[26]

Unlike many other people in positions of power, *The New Yorker*'s editors and contributors refused to accommodate the anti-Communist right at a time when this kind of refusal was widely regarded as an act of subversion. They held out against the tide, in their own way. Readers who combed through their own histories, fearful that they had once joined a questionable organization, "entertained a bubbly thought (or a second cousin at dinner)" or wore "a hat backward" could find succor in *The New Yorker,* which, in the words of one reader, had "the support of many thousands," and the distinction of being "one of the few magazines which, in this period of crisis is hitting back for democracy."[27]

In a paragraph that came as close to a overt statement of political policy as the magazine had ever made, White wrote:

We on this magazine believe in the principle of hiring and firing on the basis of fitness . . . we also believe that some of the firings in this country in the last eighteen months have resembled a political purge . . . and we think this is bad for everybody . . . In-directly, [this] abets Communism by making millions of highly fit Americans a little cautious, a little fearful of having naughty 'thoughts,' a little fearful of believing differently from the next man."[28]

In this magazine, those were fighting words.

SLOUCHING TOWARD ANTI-COMMUNISM

With the onset of the Korean War, *The New Yorker* moved from stout resistance against the anti-Communist warriors to a lukewarm acceptance of the assumptions of Cold War foreign policy, a shift similar to that undertaken by many American liberals in the postwar years. Thus the magazine's change of heart was symptomatic of a larger intellectual transformation within the liberal community concerning the underlying mission of American democracy. The change was about the concept of national virtue and with it the shape of democratic idealism: from a largely antinationalistic liberalism that had concerned itself with internal injustices in the United States, to a kind of progressive imperialism in which the United States was seen as an intrinsically just, ideal democracy—a model for the larger world to emulate.

After World War II, Americans were exposed to two competing blueprints for the shape of the political landscape. The first, a nationalist scenario, was promulgated by much of the conservative and moderate press as well as the federal government. This narrative was a Manichean construction in which the evil Soviet Union competed with the good United States for control over the hearts and minds of the world's population. In the second version of postwar reality, nationalism was seen as a fatal game, and mankind's only hope resided in the kind of globalism represented by the fledgling United Nations. This was the version of reality behind which the *New Yorker* editors had thrown their considerable weight immediately after the war.

For many mid-century liberal intellectuals, the fear of nuclear holocaust cast a shadow over the dream of world federation. *The New Yorker's* E. B. White took his stand at the center of the array of "permissible" liberal convictions concerning the postwar world. White, who clearly saw himself as one of many "free men who don't think the liberal's work is done," claimed that liberalism had given the republic both "its benign inconsistency" and "its indisputable grace," and wrote that the liberal ardently welcomes "the fact of the journey, as a dog greets a man's invitation to take a walk." Also like the dog, the liberal "leaves a crazy trail," "racing ahead, doubling back, covering many miles of territory" that his owner will never see, "all in the spirit of inquiry." Carrying his dog analogy a bit further, White added that when master and dog return home exhausted, "it is the liberal—the wide ranging dog—who is covered with burdocks and with information of a special sort." This goodnatured liberal dog is not effective as a political strategist, because he "never feels he knows where the truth lies, but is full of rich memories of places he has glimpsed it."[1]

White left us a "crazy trail" of his own concerning postwar politics. He deplored the paranoia that fueled the hunt for domestic Communists. He tried to promote détente between the U.S. and the U.S.S.R. by depicting the superpowers as only superficially different. He seemed both to decry nationalism and to accept as natural the idea that the United States had a moral mission to lead the world. He hated war, loved peace, and longed to be a citizen of a federated world. He had hailed the arrival of the United Nations, brooded over its potential failure, and eventually found a way to square its initial intentions with its role in Korea. While he displayed contempt for the hawkish General Douglas MacArthur, he came with some reluctance to the conclusion that the Soviet Union was, in fact, to blame for shattering the dream of worldwide peace.[2]

Immediately after the end of World War II, *The New Yorker* spurned the road leading toward the national security state and led its readers instead along the rocky route to world federation. White and other contributors contended that peaceful coexistence with Russia was the order of the day and that nationalism, in a nuclear age, was a lethal option. Most of the magazine's efforts at countering the idea of the inevitability of ideological conflict between the United States and the Soviet Union relied upon universalist tactics in which readers were asked to accept that the United States and the Soviet Union shared certain fundamental human goals—the desire for peace, prosperity, and personal happiness—and were simply two halves of a coin minted by the quest for global domination. For several years after the war, *The New Yorker* published light-hearted "Notes" and "Talk of the Town" pieces full of "nyet" jokes and caricatures of the Russians as bull-headed, fur-hatted blowhards who claimed to have invented absolutely everything. Assuming a voice of frisky neutrality, *New Yorker* writers poked delicately at the Iron Curtain and suggested that the United States and the Soviet Union, although at odds, were equals in general silliness.

A 1947 "Notes and Comment," for example, saw recent developments in beekeeping in the USSR and the United States as metaphors for the differences between the two super powers. In Russia, Eugene V. Arafev had been awarded the Stalin Prize for "speeding up honey production by the artificial insemination of queen bees," and for the discovery that "bees can exist in a hive without ventilation." In California, on the other hand, C. Close had applied for a patent for producing honey in "six delicious flavors and colors—strawberry, maple, chocolate, lemon, pineapple, and mint." This was archetypal *New Yorker* anti-anti-Communism, designed to flatten out ideological distinctions between the superpowers by making them into national idiosyncracies on a par with wearing kilts or living in yurts. By characterizing the differences between the United States and the Soviet Union as national quirks, *The New Yorker* was able to guide its readers through a public discourse in which the enmity between the two systems was an inevitable part of postwar reality.[3]

Writing in 1948, White explained that the chief conflict between Russia and the West "is in the emphasis each places on responsibility." Socialism takes responsibility for the use and distribution of resources, and that may lead "(as it has in Russia)" to the management of "everything, including the citizen's private life, his thoughts, his arts, his science." Democratic capitalism, on the other hand, takes responsibility for "guarding civil liberties and is notably cavalier about private concentrations of economic power." These differences fueled the antagonism between the two systems, each growing daily more "ambitious and fearful, largely because of the presence of the other." White concluded that the debate about responsibility seemed about to erupt into "a mess that, for utter irresponsibility, would make the gaudiest robber barons of capitalism and the most ruthless tyrants of Communism look like pikers."[4]

In order for Soviets and Americans to acquire an "insight into the other's culture and folkways," White suggested that it might be a good idea to hold the Democratic Convention in Belgrade and Tito's Party Congress in Philadelphia. In this way the Yugoslavs could, for example, "study the monumental platitudes of a keynote speech" and learn that after the shouting is all over, the victor must "still subject himself to the disagreeable uncertainties of a popular election." "We," on the other hand, could observe Communists in the act of "throwing the book of Lenin at each other," and could witness how the "fervor of the crowd follows the political whims of the head of the police."[5]

Decrying the intensification of the Cold War, and blaming each of the super powers equally for its escalation, White wrote in his most melancholy trope that the United States had developed a warplane that holds a "baby plane" in its belly, and that Russia had built a new artificial arm that was so efficient that a wounded veteran could "use a machine gun again." Out of these new inventions, he announced sadly, "emerges the pattern of a new war, the perfect demonstration of war's fecundity: a flying machine ... giving birth to an infant plane in air, and the young plane shot at by men whose arms were lost in other wars ... but who fight on mechanically, confident that if they are hit in the arm no blood will come."[6]

However, by the end of the 1940s, journalists found it more and more difficult to tease the two superpowers for their quirks and gently chide them for their hubris. The path of peaceful coexistence was increasingly littered with bodies. In 1948, when one-worlder Henry Wallace ran for president on the Progressive party ticket, he received less than three percent of the vote. By 1950, Alger Hiss had been convicted of perjury, and Klaus Fuchs, a German-born nuclear physicist who had worked on the atom bomb at Los Alamos in 1944, had been arrested by British officials and accused of passing atomic secrets to the Soviets. America's nuclear monopoly was at an end, and Americans of all political stripes had witnessed the erection of the Berlin Wall, the fall of China to the Communists, and the Soviet style of administering its spheres of influence. One-worlders began to seem rather *other*-worldly as the small minority of Americans who had resisted the Cold War scenario became even smaller. The voices of those who opposed a monolithic *Pax Americana* grew increasingly faint, and *The New Yorker,* along with many other moderate publications and individuals, reconsidered its course.[7]

Many of those who eventually enlisted in the ranks of the liberal anti-Communist consensus had once been firmly rooted in the Left. In 1932, for example, large numbers of American intellectuals and artists, among them Richard Wright, Edmund Wilson, and Ernest Hemingway, had endorsed the Communist party's presidential candidate. By 1954, when the CP was outlawed in the United States, it was difficult to find a credible intellectual willing to challenge this interdiction. The sway of the anti-Communist consensus was enormous, stretching from Americans for Democratic Action all the way into the corporate hierarchy.[8]

Many *New Yorker* writers in this period joined this consensus, demonstrating an allegiance to a belief system that supported competitive individualism in social life, private property in economic life, and the right to have rights in political life. Certainly by the beginning of the Korean War, the Soviet project increasingly seemed inimical to these beliefs, and *The New Yorker* found itself resting in the ample lap of liberal anti-Communism. And so, by the early fifties, the magazine's approach to the Cold War had shifted toward the notion that Communism was indeed a threat to the United States but was not a threat in the United States. Anti-Communism was strictly an export good.[9]

In fact, *The New Yorker*'s brand of anti-Communism and its prevailing attitude toward the role of the United Nations in Korea were of a piece with the brand of global meliorism that was the credo of many members of the foreign policy establishment, like Adlai Stevenson, George Kennan, Chester Bowles, and Averell Harriman. These men saw themselves as displaying "pragmatic wisdom, avoiding ideology, and steering the middle course between the ignorant yahoos of the Right and the impractical sentimentality of the Left." The convictions of these experts concerning the United Nations bore a resemblance to the religious beliefs of the not-very-devout. They prayed (in a pinch) and went to church on Sundays, but ultimately took matters in their own hands. These proponents of American exceptionalism expressed confidence in the U.N. while continuing to believe that it was the duty of the United States to take up the mantle of moral world leadership that had once been worn by Britain.[10]

Like these defense intellectuals, *New Yorker* contributors wished to distance themselves from the anti-Communist paranoia that was the peculiar provenance of the right wing. They often invoked the sharp distinction between the liberal and the illiberal versions of anti-Communism. The illiberal variant was visceral rather than ideological, characterizing Communism as a kind of overriding evil that defied reasoned argument or intellectual debate. This "better dead than red" form of anti-Communism was not a logical reaction to serious foreign policy dilemmas, but was rather a primitive organizing principle—a way to understand the entire political and moral world.[11]

The liberal construction of anti-Communism, on the other hand, was more of a series of ad hoc responses to events than an overarching belief system. This would be the kind of liberalism that E. B. White described as the ramblings of a dog, a creature that roams far and wide in search of truth, never claims to have found it, and subscribes to no orthodoxy. The liberal dog was not an ideologue.

What is perhaps most striking about *The New Yorker*'s drift toward anti-Communism is not that it happened, but how long it took. Even after the Korean War, when historical changes sent the magazine along the path of anti-Communism, it displayed no particular fondness for it. The magazine's anti-Communist voice lacked the vociferous energy of either the Right or of the disenchanted former leftists who had railed against the "God That Failed." But as *New Yorker* contributors started to underwrite the rhetoric of intelligent anti-Communism, snippets of a broader Cold War rhetoric began to make their appearance in the magazine. More and more frequent references were made to the Iron Curtain; the phrase "free world" crept into the magazine's political vocabulary; and portrayals of Russians as globally ambitious, ill-mannered liars became commonplace. While *The New Yorker* continued vigorously to oppose jingoistic nationalism and scorned the domestic search for spies, by the end of the Korean War it had joined a growing liberal-conservative consensus that reached its peak in the late 1950s.[12]

One of the shared assumptions of this national consensus was a dread of Communist totalitarianism. By the early fifties, many members of the information bureaucracy had begun to describe Soviet Communism as a Marxist-Leninist version of Nazi Germany. This fusion was consolidated in the concept of Red fascism. In this scenario, any system with an internally consistent world view risked political fanaticism and hence totalitarianism. By the beginning of the 1950s, the central assumptions of Red fascism were increasingly supported by dispatches coming out of the Soviet satellite countries about the terrors of life under Soviet rule. This equation was compelling for several reasons, one of which was that it appropriated the language and emotion of anti-Nazi sentiment. The invocation of Red fascism also served to minimize the weaknesses of American democracy, which were dwarfed by the genuine horrors of totalitarianism.[13]

During the early postwar years, *The New Yorker*'s "Letters" from Europe had contained very little Cold War rhetoric, and had matter-of-factly reported the rise of Socialist and Communist parties in Italy, France, and England as historical events that intelligent readers would want to follow. In dispatches from Rome, Vienna, and Germany, *New Yorker* reporters described, for example, the Trotskyite leanings of Italian Communists and wrote about Russian refugee camps. Andy Logan, writing from Vienna, claimed that relations between members of various occupying armies had a "cousinly air": "[A] barroom brawl between a G.I., say and a Russian private, each under twenty and newly arrived in Austria from his respective Georgia, is still treated as a barroom brawl rather than as an occasion for tank maneuvers."[14]

By 1950, however, many of the letters from abroad contained remarks disparaging Soviet and European Communists. In a 1951 "Letter from Paris," Janet Flanner (writing under her pen name, Genet) discussed a recent French election won by the Communists, explaining that "the thing they [the Communists] wanted most was to see France turned—by votes, if necessary—into a Soviet Satellite." The following year, Flanner quoted the leader of the Communist riots in Paris, as he was manacled and led off to jail: "There's your bourgeois democracy, Messieurs! Admire it!" Genet commented tartly that "As it happens, there was much to admire in democracy at that moment: although arrested on a charge of plotting against the internal safety of the state, [the leader] had just been permitted by the police, to consult his lawyer without eavesdroppers, rather more than his Soviet Democracy might have offered him in Moscow had he been caught leading an anti-Stalinist riot." Decrying the monolithic nature of Communist thought, Flanner also criticized the World Congress of Partisans of Peace, featuring such Communist luminaries as W. E. B. Du Bois, Pablo Picasso, and Paul Robeson, as inflammatory and anti-American.[15]

During the same period, Joseph Wechsberg, who had been born in Czechoslovakia, was writing "Letters" from Eastern Europe that were compelling accounts of the grimness of life lived under the Soviets. In his opinion, citizens in these countries exchanged the terror of Nazi hegemony for the terror of life under the regime of their Soviet "liberators." In "Howling with the Wolves," Wechsberg wrote that in order to maintain a modicum of comfort and privilege, middle-class Czechs had found it necessary to join the Communist party. "You've got to howl with the wolves or they will devour you," Janda, one of Wechsberg's childhood friends, told him. To resist joining the Party was to sacrifice one's middle-class status. "Party members get jobs, vacations, seats at the opera." Middle-class people who refused to join the Party were "proletarianized into the new working class"—a class "that has only duties and no privileges." A case in point was Dr. M., a lawyer who had once "spent every Spring in Monte Carlo," and had refused to join the Party. "They came for him at dawn," Janda said, and he was undoubtedly sent to a labor-and-correction camp where he would be transformed into a model citizen of a "Marxian Society," proletarianized and made ready to work in a factory. Wechsberg delineated a world in which middle-class cosmopolitans were forced to exchange their political principles for scraps of privilege, and schoolchildren studied Russian grammars and denounced their own parents as reactionaries. This particular account, in which bourgeois Eastern Europeans lived under the threat of proletarianization, might have had especially nightmarish overtones for those *New Yorker* readers who had feared the oppressive intrusion of the government into their private lives during the HUAC investigations.[16]

While a dawning awareness of the emiseration of life under Soviet rule certainly played a major role in modifying *The New Yorker*'s political path, it was the Korean War that ultimately rerouted it. The magazine had welcomed the United Nations to Turtle Bay with great fanfare. Early pieces about the peacekeeping institution were optimistic, though they cautioned against the intrusion of nationalism into the utopian globalism of the U.N. experiment. At the beginning of 1946, E. B. White had issued a series of instructions to U.N. delegates, suggesting that they avoid being mere instruments of their own nations' foreign policies ("domestic policy with its hat on") and reminding them that they were gathered together only in order to "make common cause" in order to "save the world." In a similar vein, a 1947 Jessamyn West poem compared the political and geographical limits imposed upon U.N. delegates by their national origins with the unfettered purity of birds. Being "pure democracy . . . / He sings no anthem but his own. No craft but bird / by him is flown."[17]

A year after its inception, the U.N. looked far less hopeful. On the occasion of the organization's first birthday, E. B. White wished it "many happy returns" and listed some of the major problems the youthful institution had taken on during its first year. The delegates had "recommended that genocide be outlawed, armaments be reduced, troops be counted, atomic energy be controlled, culture be exchanged, Franco be unseated, children be fed . . . and a universal bill of rights be drawn." While White praised the United Nations for its willingness to set lofty goals for itself, he also expressed grave doubts about its ability to achieve them, comparing the U.N. to a one-year-old child who had succeeded in pulling down "every book from the bottom shelf in the living room" and was "sitting among them in happy confusion, shoving them about and vaguely conscious of some personal inadequacy somewhere."[18]

Along with policy makers and most other news media, *The New Yorker* regarded the Korean War as a critical turning point in the history of the United Nations. Some members of the *New Yorker* community lost their early hopes about the organization. The U.N. Police Action in Asia turned their anxious optimism into disappointment, after they realized that the international peacekeeping body had been coopted by the exigencies of U.S. foreign policy. Others, like White, found a way to reconcile the U.N. military presence in Korea with its role as an instrument of international peace. The notion that continuation of the United Nations depended on its willingness to act in Korea—to perform the "duty of government without at all possessing the shape and characteristic of government," was a frequent refrain of *New Yorker* editorials concerning the Korean War.

Many of the editorial pieces about the U.N. role in the Korean War conflated the United States and the United Nations and charged this entity with the exceptionalist responsibility of leading the world out of the darkness and into the light. White, for example, argued that Korea was "the perfect testing ground for brave new techniques and brave new intentions," and that failure to give Korea "the full treatment" would mean that the U.N. was "passing up the finest chance it has had." In a moment of hyperbole, he explained that the Korean crisis offered the U.N. an opportunity to "prove that freedom and civil liberties and modern science have a direct relationship to private health, individual well-being, public education, and soil fertility." Its efforts, he continued, "should not stop until the roofs no longer leak, and until the sick children are the well children."

A 1950 "Notes and Comment" expressed White's effervescent faith in the United Nations' efforts in Korea. Commenting on a "pivotal" address to the U.N. General Assembly by Truman's Secretary of State, Dean Acheson, the editor claimed the speech offered hope to those who had, since 1945, endured the rising and falling fortunes of the United Nations. As Acheson put it, "The world waits to see whether we can build on the start we have made," and the "place to begin . . . is Korea." Wrote White: "We think it is the place to begin, all right . . . Korea should be made to bloom like the rose. It should be restored until it makes the Tennessee Valley look like Tobacco Road." By doing this, the U.N. would "not only recreate a demoralized nation"; it would "recreate itself." Although Korea's benefactor was allegedly the United Nations and not the United States, White's statement contained a strong current of national pride. America, he seemed to be arguing, no longer needed to focus its apparently boundless ameliorative energies on domestic problems. We were now in a position to turn our hand to recreating "demoralized nation[s]." This was an expression of American exceptionalism, only slightly obscured by White's invocation of the United Nations. We had successfully transformed the Tennessee Valley, and now we had the capacity to transform the world.[19]

In order to tell the story of the military intervention in Korea as a bona fide international effort toward world peace, it was necessary to dispel the "myth" that the U.N. Complaint of Aggression Against the Republic of Korea and the ensuing "police action" had made the United Nations into an instrument of American foreign policy. White, for example, contended that Acheson's U.N. speech was far more than a diplomatic exercise. It was a "solid, detailed indication that national policy from now on is impotent unless it contains the fertilizing agent for world policy, unless it is a sperm entering the world's egg." In this way, White managed a seamless metaphoric segue from his support of world federation to his support of the Korean War. He achieved this magical collocation by claiming that world federation depended upon world peace and that the only hope for world peace was an international peacekeeping body such as the United Nations. White's affinity for wishful metaphor, his sheer writerly deftness, allowed him to make convincing arguments out of what may well have been huge leaps in logic. In fact, in contending that our national policy was now sterile unless it was impregnated with a larger "world policy," White was wrapping U.S. nationalism in the U.N. flag and thereby offering readers an argument for a progressive version of American imperialism.

Phillip Hamburger, who was, among other things, the magazine's first television critic, supported White's notion that the United Nations' involvement in Korea was a matter of life or death, both for the credibility of the institution and for world peace. In an essay that offered a step-by-step chronology of U.N. involvement, Hamburger wrote that before July 1951, many old U.N. hands "privately felt that the organization was, if not actually moribund, at least in an oxygen tent." The same expert witnesses noted that it had taken "a shooting war some seven thousand miles to the west to bring the patient hopping out of bed, within twenty-four hours, almost as good as new." Arguing that the organization acted "with a keen consciousness of its overarching duty" to its peaceful member nations, Hamburger dismissed the idea that the U.N. had moved precipitously in Korea without first gathering adequate information, and denied that it had allowed itself to "become a tool of the United States State Department."[20]

According to Hamburger and White, the United Nations' very existence depended upon its ability to act swiftly and decisively in Korea. The "police action" fought under the U.N. flag in Asia was the last best hope for world federation of any kind. And "this business" in Korea was "not exactly a war, no matter how bloody it looks to the naked eye." Explaining that a soldier in Korea "is not one man but two," White illuminated the divided allegiances of these servicemen. On the one hand, he explained, they were engaged in "the first police action ever attempted under a universal banner," and constrained by "all the restrictions that go with a cop's duty." On the other hand, these "double-barrelled" soldiers were participants in the "power struggle between nationals— between the United States and Red China, between East and West, between Communism and free democracy." Distinguishing between the "quick victory" of war and the "slow, tough, gradual victory" of a police action, White reminded his readers that "a policeman's lot is not a happy one," largely because in his "unhappy world, there is no substitute for patience." Even when a "cop is beating a rioter over the head," his primary purpose was not to win a victory for the police department, but to "restore order" to his community.[21]

White, though he sometimes seemed an apologist for the Korean venture, regretted most of all the necessity for that intervention and wished that nonbelligerent world cooperation had prevailed. Although he had once divided the responsibility for the Cold War equally between the United States and the Soviet Union, he now blamed the collapse of hopes for world government on Russia's "private attempt to set up a cozy world government of its own along Communist-Fascist lines." Sadly, collective security seemed to be "our best . . . and only bet" for world peace. Comparing the Korean war to a bulldozer that raises "a lot of local hell" when it is brought in to dig a foundation, White characterized the rout in Korea as a necessary and temporary evil. What worried White the most about collective security was that it was "the security of arms meeting arms," and that it used force to "make good a majority decision of independent nations." This was fine, he argued, as long as it worked in the service of free nations (as it did in Korea), "but it would be all wrong if it were to work to the advantage of tyrants." It is White's pieces about the Korean War, perhaps more than any of his other writing, that expose his amazing ability to use the slipperiness of language to dissolve geopolitical problems. White waves his metaphoric wand and transforms armies into cops, war into a bulldozer, and national policy into sperm for fertilizing "the world's egg."[22]

Richard Rovere, the magazine's man in Washington, in direct contrast to Hamburger and White, saw the U.N. actions in Korea as an indication that the peacekeeping body had abandoned its internationalism and become an agent of U.S. foreign policy. Rovere directly attacked the notion of a reconstituted Korea as an example of hegemonic utopianism. Writing in February of 1951, he pointed out that the dream "that Korea could be made over into a model community on the borders of the Communist world" was little more than the "unfortunate fantasy of a nation bewitched by hygiene, civil engineering, and democratic dogmas."[23]

Commenting on a vote in the General Assembly on an American resolution to censor the Chinese Communists' intervention in Korea as "unprovoked and unpardonable aggression," Rovere offered his interpretation of a once idealistic institution compromised by America's economic clout. "Yesterday's vote," Rovere explained, is a "tribute not to the vigor of our diplomacy or to its moral soundness but to the goodies our industries provide and to the realization that while it may be hard at times to get along with the United States, it would be even harder to get along without her." Rovere, more than any other *New Yorker* writer, was consistently critical of the way the United States delegation used its economic power to dominate the United Nations and make U.S. national policy into international policy. "A half hour in the broadloomed, alcohol-scented Tower of Babel called the Delegates Lounge" gave Rovere a "distressing conviction that most of the civilized world felt American intransigence to be of the very same stuff as Communist intransigence."[24]

The coexistence of Rovere's dissonant voice with White's metaphorical comments and Hamburger's restrained exegesis reflects not only the capacity of the magazine to present an array of positions, but also mirrors ruptures in the liberal community itself—a confused and unruly dog bounding uncertainly toward Cold War consensus. If, in fact, Richard Rovere's argument that the United Nations had become little more than an instrument of U.S. foreign policy was true, then White's occasionally rhapsodic acceptance of its goals was exposed, in his own forum, as a version of the very nationalism he had long shunned. It is worth noting, however, that the utopian anti-Communism of "Notes and Comment," with its optimistic view of America's global mission, ran in the front of the magazine and was tacitly understood to be *The New Yorker*'s editorial voice, while the more critical, analytical discussions of the crisis tended to appear in the back of the book, buried amidst advertisements for ski holidays and tinned paté. Yet the persistent presence of Rovere's dissenting position does put into question the wholeheartedness of *The New Yorker*'s endorsement of the Korean War. While the magazine made a place in its pages for a temperate variant of Cold War vernacular and accepted involvement in Korea as a necessary price to pay for world peace, the magazine's contributors were careful to reserve their approval for the war only as a United Nations "police action," and balked at the demands for escalation issued from the camp of General Douglas Mac-Arthur and his champions.

President Truman's firing of the insubordinate General MacArthur in April of 1951 was an occasion that sharply illuminated the polarization of the illiberal and liberal versions of anti-Communism across America. Billy Graham described the firing as a blow against Christianity, and Senator Joseph McCarthy called it "the greatest victory the Communists have ever won." MacArthur's interpretation of the purpose of U.S. intervention in Korea stood in direct conflict to that of most liberals, who were, along with *New Yorker* contributors, unanimous in their support of the President's decision to fire the rogue General. In the magazine's opinion, MacArthur was the personification of the nationalist warrior and the natural enemy of world peace. For White, MacArthur's belief that there was "no substitute for victory" proved that the

General saw the Korean crisis as a conventional nationalistic rout, rather than an unprecedented international peace effort. In a thoughtful decoding of the popularity of the military leader's plan for ending the Korean situation, Richard Rovere explained that MacArthur promised "victory and an eventual end to the crisis," while Truman was offering only a "sweaty, unglamorous program of caution and compromise." Rovere noted that it was quite likely that the public and the Congress would find MacArthur's "program for knocking the Chinese cold" far more appealing than Truman's "plan to negotiate a peace in some uncertain future." Although, Rovere explained, MacArthur might ultimately triumph, there were many people who "put a pretty sordid construction" on the General's insubordination, raising the possibility that MacArthur had forced Truman into the confrontation in order to "redeem the political currency" that had been "piling up in his domestic account," and improve his chances of a presidential nomination in 1952.[25]

Damning MacArthur with queer praise, E. B. White told readers that the General, who had "more personal magnetism than a baby seal," had made a speech before Congress in which he declared "that war should be outlawed." Noting that "we have been outlawing the hell out of war" for thirty years, White wrote that war was simply "not amenable to law." Peace, he added, "will not arrive through the abolition of war by independent states, it will arrive in the shape of a federation of nations." Placing himself and *The New Yorker* in flagrant opposition to MacArthur and all others who rhetorically denounced war, White declared: "This magazine takes a firm stand against outlawing war by fiat, for the same reason we are against trying to operate Madison Avenue buses by feeding them oats." White reported that when the General returned home, he announced "in a moment of natural emotion, 'The only politics I have is God bless America.'" This statement, White avowed, was an expression of an "ancient school of politics" that was nationalistic to its core. It could, he said, be translated into "God bless Poland, God bless Iran, God bless Italy," and this kind of prayer would not constitute a foundation for a peaceful world.[26]

Although the magazine generally blamed Soviet intransigence for driving otherwise peaceful (and nonexpansionist) nations to engage in the fighting in Korea, it demonstrated no real appetite for the ensuing fray. In its straight reporting about the war—"Letters" from the front, as well as casuals, short stories, and cartoons—*The New Yorker*'s overall tone was more rueful than belligerent.[27]

Christopher Rand's impressionistic 1951 "Letter from Korea" was a war piece that demonstrated the vast differences between the magazine's World War Two and Korean War reporting. In this piece Rand tried to capture the peculiar quality of a war in which the United Nations forces were fighting in the air against an earth-bound enemy. "To our people," Rand wrote, "the Reds must seem nearly as unaccountable as animals must seem to birds." The U.N. planes could "soar at will, scanning the ground for telltale signs of life." The enemy, on the other hand, "must imitate the fur bearers—going abroad by night, freezing motionless when something is overhead," and "wearing protective coloration." The front was "easy to place at night" from aloft, because it was "nearly always a grim festoon of burning villages or cottages that have been fired by our planes and artillery" on the chance that they might shelter Communist troops. Rand saw the Korean crisis as an amalgam of three separate conflicts: "misunderstandings between East and West . . . Communism and anti-Communism . . . ground and air." He claimed that this "aerialist view of ground life" had the effect of detaching fliers from the humanity of their targets. Pilots began to see Korea as a kind of "shooting gallery," and gave little thought to "the mortals broiling in the napalm below." It was, Rand argued, the "difference of elements" (earth and air) that gave rise to the detachment. "Distance lends more than enchantment to the view out here." The dirge-like tone of this report in comparison to the magazine's dispatches from World War Two showed that the world had changed, and so had *The New Yorker*.[28]

Neither the magazine's resistance to the Cold War consensus nor its eventual concessions to it were products of political orthodoxy. The magazine, liberal dog though it was, trotted alongside no one political master in the postwar period. Both its un-Communism and its later moderate anti-Communism were what *New Yorker* writers saw as even-handed journalistic representations of the truths of a changing world. This shift in the magazine's political orientation was not so much a capitulation as a reconsideration and was accomplished with a lot of foot-dragging. The innocent dream of turning in one's passport and living freely as a citizen of the world had apparently turned out to be just that—a dream. In the light of more accurate knowledge about life in the Soviet satellites and of detailed dispatches from the Korean front, to ignore Soviet totalitarianism would be to position oneself on the wrong side of history.[29]

Although the shift in *The New Yorker*'s political posture represented a genuine reappraisal of political reality, this ideological alteration also enhanced the magazine's almost alchemical ability to fuse the twin values of postwar liberalism—economic privilege and social justice. By the beginning of the 1950s, despite the postwar economic boom, the United States continued to be riven with inequities. The fact of economic discontent within the United States greatly heightened the appeal of a Cold War rhetoric in which American democracy was made exemplary through its juxtaposition with Soviet totalitarianism. Both in *The New Yorker* and in the larger culture, the ideology of anti-Communism served to camouflage the continuing presence of poverty and inequality in the United States and amplify the benevolent aspects of American style democracy. America was good, America was rich, and America had a mission to deliver democracy to the world in order to counter the repressive antidemocratic nature of Soviet Communism. The focus moved from active engagement with the problems of underprivileged or disenfranchised Americans (as had been the case during the Depression) to advertisements for the Foster Parents' Plan for War Children, which depicted hungry and maimed European war orphans like Varvara, "a twelve-year old Greek child" who lost her eye to a mortar shell; or Armandino, who lost his right arm and his entire family in a bombardment, and who promises his foster parents that he "shall try to be a good child." For fifteen dollars a month, *New Yorker* readers could demonstrate an active engagement with the problems of the larger world. Considered from a vantage point in which a missionary America was rendered utopian by comparison with Soviet totalitarianism, it seemed possible to be both privileged and truly democratic, a state of being that was particularly compelling to *New Yorker* readers.[30]

5

THE NEW YORKER IN BLACK AND WHITE

Although members of the professional upper-middle class certainly acknowledged the presence of social injustice in the postwar American landscape, they had compelling personal and political reasons to wish it away. The very fact of their own often relatively new privilege kept many of these upper-middle-class liberals from comprehending in any visceral way the entrenched and structural nature of these inequities. Their sense of living in Eden was enhanced by Cold War rhetoric, which emphasized the totalitarian injustices of Soviet Communism and presented a democratized America as a fait accompli. Yet there was a troubling fly in the liberal ointment: the problem of race. Its intractability belied some of the optimism regarding the virtues of American style democracy that was one of the major underpinnings of postwar American ideology.

A study of *The New Yorker*'s treatment of the race problem illuminates the views of a significant segment of postwar American culture. Its readers and contributors, by and large, saw themselves as liberal exemplars of the American conscience. At the same time, they often lived in privileged enclaves in a privileged country and rarely interacted as equals with people of color. The dissonance between the world of evolving egalitarianism they believed in and the world they actually inhabited was a troubling fact of life in the *New Yorker* village.

In "On the Rocks," a humorous short piece published in *The New Yorker* in 1952, St. Clair McKelway tells the story of a fellow who drops in at a bar for a drink and is delighted to find that the bartender is a "pleasant-looking colored man," and that the only other patron in the saloon was "also a pleasant-looking colored man." ("Kindly" and "pleasant-faced" Negroes seem to abound in the postwar *New Yorker*.) The white patron thinks: "How wonderful it is that in New York a colored man can sit at a bar like this and know that nobody is likely to make him feel uncomfortable! . . . If some of my relatives and friends in the Deep South could be here right now and could know how I feel about this, and how that colored man feels about this, they might perhaps begin to understand why I have so frequently badgered them about their unreasoning prejudices." Unfortunately, the patron's delight in the equality of it all leads him to make what he thinks is a terrible faux pas. When the bartender asks him what he is going to drink he says: "Black Horse on the rocks . . . I mean White Horse . . . Black Horse is the ale, isn't it? I'm always getting them mixed up." Immediately his good mood vanishes. He stumbles home and takes "three grains of Nembutal" hoping to find solace in sleep. The following day he briefly succeeds in cheering himself up by savoring the plight of A. Hyatt Verrill, author of *Strange Insects and Their Stories,* which has just been rejected by the New York Board of Education because of its "invidious reference to the superiority of white ants over black ants."[1]

McKelway's bar hopper, ashamed of his failure to be genuinely color-blind, ridicules his own dilemma by poking fun at another author's public failure to be adequately sensitive to black/white issues, albeit concerning bugs. The following day, finding himself "refreshed," the narrator heads back to the same bar thinking "We are all too sensitive about this whole matter! . . . It is only by progressing one step farther in our march toward the end of all discrimination, all prejudice, and actually ceasing to be sensitive, that we will reach our goal." Then he orders a Cutty Sark.[2]

At midcentury, an expanding sector of the American population experienced a newly heightened sensitivity to ethnic and racial stereotyping that is highly reminiscent of the current discourse concerning political correctness. To take notice of race had become something socially inept. McKelway's narrator, like other members of the liberal intelligentsia, tried to make himself color-blind by fiat. The problem with this was that he was acutely aware of racial differences and this contradiction produced a chronic tension surrounding the very fact of color or ethnicity. "On the Rocks" serves to illustrate both the earnest efforts to conform to correct postures concerning color and a certain crankiness about the whole matter. The narrator is delighted to find people of color in his purview, but his delight is compromised by his lack of experience in actually coexisting with them. He wants black people in his world, he congratulates his world for allowing them in, but he is disconcerted by their unaccustomed presence.

McKelway's story typifies some of the overarching concerns of a potent subculture of middle-class liberals in this period who perceived racism as a troublesome shadow over the dream of American democracy. This concern revealed itself in a number of ways. In pursuit of the liberal ideal of color-blindness, the magazine practiced a partial erasure of African-Americans from the magazine's pages, the transfer of racist stereotypes from America to Africa and the South Sea Islands, and the evolution of a new stereotype—the villainous racist.

The New Yorker's racial revisionism took place during a period in which race relations in the United States were undergoing a number of alterations, some gradual, others more volcanic. World War Two had raised both uncomfortable questions and expectations of change concerning the racial divisions in American society. The struggle between democracy and fascism, the ideological basis on which the war was fought, promised to deliver a new pluralism, promote consensus, and reinvigorate the democratic principles of equal opportunity. During wartime the Office of War Information had successfully disseminated a picture of an idealized America that came to be widely accepted by white middle-class citizens. This America was a sort of Norman Rockwell Thanksgiving painting in motion—a place in which African-American soldiers stood shoulder-to-shoulder with their white comrades in the service of democracy against a foe who was both antidemocratic and racist. Yet the picture cannot be dismissed simply as the product of war propaganda. Knowledge of Hitler's Final Solution had forced America's liberals and radicals to face the dual issues of racial inequality and racist stereotyping in their own society. Monographs and books abounded, both scholarly and popular, about tolerance, religious prejudice, and diversity. The conflict between America's belief in equality and its continuing history of racism became a focal point of postwar American intellectual life. Social scientists, among them anthropologists Franz Boas, Ruth Benedict, and Margaret Mead, who had long been engaged in the struggle against racism in America, now found themselves in great demand as lecturers before large audiences earnestly seeking psychological and sociological explanations for the problem of prejudice.[3]

In 1944, at the behest of the Carnegie Corporation, the Swedish economist Gunnar Myrdal made a study of America's race problem and published his findings under the title *An American Dilemma*. Myrdal argued that America's critical "Negro problem" was not a Negro problem at all, but rather a white moral dilemma. When the book was published, one-third of the states still excluded people of color from schools, restaurants, and public spaces like pools and parks. African Americans served in a segregated army and traveled on segregated buses and railroad cars. They often could not vote, or use a public water fountain or restroom; they earned their living largely from menial labor.

Emblematic of this inequality was the fact that even in 1945 a black person could not attend a movie in the nation's capital.[4]

By the mid-fifties the army had been desegregated, the Supreme Court had declared school segregation unconstitutional, and African Americans were in the process of integrating the bus system in Montgomery, Alabama. However, Congress had not passed a civil rights act for seventy-five years, and the majority of Americans remained largely insensitive to the scope of racial injustice. National politics focused principally on foreign policy issues, especially the export of American democracy, and even with the liberal Adlai Stevenson as the Democratic nominee, civil rights were barely mentioned in the 1952 presidential election.[5]

At *The New Yorker,* as in the nation, a variety of levels of consciousness about race coexisted. Harold Ross represented what was perhaps the nadir of the magazine's racial awareness. Ross, whose attitudes about race were shaped by his nineteenth-century upbringing in and around Colorado mining camps, had long refused to hire black people at the magazine even in menial positions, claiming that "Coons are either funny or dangerous." And even though a number of the magazine's editors and contributors were Jews and Catholics, these groups also came in for their fair share of abuse from Ross. The editor was, for example, dismayed in 1934 when St. Clair McKelway expanded what was meant to be a one-part "Profile" of the dancer Bill Robinson into a two-part essay about both the dancer and his relationship to Harlem. "Jesus Christ," Ross moaned, "two parts on a coon."[6]

Until 1945, *The New Yorker* had not been particularly sensitive about the matter of race. A survey of the magazine between 1930 and 1945 reveals a plethora of cartoons and short stories containing crude dialect and stereotypical representations. *New Yorker* covers before 1945 depicted American blacks in a variety of roles. A 1934 cover portrayed elegantly dressed members of black cafe society (women in furs, men with yellow kid gloves), in a style reminiscent of the hyperbolic chic of the Harlem Renaissance. One 1936 cover shows a wide-eyed black man meeting the gaze of the terrified chicken he is in the process of stealing, another cover of the same year portrayed a very black-skinned elevator operator squeezing a throng of white shoppers into his car. A wartime cover depicted a big-lipped black hobo standing in the snow staring wistfully into a shop window featuring resort wear and a sign that asks: "Going South?"

As John Updike has explained in his introduction to *The New Yorker Book of Covers,* after the war "[t]he population of the covers becomes one class, the prospering middle class, and one color, white . . . There is something racist . . . about the virtually absolute postwar disappearance of black people from *New Yorker* covers. To judge from their evidence, blacks might be found in the Caribbean but nowhere in New York City. True, in all the arts, from short stories to the movies, a commendable wish not to give offense led to a suppression of the ethnic emphases of a ruder America."[7]

It was not, however, just the "commendable wish" to suppress racist stereotyping that kept African Americans from the magazine's pages. The crude reality was that in the late forties and early fifties African Americans' status in postwar society had not altered enough to allow them equal footing in the *New Yorker* world. Black people could not realistically be shown drinking Scotch in elegant restaurants, flying to Europe, or joining the ladies' gardening club. At the same time, it was no longer considered acceptable to present (without editorial comment) an American Negro as a hapless domestic, a wide-eyed hobo, a chicken thief, or a grinning pullman porter. Because the magazine's pictorial elements lagged far behind its written text, a few smiling black barmen, caddies, and waiters continued to appear in advertisements and casual drawings. However, by the mid-fifties, as mammies and shoeshine boys and even many black domestics were excised from the magazine's pages, they took with them most representations of black Americans as genuine inhabitants of the *New Yorker* world.[8]

This near disappearance lasted for a decade. As actual American black *people* faded from the magazine's pages, the problem of blackness in America took their place. In this period the magazine did publish a few interviews with African-American entertainers and some uplift pieces such as E. J. Kahn's laudatory profile of Walter White, and an occasional "Talk of the Town" concerning Paul Robeson's troubles with the U.S. government. Many of the remaining stories about people of color in the magazine were focused on the relationship between upper-middle-class people and their servants (the situation in which members of the *New Yorker* circle were most likely to encounter African Americans) but even these were informed by a certain sensitivity to matters of race, which meant that they too were often *about* race. Thus when a piece of fiction or journalism highlighting an African American turned up in the post-war magazine, whether it concerned a domestic servant, a sports figure, or the rare black person who actually made his or her way into the *New Yorker* world, it was invariably focused either upon the nobility of its subject or the dilemma of race itself. Musicians, maids, athletes, Ralph Bunche, and Paul Robeson were among the only African-American survivors of the postwar *New Yorker*'s anxiety about racial stereotyping. It is therefore enlightening to examine these portraits closely.[9]

Often, stereotypical African Americans were replaced by stereotyped South Sea Islanders, Africans, and jungle denizens. This sleight-of-hand offered many *New Yorker* contributors a way to continue doing what they had always done (produce stereotypical representations of black people) without seeming to do so. It is difficult to find a single issue of the magazine that did not contain at least one cartoon depicting a swarthy caveman, a cannibal, or a grass-skirted South Sea Islander up to some antic caper. The humor in these cartoons was derived from a kind of juxtaposition in which jungle types were shown participating in the common rituals of Western European cosmopolitan culture. But while the humor of this was built upon the back of the culture's hegemonic assumptions, its spin declared a sense of the foolishness of those assumptions. This one-two punch was accomplished largely through the use of a homogenizing technique at which the magazine's editors and contributors were most adept. *New Yorker* humor about savages used the amalgamation of disparate societies both as a demonstration of universal norms and the idiocy of this idea. If there was an arrogance in this tricky fusion, it was the same one that was at the core of much of the magazine's writing about One World—the notion that if every nation would just reconstitute itself along the lines of American-style democracy, well then, we could have one world: our world, only bigger. In the postwar period liberal intellectuals produced a vast species-centered discourse which invoked the image of a generic "humanity"—a humanity which, at times, bore a rather striking resemblance to E. B. White. This confusion of the particular with the universal was such a widespread practice that Clifford Geertz has even given it a name: "UNESCO cosmopolitanism."[10]

The New Yorker can be placed in the center of the UNESCO cosmopolitan camp. While appearing to play gently upon the differences between cultures (the difference, let us say, between a witch doctor and a pediatrician), *The New Yorker*'s cartoons about ethnic asymmetries trivialized particularisms, making them only skin deep—matters of style, not substance. The importance of superficial differences between individual others and members of the *New Yorker* community—a red dot between the eyes, loin cloths, fuzzy hair, was played down in an effort to universalize certain human values. By defusing the problematic of real inequities of power between peoples or the possibility of turbulent cultural collision, the magazine succeeded in creating a happy global village in which people—some in tiger-skin loin-cloths, others in Lord & Taylor suits—merrily co-existed.[11]

The comic witch doctor as a dark-skinned mirror of the Park Avenue internist was perhaps the most frequent cartoon motif in the homogenization-of-savages genre. A very sick, loin-clothed native lies on a mat on the floor, tended by his bare-breasted, anxious wife. A messenger stands in the door of their grass hut saying: "The doctor has to make a few other calls. He says to make horrible faces every fifteen minutes until he gets here." A debilitated native in a grass skirt faints at the sight of a scary jack-in-the box that the witch doctor has just pulled out of a kit labeled "First Aid." A fat black witch doctor in a grass skirt shakes a frightening mask at a prone patient, explaining: "Now this may frighten you a little bit."[12]

On the surface it seems that the point here was commonality—a way to relate to the customs of others by rendering them more like us. Hence at one level the customs of Africans, Eskimos, and South Sea Islanders were shown to be not so exotic after all. They were, in fact, really just less evolved, more "primitive" versions of our own customs and rituals. Witch doctors made house calls, had bedside manners, and kept patients waiting. Instead of stethoscopes and X-ray machines, the tools of their trade were scary masks and weird incantations. Native newsmen beat on drums instead of typewriters, and their royalty wore loin cloths, double-breasted suit coats, and silk tophats. Primitive peoples are like us, but they haven't quite got it right. The joke and the point here was always that familiar civilized customs were played out by natives in exotic settings. The primitives in these cartoons were thoroughly samboized—fuzzy-haired and fat-lipped. For more examples, a pitch black African woman with woolly hair, many rings around her elongated neck, and huge white lips lies on her pallet and tries to lull herself to sleep by counting giraffes; a young Fiji Island bridal couple stands in the center of an enormous throng of revelers, all brandishing torches, spears, baskets of fruit. The irritated groom says to his bride: "I thought your folks said it would be just a simple ceremony."[13]

Another related subgenre concerning savages played upon moments in which modern culture and "primitive" life intersected. In such stories and cartoons a white observer was often provided—someone for readers to identify with, someone to legitimize the proceedings. A fat black cannibal in a grass skirt stirs a little wine into a boiling cauldron, while his colleague asks the white man who is presumably about to be thrown into the pot: "Do you still maintain that we're nothing but barbarians?" As one big-lipped native beats on a drum, another explains to a plump white man in Bermuda shorts and a safari hat: "Momboango gives the news behind the news." A travelogue featuring bare-breasted "native" women wearing their hair in buns high atop their heads plays to an audience of New Yorker types. A woman in the audience whose hair is coiffed in exactly the same style reacts in horror as the narrator of the film says: "Notice the hair-do on these beauties. The men of the tribe go for it. Ha, ha! Everyone to his taste." While the white narrator here serves an amanuensic function, the contrast of sloppy Westerners with their leaner, less decadent native counterparts calls for a snicker at ugly American cultural imperialism.[14]

A 1947 Charles Addams cartoon depicted a South Sea Islander placing an offering of food at the foot of a huge carved totem of an American military policeman. While this can be seen as a veiled critique of American imperialism, the cartoon also assumed the utter simplicity of these people who would, in effect, worship anything. In another Charles Addams cartoon, a disgruntled-looking white man in a safari suit stands beside a grotesque pygmy woman who gazes up at him tenderly. Another pygmy stands behind him aiming a poison dart at his head while a third pygmy asks: "Do you, Oliver Jordan III, take this woman to be your lawful wedded wife?"

More than half a century later it is sometimes difficult to discern just what is supposed to be funny about this. At first glance one assumes that the humor was derived solely from the participation of an exotic in that most familiar of comic set pieces—the shotgun wedding. But the real comedy here was the incongruity between the bride and groom—the notion of sexual congress between a white man with the WASP name of Oliver Jordan III, and a fat, tiny, black troll.[15]

In spite of the conscious vigilance of the magazine's editors and writers concerning overt expressions of bigotry, they were unable to repress what they did not see, and they were blind to the cultural biases that appeared "natural" to them. The idea of dark-skinned peoples as comedic primitives cannot be laid to rest by fiat. Paradigm shifts take place haltingly and consciousness is never raised in unison. The persistence of these stereotypical images in the magazine suggests that they may have helped resolve the tension between contributors' genuine desire to avoid racial insensitivity and their reluctance to give up any old creative ground. After all, one can hear them say, this stuff is funny! Dark-skinned "savages" did more than provide the shorthand of stereotyping for comic effect. They also moved the problematic of race to a global arena and solved it by downplaying cultural disparities.

In an essay about *The New Yorker* in the *Partisan Review*, Dwight Macdonald argued that in societies in which the social norm is essentially unchallenged, humor serves to validate the existing social order, functioning rather "like the police force." Simply pointing out a departure from the norm will provide a humorous effect. In comparison, a society that is in a state of confusion about its values tends to produce a more complicated kind of humor. *New Yorker* humor, claimed Macdonald, was an example of this second phenomenon. Certainly the magazine's savage cartoons criticized both the social norm and the comic object, in this case New York upper-middle-class society and dark-skinned primitives in loincloths. The drawings ridiculed universalist assumptions at the same time that they perpetuated them. The whites who appeared in them were inept and unable to cope. At the same time, however, the natives were portrayed as less-than-human grotesques.[16]

Another tactic the magazine's contributors used to avoid complicity in the practice of racism was to depict florid examples of racial bias occurring in an earlier, less enlightened time. *New Yorker* reports of the troubles of black sports figures, for example, were often about injustices in the past and could function doubly as vehicles for antiracist sentiment and self-congratulation. By looking back to an earlier, less sensitive world in which concepts like the "color line" and "the White Hope" dominated the racial politics of sports, these pieces highlighted the great strides black athletes had made in the postwar years.

Much of the magazine's sports writing during these years was about prize fighting. Many of these pieces characterized the rise of Joe Louis to the heavyweight throne in 1937 as the supreme example of sporting success as well as a proof that overt racism in the fighting world (and parts of the larger world as well) had been laid to rest. To remind us of the bad old times, a regular column called "That *Was* Pugilism" (emphasis mine) often focused on black fighters and their historical struggles.

In a 1949 piece about black heavyweight champion Jack Johnson entitled "The White Hopes," John Lardner untangled the history of the phrase "white hope." The term, which "enjoyed its first and last real vogue when Johnson was champion from 1908 to 1915," was used "to describe an athlete of so-called Caucasian background who might retrieve the heavyweight championship, for the honor of his race, from a Negro incumbent."

Jack Johnson's story, in Lardner's telling, had a tragic trajectory. Unlike Joe Louis, Johnson was "haughty, articulate, stubborn." He was determined "to assert all his rights in the face of prejudice." His fondness for white women and his lavish life style got him in trouble with various "watch-and-ward" societies and he was railroaded into a Mann Act trial that forced him to leave the United States in 1912 and spend eight years as a fugitive from justice. "Considered in the light of advanced views today on race relations and tolerance," Lardner, explains, "the country was in a callow and bumptious state."

The occasion of the Johnson piece was the end of Joe Louis's reign as world champion in March of 1949, a reign which Lardner described as not only "the longest in boxing history," but "one of the most popular with the public." The piece was essentially a story of racial progress. Lardner took pains to explain that the term "white hope" had lost any genuine racist connotation even before Louis's ascension to the boxing throne, and illuminated this point by recounting a story of one fight promoter Walter (Good Time Charlie) Friedman, who "went to China to look for a white hope among Chinese peasants."

Lardner ultimately placed the entire "white hope" notion into the context he felt it deserved: "The last publicist to invoke the idea . . . was the late Dr. Goebbels, when he billed Max Schmeling's second fight with Louis, in 1938, as a mission to restore the championship to Aryan control."[17]

In a November 1949 "That Was Pugilism" column, called "Battling Siki," Lardner used the story of Siki, a famous Senegalese boxer who held the world's light-heavyweight championship for six months in 1922 and 1923, to reflect on the difficulties encountered by black fighters in the years after World War I. Siki was a ten-year-old boy plucked out of his native Senegal by a visiting French actress. She took him with her to the French Riviera, dressed him in a little bottle green suit, and made him her personal servant. He began boxing when he was just fifteen and soon became a champion. Describing Siki's difficulties with the Boxing Federation, Lardner argued that these difficulties were solely because of the color of the young man's skin. "My own opinion," he wrote, "is that being champion constituted Siki's chief sin in the eyes of the Federation."

Lardner ridiculed the sports press (circa 1920) for making Siki into a cartoon of the noble savage. "During the three years of his life in which he received international publicity—the last three—he was referred to repeatedly as 'a child of nature,' a 'natural man' . . . 'a jungle child,' and at least once as 'the black Candide.'" One reporter in Paris praised Siki's "strength and simplicity," but then went on to describe him as "very black and very ugly." Even Siki's manager embraced the notion of his able young fighter as a noble savage, saying that he "was a fine lad but just a little bit crazy."[18]

Describing these "tributes" paid by "civilized people to a 'natural man'" as "patronizing," Lardner tries here to offer the reader a more authentic, less aestheticized version of Siki's bittersweet life story. Insisting that Siki was crazy only when he drank, Lardner told the sad tale of the fighter's final years in New York's Hell's Kitchen.[19]

Although Lardner intended to relate the tale of Siki's rise and fall in a finely calibrated variant of gritty social realism, Lardner ultimately succumbed to the very version of Siki's story he was attempting to depose. Siki, who "was killed by gunfire," could not master the customs of the West Side of New York City. Although Lardner ridiculed a fellow sportswriter for referring to Siki as "the black Candide," he himself explained the twenty-eight year-old athlete's untimely demise by saying: "Voltaire has shown when civilization gets its hands on one of these natural men, it pushes him about at random from curious place to curious place." While Lardner was trying to turn the myth of the noble savage on its head, what he did, in fact, was to retell the age-old tale of the corrupting influence of civilization on an innocent citizen of some purer clime.[20]

The historicism of "That Was Pugilism" served to illuminate progress, demonstrating how far America had come in finding a solution to its race problem. Both Siki's story and that of Jack Johnson were part of the shameful past of American sports, a past that had purportedly been laid to rest by the ascension of Joe Louis to a twelve-year reign as heavyweight champion of the world.[21]

In writing about the 1952 Olympics in Helsinki, A. J. Liebling pointed out that the "omnipresent Negroes of the United States team, by their bearing in competition and in the streets were about the most effective political exhibit we had at the Games." There was, he insisted, nothing deliberate about the Negro presence at the Games. "Each of them had simply earned his or her place as a competitor, usually a good one. But the way they handled themselves was a stunning refutation of the perpetual European Communist theme that in the United States the colored man is a resentful peon, constantly in flight from a lynching party or a chain gang."[22]

An important exception to the tendency of *New Yorker* sports pieces to present racial prejudice as a thing of the past was Liebling's "One Hundred and Eighteen Pounds." Here, by examining the relationship of prize fighting to poor immigrant populations and minorities, Liebling indirectly confronts the entrenched economic oppression of African Americans. Describing the illustrious history of Jews in American boxing, Liebling explains that they disappeared from the ring as their fortunes improved. At Stillman's Gym in Manhattan, a fight manager bemoans the toll taken on boxing by postwar affluence. Even the Irish had defected from life in the ring. "The good white fighters you got coming up, you could count them on your fingers," the manager explains. "When the kids didn't have what to eat, they were glad to fight . . . Now that any kid can get a job, they got no ambition . . . The kids we get now, even the Italians, they just want to have a couple of fights so they can say they were fighters . . . The only ones who work hard are the colored boys . . . because for them its still tough outside."[23]

"One Hundred and Eighteen Pounds" is a microeconomic essay on structural poverty. Here Liebling conceded that African Americans in large part had not benefited from the postwar affluence that was assumed by many to have reached every corner of national life. This piece also undercut the self-congratulatory tone of many of the magazine's essays concerning athletics, which stemmed from the assumption that the "color line" had vanished from American sports and American life. Liebling's "One Hundred and Eighteen Pounds," while it was not of a piece with much of the writing about race and class in the early Cold War period, does suggest the shape of things to come. By the early 1960s, with the publication of Michael Harrington's *The Other America* (and the review of it in *The New Yorker* that brought the book to President Kennedy's attention), the idea of the structural nature of poverty, as it had been presented in Liebling's boxing piece, was being "discovered" by intellectuals and policy makers.[24]

It was on those rare occasions when *The New Yorker* tried to bridge the enormous distance between its own culture and that inhabited by Black Americans that the size of this gap was at its most conspicuous. A long profile of the acclaimed musician Dizzy Gillespie entitled "Bop," by Richard O. Boyer, illuminates the scale of this cultural gap between white author and black subject. In this piece, in which Gillespie was described as "a husky young man with the chest development of a middleweight boxer and the bandy legs of a cowhand," the author made a valiant effort to deliver to *New Yorker* readers the flavor of the language used by aficionados of bebop, with predictably humorous results. He explained that Dizzy's fans often exclaim that "Dizzy is 'it,' that he is 'real crazy,' 'a bitch' and a 'killer.'" Boyer pointed out with some dismay that the citizens of Gillespie's world call one another "Pops, Daddy, and Dick," say "Cool!" to express approval, and "use the word 'eyes' oddly, as in 'Have you eyes for a sandwich?'"[25]

New Yorker contributors were certainly not unaware of the disjuncture between the white bourgeois world and that of most people of color. Often the magazine's fiction displayed a preoccupation with the way in which white people responded to these disparities. The central claim of these pieces was that prejudice was the ultimate expression of bad manners—a proof of vulgarity—which inevitably transpired in other climes, in other times and among other kinds. By and large *New Yorker* writers categorically declared themselves unracists—people for whom making an ethnic slur would be as unlikely as drinking Southern Comfort, reading *Forever Amber,* or having plastic slipcovers. Racism was the appalling purview of lower-class people, boors of all stripes, the tasteless, the igno-rant, the misbegotten and, of course, the Southern. It was not a com-monplace in the *New Yorker* world.

A 1946 "Talk of the Town" item described an encounter between a "high principled young woman" who was visiting the Friends of Democracy building on East Fifty-Seventh Street, and the building's "kindly-faced Negro" elevator operator. When the young woman steps into the elevator, she is shocked to see that the man is "fixed into place on his stool by a short, thick chain which [runs] from his belt to one side of the car." Horrified, she asks the man to explain this "indignity." "Well Ma'am . . . seems like in the old days, when I got to napping, I used to fall off this little old stool. Now the chain catches me when I start to go." Racism, the piece seemed to say, may still be a problem in our society, but certainly not among our kind and certainly not on Fifty-Seventh Street.[26]

The American South, on the other hand, was singled out as the na-tional repository of unreconstructed racist sentiment. Often the South-ern racist functioned in *New Yorker* fiction as the ideological counter-point to the enlightened Northeasterner, assuring readers of their own greater enlightenment concerning the question of color. The magazine was peppered with references to Southern bigots: Elmer Gantry types, vulgar Southern bumpkins, and, perhaps worst of all, the *New Yorker* readers' Southern counterparts, white-upper-middle class *educated* pro-fessionals who incomprehensibly indulged in the kind of wrong thinking commonly held south of the Mason-Dixon line.

Thus the South was often used in much the same way that the U.S.S.R. or Eastern Europe was used, to invoke a geography of political incorrectness, a place utterly resistant to democracy. It was comforting to contemplate places in which totalitarianism or racism persisted. By having their focus directed to a more remote intransigence, readers were given an opportunity to excuse smaller inequities in their own world.

Frances Gray Patton, *The New Yorker*'s spy-emissary into the enemy camp of the American South, was particularly adept at offering the magazine's readers a narrator who was in but was not of Southern culture—someone who could take them inside the polite racism of high bourgeois Southern life but who was not entirely tainted by its values.

Patton's "A Nice Name" was exemplary in this regard. Its central figure, Josephine Archer, is an upper-middle-class Southern housewife. Josephine's best friends, Jane Banks, Amy Webb, and Kate Honeycutt, all age "forty-odd," are trying to make a little extra money to help out their affluent husbands, "on account of the inflation." Josephine, "the highbrow of the group," tutors other children now that her own are away at boarding school. Amy has "taken up . . . the beauty business." Every Friday "the girls," assemble to gossip and purchase cosmetics from Amy.[27]

Josephine also has a pen pal, a Mrs. Marshall from Virginia, whom she has never met. Their correspondence began over a letter that Josephine had written to a local newspaper "advocating a reformed technique in the teaching of beginner's Latin." Soon the two women were writing to each other about "food and religion and art," and even disclosing bits of their inner lives. Whenever Josephine received one of Mrs. Marshall's letters, she found that her "vision seemed to widen, to brighten, and all the accustomed details of her life seemed more important than they really were."[28]

The dénouement of the story is the moment when "the girls" tell Josephine what they have discovered—that "her" Mrs. Marshall is "colored." Shocked at this revelation, Josephine begins to reconstruct Mrs. Marshall in her head. She attributes her correspondent's use of certain "hackneyed expressions like 'noble words' and 'richness in their minds'" to the fact that she is "colored." She also tries to picture her friend, but her frame of reference is limited by her circumstances. For Josephine the idea of a "colored" woman and a domestic are synonymous. She thinks of her own maid, Liza, "a treasure," who was "humble and self-respecting," proof that "it was plain silly to say that all darkies were spoiled by prosperity." She pictures Amy's maid, Mossy, a "fat oily-black woman," whom she loathes. Josephine "disapproved of familiar servants and suspected [Mossy] of playing professional darky."[29]

After "the girls'" malevolent revelation of Mrs. Marshall's secret, they further demonstrate their narrow-mindedness by joking that they should now start calling her by her first name, Hannah, and that *if,* God forbid, she ever tried to visit Josephine, "There needn't be any embarrassment . . . she can go home with Liza. Or she can come out and stay with Mossy. Mossy has a double bed, with an inner-spring mattress."

Josephine, stung by their insensitivity, begins to wonder what she is doing "with these silly women"—they are now in the middle of painting their toenails and discussing the relative merits of "Tropic Pink and Forbidden Apple" polish. She imagines her Mrs. Marshall sharing a bed with "fat Mossy," and thinks: "I couldn't have heard that." But even as she is telling herself that she can just get up and go home and "write a letter to [her] friend Hannah Marshall," she allows herself to submit to the wet compress Amy is placing on her eyes.[30]

In her story Patton illuminated more than the muffled illiberalism of their middle-class Southerners. On her way to Amy's house on the day the revelations about Mrs. Marshall are made, Josephine feels "pleasantly liberal" when she thinks to herself that it is character, not color, that really matters. She even resolves to discuss this idea with her friends, who need "shaking out of their fixed ideas." Patton's narrator, as one who felt superior to the racism surrounding her, was a sly creation that may well have had a disquieting resonance for *New Yorker* readers. Not only could they identify with the self-congratulatory aspect of Josephine's consciousness about race, but they could also relate closely to its limitations. In spite of Josephine's tendency to separate herself intellectually from her peers, she was after all, just one of the girls, enjoying all of the privileges and comforts of the life to which she condescends. Like many socially conscious members of the *New Yorker* community, Josephine's knowledge of black people was limited to contact with domestic servants. While her relationship with Mrs. Marshall broadened and deepened her (even before she learned of her color), it promised to have no genuine transformative effect on her life. Ultimately she will remain an ineffectual liberal in an illiberal society. As she sinks back on the massage table and "lets her little muscles go slack," she is surrendering to her milieu. Josephine's failure to make a place in her world for Mrs. Marshall suggests the ultimate power of privilege over principle, comfort over confrontation—a hierarchy that was certainly familiar to *New Yorker* readers.[31]

Depicting racial discrimination as something confined to a remote region or time placed the problem at a comfortable distance from readers and eliminated the danger of contamination. Contamination became a distinct possibility, however, when racist sentiments were played out in milieus that were familiar to *New Yorker* readers. In the postwar period, anyone in a *New Yorker* short story who expressed racist sentiments was waving a red flag, signaling ruin or hopeless decadence. This dereliction was particularly conspicuous if the character was neither Southern, nor lower class, nor a historical actor from an earlier era.

John O'Hara's "Ellie," which describes a brief flirtation between a cosmopolitan New Yorker and a glamorous Texan, illuminated the notion that Southern racism was a moral failing—a rottenness eating at the core of those who inhabited the American South. In this story Jim (the narrator) and his sister take Ellie and her husband, visitors from Texas, out for a night on the town in Manhattan. Ellie's husband, Ham, is a cartoon Texan who wears a Stetson with his evening clothes. Jim, however, is utterly charmed by Ellie. When he looks at her she smiles and it is clear to him that she was "quite happy just knowing that she had an effect on" him. "Admiration was something she breathed in." After dinner, at Ham's request, the party heads for the Dorchester Ballroom in Harlem, a place that is clearly a frequent haunt of Jim's. He knows the maitre d' quite well and describes Al Spode, an old Negro heavyweight who acts as the club's bouncer, as "another old friend." Eager to get Ellie out of earshot of her husband, Jim steers her onto the dance floor and before the first dance is over, he has made a date with her for the following day.

When Jim and Ellie sit down, a boy and girl—"surely the best dancers in the ballroom"—came over to the railing near their table. The girl leaned against the railing, and the boy, "who was very black," faced them. Suddenly Ellie turns to her husband and says: "Ham, that niggah's lookin' at me" "'Which one, honey?' asked Ham." Before an incident can occur, Jim calls Ham "a silly son-of-a-bitch," grabs Ellie's wrist, and hustles them all out of the club. Jim goes to bed that night "with [his] mind made up that was the last [he'd] ever see of Missy Ellie." His resolve weakens the following day however, and he drives to meet her at the appointed spot. But when he sees her "walking down Park, keeping her date," he became "old and cautious, and . . . drove away from her and trouble, her kind of trouble."[32]

Jim sees Ellie's racism as a key to her character. And, more important, he sees his own unracism as a critical component of his own. While he is drawn to Ellie sexually, her use of the word "niggah" is a potent repellent. It actually dampens his desire and alters his behavior. While the fact that she is married and that she and her husband are friends of his sister does not inhibit Jim from pursuing her, her bigotry does. Jim's sense of himself as unprejudiced is more than just an idea here. It is rather an internalized value with the power to influence his actions.

Because she was a Southerner, Ellie's racism, however offensive, was well-charted territory on *The New Yorker*'s map of the world. The expression of racist sentiments among Northerners, on the other hand, would be somewhat astonishing. In J. D. Salinger's "Uncle Wiggily in Connecticut," for example, Eloise, a young, emotionally bankrupt suburban housewife gets together with her former college roommate. In the course of a long, drunken afternoon, she goes over her husband's various idiocies and abuses Grace, her black housekeeper. "Wuddya think [Grace] is doing out there?" Eloise asks her guest. "She's sitting on her big black butt reading *The Robe*. I dropped the ice trays taking them out. She actually looked up annoyed." When the maid asks Eloise if her husband can spend the night in her room because the roads are icy, Eloise demurs, telling Grace that she is "not running a hotel." In fact, Eloise is running more of a hotel than a home. Because she is so disconnected from the life that surrounds her, she keeps everyone out in the cold. Her own husband is a shadowy offstage presence, her lonely child has formed an alliance with an imaginary playmate—Jimmy Jimmerooney—and her housekeeper's husband is banished. Ultimately, Eloise's mistreatment of Grace is just another sign of her emotional barrenness. While Ellie's racism can be attributed to geography, Eloise's suggests a kind of banal ruin.[33]

Jean Stafford's 1949 short story "Pax Vobiscum," about a man whose racism was so virulent that it bordered on caricature, offered a complex diagram of racial attitudes in the *New Yorker* set. By placing her cartoon racist in the midst of a group of affluent New York women, Stafford was able to extract a veritable Greek chorus of liberal outrage from the postwar conversation about bigotry.

"Pax Vobiscum" takes place at a Caribbean resort where New York women awaiting their divorce decrees come to idle "through their six weeks' quarantine," swim in the sea, and "drink, and haunt the shops for tax-free bargains in French perfume." The owner of the hotel where the divorcees are staying is a "lumbering fourth-generation Dane," the kind of man who "crow[s] concupiscently" when he describes himself to women as "a gourmet and a sybarite." He is also an unreconstructed racist whose ideas about the native population are utterly offensive to his guests—women like little Mrs. Fairweather, "a high-principled girl in her middle twenties, who had fanatically learned tolerance in college," and who weeps as she knits argyle socks for her soon-to-be-ex-husband. Then there is Sophie Otis, so paralyzed by the indolence of this "place so wanting in shadow" that she cannot "project herself beyond [her] present anesthesia." And Mrs. Baumgartner, "a delicious blonde" whose husband "had beaten her with a ski pole in the railroad station in Boise, Idaho," who is nevertheless already planning her next honeymoon as she awaits her decree. The Dane enjoys offending these Northern women with tall tales of his erotic and racist adventures. He describes an incident in which a Liberian sailor had a fatal accident while his ship was anchored in the harbor. The health authorities agreed to embalm the body so that it could be shipped back to Africa by plane. "But then," the Dane says, "they found . . . that the nigger's head was such a mess that the embalming fluid wouldn't stay in, so they had to plant the bugger after all. We haven't got enough of our own coons, we have to take care of this stray jigaboo from Liberia, what?"[34]

When this sally draws merely silent disapproval, the Dane goes a step further, telling his guests that he is involved in a biological warfare project in which he is "hunting for a virus that will kill off all the niggers but won't hurt anybody else." At this little Mrs. Fairweather actually starts to cry.

Mr. Robertson, a former rumrunner, outdoes the hotelier by telling the women about the night that he and the Dane almost got to eat a "broiled pickaninny." Claiming to have found a perfectly cooked black baby in a house fire, Robertson explains: "It was charred on the outside, naturally, but I knew it was bound to be sweet and tender inside." The visitors respond to this tale with "reproachful eyes" which seem to say: "There are limits." One of the guests, a Coca-Cola salesman who is stopping for a few days on his way to Argentina, is visibly shaken and says: "What's the matter with you people here? You ought to shoot yourself for telling a story like that."

The world of "Pax Vobiscum" was divided and conflicted without easy moral resolution. The men were vulgar and robust, the women were either silly, passive, or calculating. The narrator's imagination was divided by geography into North and South: the lush tropics seemed to trespass upon even the memory of "another landscape . . . the sober countryside of Massachusetts under snow . . . the decorous smell of pine forests." In the imagination of Mrs. Otis the tropics, like the American South, were a tainting climate—one that intrinsically bred wrong thinking. The "broiled pickaninny" story made it clear what the place of the natives was for these venal white islanders.

While the Dane's strident chauvinism marks him as a vulgarian, the reactions of his guests are also suspect. Mrs. Fairweather's tearful leaps at the Dane's vile bait are seen as the knee-jerk reactions of a liberal simpleton. Her objection to racism is just another reason to cry. In comparison, Sophie Otis, Stafford's narrator, who is nearing "the end of her exile," remains entirely aloof from the inharmonious proceedings at the hotel. The verbal atrocities committed on the porch are only "the voices of strangers thrumming behind her." Sophie cannot find the necessary energy to challenge the hotelkeeper. She blames her torpor on the tropics, but her failure cannot be laid entirely to the climate. Like Josephine in Francis Patton's "A Nice Name," Sophie's privileged status reinforces her passivity.

The conscious intentions of this story were complex. Stafford was depicting a somnolent interlude in which Mrs. Otis, clearly Stafford's stand-in here, was forced to endure the indignity of a world of interlocking evils. To be sure, the Dane's venality was as plain as the huge nose on his face. But there are, Stafford seemed to be claiming, degrees of evil. The weeks spent entrapped in the hotelkeeper's awful hospitality were a season in Hell, in which everything base in his guests was exposed in the harsh tropic light. The entire project of awaiting divorce—the days of shopping and drinking and sleeping in the sun enjoyed by the privileged enclave of women—suggested a moral flaccidity, a noxiousness which, while less pronounced than that of the Dane, was nonetheless reprehensible. The lack of rigor in Mrs. Fairweather's weepy liberalism, the crass marital manipulations of Mrs. Baumgartner, and Mrs. Otis's own detachment were all evidence of bourgeois sloth, passivity, and privilege, corruptions of another kind.

Just beneath the surface of Mrs. Otis's nonresistance, however, lurks a significant subtext in which dark-skinned people were imbued with a nobility, purity, and authenticity that was sorely lacking in their paler observers. Mrs. Otis romanticizes the black children she sees playing on the beach. She observes the black house boy and thinks: "Angels and ministers of grace defend you." She is "humbled" by the boys's "great dignity," his "sagacious patience" in "an improbable world." "His," she thinks "was all the sufferance and suffering of little children."[35]

"Pax Vobiscum" was consciously commenting upon the social disjunctures created by the confrontation of passive liberalism with malign racism. While its unconscious content summoned up a social context (the enlightened North) in which racial stereotyping had been successfully suppressed, a kind of compensatory racism emerges in its place—one in which dark-skinned people are aestheticized as innocent victims, endangered children in an "improbable world."

It was difficult for privileged socially conscious men and women to find their bearings in the confusing terrain of postwar race relations in the United States—a place over which the brave flag of equality waved but material equality was little more than a dream. One of the cultural functions of *The New Yorker* was to offer its contributors a stage upon which they could act out their contempt for race prejudice while distancing themselves from the perpetrators of it. The genuine desire to eradicate racism from their world shared by many *New Yorker* contributors, editors, and readers after the war, coupled with the intractability of structural inequality, produced a peculiar discourse in the magazine concerning race in which the problem was located in the past, in distant climes, or in people of bad character. If the wishes of affluent liberals had prevailed, then minstrels, mammies, and shoeshine boys would have vanished entirely to be replaced by a parade of dark-skinned statesmen, lawyers, academics, and doctors. But wishes alone were insufficient to the task at hand, and white upper-middle-class Americans, whatever their democratic hopes, continued to encounter people of color primarily as domestic servants and remote others well into the 1950s.

The dissonance between the egalitarian world they wished to live in and the realities of American race relations at midcentury was a thorn in the side of American liberals. This discomfort was particularly keen in light of the global image of America as an ideal democracy. *The New Yorker* sought to allay some of the uneasiness produced by this troubling anomaly. Readers could take comfort in its depictions of racist sentiment in other geographies, other sorts of people, and other times. These descriptions offered the reassuring suggestion that most signs of overt racial prejudice had been expelled from the *New Yorker* village—that at least one corner of the American landscape was worthy of emulation.

6

THE ROMANCE OF THE OTHER

It is difficult to know with any certainty the cultural function of a stereotype. Yet the frequent presence of the image of the ethnic other as an idealized figure in the postwar *New Yorker* raises compelling questions about how the magazine's contributors saw themselves. What does it mean when members of one culture consistently portray members of another as deeper, livelier, and more spiritual than themselves? *New Yorker* writing about ethnics may not tell us much about its actual subjects, but it reveals a great deal about the society that produced it. While the way *The New Yorker* treated the subject of African Americans suggests the extent to which contributors were morally troubled by the shadow cast by racism over the sunny vista of postwar American democracy, the treatment of Asians, Hispanics, and Native Americans suggests another, more internal and self-reflecting debate concerning the moral cost of affluence.[1]

Postwar American culture was rife with fears about the morally corrosive effects of affluence, technological development, and mass consumption. Economic comfort seemed to be linked with a strange kind of malaise. Sociologists and cultural critics in this period operated on the assumption that problems of "material inequality had been solved" and focused their attention upon the discontents of abundance. Pointing to the bland conformity and the flavorlessness of contemporary American life, they asked: "what went wrong?" David Riesman, in his best-selling *The Lonely Crowd,* rebuked Americans for their "outer-directedness." Allen Tate saw a sated America unable to resolve its ethical dilemmas in the thin moral air of excessive abundance. In *Asylums,* the sociologist Erving Goffman described the loss of autonomous selfhood that occurred in large-scale, highly bureaucratized institutions such as prisons and mental hospitals, and implied that America's corporations had a similar impact upon their inhabitants. Contemporary architecture critics like Lewis Mumford and Ada Louise Huxtable castigated suburbia for its cookie-cutter uniformity, its flavorlessness. In *The Organization Man,* William H. Whyte, claiming that the "fruits of social revolution are always more desirable in anticipation than fact," described a pervasive sense of disappointment amongst postwar Americans, which he linked to the deadening effects of corporate growth on cultural life and spirit.[2]

Followers of *The New Yorker* were certainly not exempt from this anxiety concerning the drift toward moral vacuity and aesthetic uniformity. In fact, the fusion of affluence and social consciousness that defined many members of the *New Yorker* community produced a particularly lively strain of self-recrimination. The uneasiness of this growing cohort of prosperous liberals had a number of sources, among them the fundamental suspicion that it might be easier for a camel to slide through the eye of a needle than for a rich man to enter the kingdom of heaven. For in spite of the material comforts with which these postwar cosmopolitans were able to surround themselves, the consolations of the spirit often seemed to elude them. In addition to spiritual malaise, the war had brought American servicemen face to face (often as "liberators") with the deprivations and sufferings of huge numbers of other inhabitants of the globe. There was some burden of guilt in being, as much of America was, an island of prosperity in a sea of poverty. And many Americans shared the terrible awareness of culpability in the mass destruction of Hiroshima and Nagasaki—a culpability that particularly plagued socially conscious liberals.

This disquiet concerning the spiritual cost of American power is supported by the sheer volume of pieces in the postwar *New Yorker* that portray admirable individuals of diverse ethnic backgrounds as a counterpoise to the materialism and complacency of the white middle class. The number of cartoons, short stories, and journalistic pieces concerning preternaturally noble or soulful ethnics does suggest the power of this perception of the other as more innocent and benign than his or her affluent cosmopolitan counterpart— as somehow superior to those who write about them. These pieces reveal a curious blend of guilt over the corrupting influence of civilization and a concomitant yearning to be returned to a more innocent time before the war, before the bomb.[3]

Because white upper-middle-class Americans most often encountered African Americans in the role of domestic servants, relationships between the two groups had a habitual and intimate quality. Encounters between white elites and other ethnics—Native Americans, Asians, Arabs, or Hispanics— because they were more likely to be occasional and nondomestic, were easier to romanticize. The very magnitude of the social distance between author and subject eased the way for the creation of a genre in which others were lionized as exceptionally pure, noble, and fierce, possessing "all the sufferance and suffering of little children." American Indians, rarely encountered in casual social situations, were particularly suited to such idealized treatment.[4]

Many of the magazine's pieces concerning ethnic others retained the

Enlightenment tradition of the Noble Savage as a figure untainted by corrupt society, and the nineteenth-century variant of the Romantic Savage as a child of nature and instinct. In these traditions Indians/ savages were more natural, more spiritual, less materialistic, and less spoiled than white people. Their purity was, however, attended by a concurrent set of less attractive traits such as childishness, gullibility, and lack of reflective intellect.[5]

Although the Indian was most often seen in the popular American imagination as a scalp-hungry obstacle to expansion—a stereotype that extended from the New England captivity narratives of the seventeenth century to the Western films of the years following World War II—there was an American countertradition that romanticized primitive people as noble children of nature. This lively intellectual tradition had its roots in the early anthropological work of Franz Boas at Columbia University. Boas's students tended to make malign comparisons between their own society and the technologically primitive peoples they scrutinized, insisting that these simpler cultures did a better job of satisfying basic human needs than did bourgeois white society.[6] *New Yorker* contributors, like these early anthropologists, were often critiquing American society when they wrote about Native Americans. *New Yorker* Indians were neither bloodthirsty nor threatening. They were rather casualties of expansionism and neglect, their only savagery a justifiable anger at their mistreatment at the hands of the white man.[7]

Edmund Wilson's two-part Profile of the Shalako—an annual religious festival on the Zuni reservation—was both an effort to understand Native American culture and an indictment of middle-class American life. Wilson's upright Zunis were observed in counterpoint to the insipid whites: they were at once spontaneously attuned to the natural world and fiercely "self-controlled, industrious, and self-reliant." Reflecting on the way that white Americans, dissatisfied with the gracelessness of modern urban life, seemed to "glance wistfully . . . toward the Indians, whom only a short time ago we were fighting, tooth and nail," Wilson describes the purity and integrity of Zuni ritual, which he contrasted with the disorder and indirectness encountered in white urban America.[8]

The second installment of "Shalako" was largely concerned with the terrible incursions of the white man's bad values and liquor upon the Native American community. Drunken Indians litter the lobby of Wilson's hotel in Gallup. One comatose Indian lay blocking the hotel's entrance. "This," he exclaimed, was his "final impression of what the white man [has] given the Indian; and of what modern white man had made of himself." Wilson was equally discouraged by his fellow passengers on the Santa Fe Railroad. White people, he proclaimed, "have been turning soft, stout and blank to a degree that is disappointing and dismaying. What do these puffy-faced doughbags do? Some, no doubt, are commercial travellers; others, businessmen, well-off and retired, who have bought themselves 'homes' in Los Angeles. The women, whether squashy or scrawny, are equally charmless and sexless. If the Zunis are human beings, these must be something else."[9]

Wilson concludes his piece with a discussion of the unrequited romance between white liberal intellectuals and Indians, noting that anthropologists "like Ruth Benedict" contrast the Indian with our "badly run" neurotic society; "the aesthete in Santa Fe admires, even adores, the Indian;" and the journalist (Wilson himself) who has reported so many "hateful and destructive events, wants to get a good look at the Shalako birds . . . before they shall have ceased to come," replaced by the "white man's bad liquor," or worse, "the worship of some white Fuhrer."

To what extent was Wilson implicating himself in the impurity and weightlessness of white urban modern life? Certainly Wilson's "doughbags" were not people with whom he identified. But were the people who "adore the Indian" exempt from the harsh charges he invoked against whites in general? While Wilson may have claimed some exemption from this harsh critique of white bourgeois society, his unequivocal assertion that members of his own race and culture seemed somehow inferior to the Zunis, along with his invocation of a "white Fuhrer," were hefty indictments of his own kind. Whiteness itself was a kind of contagion. If the Indians were "thick-tongued" and "stiff with drink," it was because they had come in contact with the white man. And the "doughbags" who so disgusted Wilson were among those of his fellows who lived "inharmoniously in cities, buying and selling" rapaciously, utterly "divorced from the earth" that sustained them. The illegitimacy and toxicity of the white man's presence in Wilson's piece is not an anomaly. Much of *The New Yorker*'s writing about Native Americans is a sustained threnody of mea culpa.[10]

E. B. White's 1951 "Notes and Comment" about Indians and their allegiance to treaties, for example, placed Native Americans on the moral high ground. Pointing out that the "world would be in better condition if nations observed covenants as faithfully . . . as Indians," White then recounted an incident at a movie location in Florida in which Indian actors "balked" at shooting Gary Cooper because their peace treaty with the United States "prohibited taking up arms against the white man." Only after "a long powwow" did the whites, who "can take a treaty or leave it alone," get the "braves" to see things their way. This détente was reached largely through the exchange of "green wampum."

White clearly admired the Indians' rigorous faithfulness to covenant, their lack of corruption by civilization. The Indian nation was superior to other nations because of its reliance upon this natural integrity. While their fidelity seemed somewhat deluded—the result of a childish inability to understand the distinction between a movie set and the real world—it also contained a critique of Euro-American civilization. Although white men did indeed control the "green wampum," they were indifferent to ethical imperatives, a dangerous failing in the atomic age.[11]

In *The New Yorker*, "primitive" societies were often rendered virtuous simply by comparing them to a technologically advanced society that had unleashed the threat of nuclear annihilation upon an unsuspecting planet. This juxtaposition is represented in a number of the magazine's cartoons about the evacuation of Bikini Island. While "childlike" natives confront "sophisticated" military officers, it is clear who holds the better moral hand. A 1946 Robert Day cartoon, for example, depicts a very befuddled looking group of saronged natives seated on a tropical beach while a naval officer points at a complex chart, instructing them in the arcana of molecular theory. A pair of uniformed officers watch this scene with dismay as one says to the other: "I don't see why he goes into all that detail. Why doesn't he simply tell them there's going to be one hell of a bang and let it go at that?" In another cartoon two dark-skinned natives confront two naval officers as they disembark from a naval cruiser, saying: "The residents have voted two to one against your experiments in this vicinity." The joke here is the arrogance of power and science in the face of the fundamental claims of humanity.[12]

Unlike the cartoon Bikini Islanders, the Native Americans in *The New Yorker* respond to the injustices done to them with outrage. These Indians are portrayed as the angry victims of a variety of indignities both at the hands of the United States government and white people in general. The magazine's cultural critics, short-story writers, and cartoonists who depicted Native Americans consistently remarked upon the hostility of their subjects, often implicating themselves as white observers in generating this rage. For whatever else these contributors were (liberals, intellectuals, ethical beings), they were all white people and this, in itself, seemed to constitute some burden of guilt, some degree of doughbaggery.

For example, an unsigned 1951 "Talk of the Town" piece told the story of Sequoyah, a man without any formal education who had created a written language for the Cherokee Nation. In elegiac style, "Talking Leaves" decried the inequity between the magnitude of Sequoyah's cultural contribution and the size of his reward. Although he had been promised a grant of five hundred dollars in a treaty with the U.S. government, after a six-year delay, he received only one hundred and fifty dollars in cash, twenty-two kettles of salt, three saddles, and bits of other merchandise. And to add insult to injury, the Indian Territory that had voted in 1907 to be called Sequoyah when it became a state, was named Oklahoma instead. The piece ends on a bittersweet note, reminding the reader that the "giant redwoods of the West were named sequoias in his honor, which is probably better than having a state named after you."[13]

Native American rage was also the primary emotion displayed in Jean Stafford's short story "A Summer's Day." In this Dickensian tale of sickly Indian orphans and the beleaguered adults surrounding them, (all with angry names: Miss Hornet, Miss Dreadfulwater) Stafford described the ordeal of an eight-year-old Cherokee orphan, Jim Littlefield, who is sent off to the Bureau of Indian Affairs school in Oklahoma. When the terrified child expresses fear about being sent to a place like the asylum out by the fairgrounds, where lame, bespectacled children march about in drab uniforms, Mr. Wilkins, the white minister who is sending Jim to the Indian School, declares: "Landagoshen, Jim boy, didn't I say you were going to be Uncle Sam's boy? . . . Uncle Sam isn't one of your fair-weather friends that would let a Cherokee down when all his kin were dead."[14]

In Oklahoma Jim comes face to face with the harsh realities of Federal Indian policy. The orphan school is overpopulated, underequipped, and understaffed. Many of the students are sick and dying from some unnamed epidemic caused by "poisonous water," the result of the failure of the Bureau of Indian Affairs to provide the school with money for a septic tank.[15]

Jim decides to escape. He is sent outside "to play" and encounters a Navajo boy with sickly red eyes who, when asked his name snarls: "Rock Forward Mankiller. My father's name is Son-of-the-Man-Who-Looked-Like-a-Bunch-of-Rags-Thrown-Down." Rock Forward's explosive anger is the incoherent fury of a child. "If I get sick with the epidemic and die, I'll kill them all . . . I'll burn the whole place up and I'll spit everywhere." At the story's end, the exhausted Jim collapses into sleep on the school's "sickly grass," surrendering to the arms of an "Uncle Sam" who is more of a jailer than a surrogate parent.

Stafford crafts her narrative around the issues of powerlessness, besieged nobility, futile anger, and ultimately capitulation. For Stafford Indian anger was a form of self-expression, rather than a strategy. She portrayed this rage as justified, and while it served no material purpose, it did steel the spirit of these Indians against the incursions of an oppressive government and a tragic history.[16]

The theme of Indian hostility toward white people was addressed more lightly in a 1948 Charles Addams cartoon, which depicted a Native American with long black braids lying on a New York psychiatrist's couch. The therapist paces nervously around the room, saying: "I think we're getting somewhere, Mr. Great Cloud Shadow. Your neurosis apparently stems from a submerged resentment against your ancestors for disposing of Manhattan Island for only twenty-four dollars."[17]

Charles Addams was perhaps the magazine's most subversive contributor. His "family" cartoons provided a ghoulish antidote to the complacent ethos of suburban, domestic family life in the postwar period. In Addams's demented world something confusing, baroque, and decentering lurked just beneath the surface of the commonplace. By juxtaposing the Native American with the Freudian and having the Freudian treat justifiable political outrage as neurosis, Addams satirized the whole notion of "adjustment," which was popularized in the period as a way to reconfigure personality so that it conformed to the demands of society. In this particular instance, getting the joke required that the reader believe that the Indian's resentment, his alleged maladjustment, was the product of actual injustice—a sane response to white colonial misdeeds. With comic incongruity, Addams's Native American patient seeks treatment from a representative of the materialism of rational scientific dogma. Part of the irony of this attempt to cure the Indian of his rage is that Euro-American civilization, of which Freudianism is a product, is what created it.[18]

The magazine's presentation of Indians consistently emphasized Native Americans' autonomy from and hostility toward white people. It is possible to argue that this was not a construction, but rather a mirror of social fact. Indians *were* angry and self-contained. It was, however, also a social fact that African Americans were often just as angry and independent. Yet rage was notably absent from *New Yorker* representations of black Americans, who were almost always presented as either "pleasant-faced colored" folks or savvy observers of white pain.

This focus on Native American rage has deep roots which can be traced to the distinctions made by European colonists. As Winthrop

Jordan has argued, European territorial imperatives shaped the colonists' view of the New World's indigenous population. Practical considerations made the idea of the Indian very different from the idea of the black in colonists' minds. Particularly in the early years of settlement, Indians could and did attack the English colonists, while the sparser black population could not. In order to avail themselves of their labor, Englishmen had to feel comfortable living alongside black people, and to do this they had to find unthreatening ways to characterize them. While portraying blacks as infinitely docile and governable, colonists attributed a fierce ungovernability to the members of Indian nations.[19]

Like those of the colonists, *The New Yorker*'s representations of Native Americans and African Americans are built upon pragmatic considerations. Readers' and contributors' contacts with Indians were limited. When they did occur, they generally took place on the Indians' turf. Conversely, the upper-middle class depended heavily upon the labor of black Americans. To acknowledge black rage and the unbearable historical burden of chattel slavery could jeopardize the comfort of privileged lives, while an acknowledgment of Native American rage exacted no personal toll.

The predicament of Native Americans was inevitably associated with certain anecdotes, in particular the purchase of Manhattan Island for a few dollars and a bunch of worthless trinkets. The popularity of this scrap of history is interesting in that it encapsulates the profound contradiction between capitalist acquisition and social justice, without invoking the notion of reparation. (Certainly, we couldn't be expected to give it back.) In fact, the version of injustice suffered by Native Americans resonated loudly for midcentury capitalists, who could readily identify with the brutality of property theft and even recognize complicity in it.

The magazine also published a number of pieces that hinged upon the ability of Native Americans to successfully navigate or outsmart white society. The legendary Joseph Mitchell's "Mohawks in High Steel" was an eloquent example of a tale focused upon Native American cultural agility. Mitchell was famous among his *New Yorker* colleagues for his painstaking craftsmanship, his attention to salient detail, and the fact that he often took months, even years to finish a piece. "Mohawks in High Steel" concerned a tribe of Mohawks, the Caughnawagas, and their extraordinary aptitude for steel work at the dizzying heights required in the construction of skyscrapers and bridges. According to the spokesman from the Dominion Bridge Company, these Indians "were natural-born bridgemen" because they seemed to lack a fear of heights. Mitchell tracked the tribe from its earliest days until 1949, following them from their Canadian reservation to a Brooklyn neighborhood, where many Caughnawagas settled with their families in search of employment in high-steel work. Caughnawaga high steel teams helped to build the R.C.A. Building, the Empire State Building, the Daily News Building, the George Washington Bridge, the Triborough Bridge, and the Waldorf-Astoria Hotel.[20]

Mitchell's essay avoided the usual angry or oppressed Indian scenario by placing the tribe at the center of its own story and following in tandem the development of the high-steel business and Native Americans' contribution to it. The Caughnawagas were presented not as pathetic victims of white society, but rather as a resourceful group of people who had turned traditional cultural skills into tools for participating in the creation of modern America. "I heated a million rivets," explains Orvis Diabo, O-ron-ia-ke-te (He Carries the Sky.) "When they talk about the men that built this country, one of the men they mean is me."

Describing the tribe members as having always "had considerable say-so in their own affairs," Mitchell pointed out their ability to convert tribal skills into conduits for the white man's money. They work in the timber-rafting industry, perform as "Wild Indians" in circuses and county fairs ("letting out self-conscious wahoos") and peddle native remedies door-to-door. Using materials from the Plume Trading Company on Lexington Avenue in Manhattan, many of the women make "dolls, handbags, and belts, which they ornament with colored beads . . . Every fall, a few of the most Indian-looking of the men take vacations from structural steel . . . and go out with automobile loads of these souvenirs and sell them on the midways of state, county, and community fairs." On these occasions the men dress in buckskins and feathers and "sleep in canvas tepees pitched on fairgrounds."[21]

Mitchell kept his focus on the enterprising spirit of the tribe and its ability to act on its own behalf in negotiations between the modern white world and its traditional culture. What little pathos there was in the piece was derived not from its subjects' ethnicity but from their humanity. His description of a Caughnawaga forced to give up steel work because "he's a little too damned stiff in the joints to be walking a naked beam five hundred feet up in the air" suggested the pain of trading the excitement of high-steel work for the narrow monotony of reservation life: "He can sit on the highway and watch the cars go by . . . or he can congregate in the grocery stores with the other old retired high-steel men . . . That is, if he can stand it."[22]

Alice Marriot's "Beowulf in South Dakota" concerned a Native American who was quite literally in control of his tribe's stories. In this comic piece, a young ethnologist studying the "worldwide distribution of certain myths" finds she is no match for the old Indian man she is interviewing to gather the ancient stories of his people. The elderly Indian is a temperamental informant, often needing to be cajoled into talking. On a day of particularly "mulish reticence," he asks the ethnologist: "Haven't the white people any stories of their own?" and demands to hear one of her "tribe's" stories, so he will know what they are like. She relates an Indianized version of "Beowulf," featuring "great white tepees," "black stone tepees," and "chiefs." The old Indian is so enchanted he makes her repeat the story so he will be certain to remember it.[23]

Near the end of her stay on the reservation, the ethnologist learns that a scholar from a rival university has also been interviewing her informant. The old man assures her that he doesn't like the other academic or his methods and promises that he will not tell him any of the stories he has told her. The punch line of the tale comes two years later, when the narrator is reading a current issue of an ethnological journal and chances upon an article entitled: "Occurrence of a Beowulf-like Myth among North American Indians." The piece is signed by the narrator's rival. The old Indian has had the last laugh here.[24]

"Beowulf in South Dakota" and "Mohawks in High Steel" circumvented the prevailing stereotype of the Native American as an angry victim of an unjust history. They offered instead a more nuanced stereotype of the Indian as culturally heroic. In "Beowulf in South Dakota," the old Indian storyteller hoodwinked a Ph.D. In "High Steel," Joseph Mitchell demonstrated the way one tribe used its cunning and its natural gifts to bridge the gap between past and present, white and native culture, traditional economic life and capitalism. (It is no accident that the Caughnawagas were described as "natural-born bridgemen.") The Indians in these pieces were in control of their lives and their stories. They gave self-conscious war whoops for the benefit of white observers, and purloined Western European legends for their own purposes. Still, the myth of the Romantic Savage persisted. The triumph of these Indians was understood to be largely the product of innate qualities. Both Mitchell and Marriot seemed to derive a degree of pleasure from depicting these larger-than-life Native Americans as wily tricksters, capable of outsmarting white people. The depiction of Native Americans as the possessors of an animal slyness, fearlessness, cat-like agility, and a superior knack for survival against all odds served to alleviate at least a portion of white guilt.[25]

If Native Americans were portrayed as purer than their white counterparts, Arabs, Italians, and Hispanics appeared in *The New Yorker*'s cosmology as livelier, more virtuous, and ultimately more humane than bourgeois white people. *The New Yorker*'s portrayals of others were often used to express a concern with the failures of postwar American society, in which, as John Kenneth Galbraith claimed, "the bland were leading the bland," an astringent comment that suggests how utterly genuine political discourse had been subsumed by questions of style and taste. Fast food (MacDonald's was founded in 1948), Holiday Inns, and suburban Levittowns, all emblems of encroaching inauthenticity, were becoming the norm. Men and women who had dreamed of writing the Great American Novel found themselves employed by Madison Avenue to churn out jingles urging people to chew Juicy Fruit and smoke Lucky Strikes. Architectural critics assailed suburban communities for their "multitude of uniform, unidentifiable houses, lined up inflexibly, at uniform distance, on uniform roads . . . inhabited by people of the same class, the same income . . . witnessing the same television programs, eating the same tasteless pre-fabricated foods, from the same freezers, conforming in every outward and inward respect to a common mold." The magazine viewed these trends with alarm, fretting about moral flabbiness, commercialization, and the tendency among its own readers toward cowardly acquiescence to cultural standardization.[26]

In Victoria Lincoln's 1946 short story "Comfort," for example, the high ground of authenticity and simplicity was clearly occupied by a dark-skinned other. Narrated by a fourteen-year-old girl who has lost both parents in an automobile accident, "Comfort" tells the story of the succor offered the grieving child by Portofiro, the family's Mexican "houseboy."

The story is set in the Edenic California of the prewar years. The deceased parents were this Eden's Adam and Eve, exemplars of a liberal bohemian innocence, as authentic as white people could be. Her father had been a rather bad, though successful, portrait painter. Her mother was a Californian who "really liked Mexicans," and laughed about the fact that Californians "gave streets and towns Spanish names" and then "pushed all the people of Spanish descent around." She often joked that it was just as if everyone "in Montgomery, Alabama, called things Mammy Road and Rastus Square and Uncle Tom Boulevard." Both mother and father were representatives of the most bohemian segment of the *New Yorker* audience, situated somewhere between the sterile inauthenticity of middle-class American life and the romantic vitality of ethnic culture.

This "happy, casual family," which resided in a private, unracist paradise, could not endure. An auto accident kills the parents, casting the narrator and her two brothers out into a world populated by middle-class neighbors who arrange a funeral service with music "like melted candy bars and a dreadful, false, cheery sermon." The child knows that there is something wrong with the way everyone tells her not to cry and to just "go on being normal." She also understands that the exclusion of the "houseboy," Portofiro, and his family from the funeral has made it into a meaningless ritual.

A few days after the funeral, Connie, the bereaved child, returns home in hopes of recovering some authentic feelings. When she arrives at the shuttered house, Portofiro is there, watering her mother's flowers. "I keep her flowers pretty. Just a while," he tells the child. Connie, the narrator, flings herself into Portofiro's arms, and as he embraces her, he utters "a droll Latin shout—surprise, love, pity, all at once." He takes her in his "thick, short, hairy forearms, so hard and real," and bursts "into tears and sobs," holding her "with love like the love that Mother and Father had always" given her—"plain, natural, open love, without notions and patronizing sentimentality."[27]

They weep together. "Poor little one," he says, "the mother dead, the father dead . . . Oh God, Oh, Mother of God." It is in this moment, with her head nestled against Portofiro's "sweaty, smelly shirt," that Connie is awakened to the enormity of her loss, "never to see them again, to touch them, never, never." Portofiro, expressive and romantic, is fully able to accommodate her grief and restore her to life. He has reconnected her to her heart. Only then can she feel her "loss and cruel grief all together, solemn and real and important, alive in [her] heart."[28]

The capacity of the other to awaken feeling was also the topic of the sequel to "Comfort," "In the Reeds by the River." In this story Connie is now fifteen and living with her aunt and uncle in a sterile Kansas suburb. Connie's only solace is the town's Hooverville, a little row of shanties near the railroad tracks, that seem to her "enchanted eyes . . . romantic and delightful and, more than that, comprehensible," as her aunt's house is not. It is here that she meets Mr. deRocca, a middle-aged Italian anarchist and carpenter, with a "fine-boned" body and much narrower shoulders than "the Mexicans with whom [she] unconsciously classed him." Like "Comfort," this is the story of a single embrace. But here the embrace of the other offered both comfort and a sexual awakening. The adolescent Connie is lured down to the river bank by old Mr. deRocca (about whom it is said: "he's liking the girl.") She allows him to caress and embrace her and wonders "if all Italians are like him, so little and handsome and wise."[29] "What had happened that afternoon, what had really happened?" she asks. "It wasn't only that I had let Mr. deRocca kiss me and touch me like that. It was something that had happened in me. There was something in me—and in the world, too— that I had never known was there before, something powerful and lovely, something powerful and new."[30] Like Portofiro's hug, Mr. deRocca's kiss is more than just a kiss. What these stories suggest is that intimate contact with an ethnic other can deliver a powerful antidote to the anonymity of bourgeois American life, with its sterile subdivisions and its "treeless communal wastes." The kiss of the ethnic is a pathway out of this monotony into a more diverse and emotionally satisfying world.

The death of Connie's parents makes her a cultural orphan. It forecloses for her their footloose, artistic, and Edenic upper-middle-class life style. She is left without defense against the inauthenticity and blandness of middle-class life in which she is urged to hide her feelings. Connie is held hostage by a culture more pedestrian and less cosmopolitan than that of her parents. Bereft, she turns to the only warmth and authenticity she can find in the barren landscape to which their deaths have consigned her—a comfort offered by a dark-skinned other.

The kiss of Manuel Ramos in Jessamyn West's "Love, Death, and the Ladies' Drill Team," like that of Mr. deRocca in "In the Reeds by the River," represented the life-giving vitality of the other. The contrast between Anglo and Mexican in this story paralleled nothing less than the polarity of life and death. The disembodied nature of middle-class Californian Anglo society, with its rigid rules of style and conduct, was on the side of death, while the bold sensuality of the other embodied life.

In "Love and Death," a group of upper-middle-class California matrons spend their mornings marching in formation as the Pocahontas Drill team. The Pocahontas "girls" are defined by the men they are with (or, as is the case of the one widow and the one spinster among their number, the men they are *not* with.) "Amy Rotunda, whose name suggests a funeral monument, is Fred Rotunda's widow." Ruby Graves (another funereal moniker) is "Milton Grave's unmarried daughter and housekeeper." Opal Tetford's husband is a bank executive, "her soft opulence . . . suited to the protection of vaults and burglar alarms." Although these women rely on their husbands for identity, they do not seem to have any amorous connection to them.[31]

This is not the case, however, with Imola Ramos, a woman from their own set who married Manuel Ramos for love (or did she marry?) and whose capers stir the girls' curiosity to a fever pitch. They cluster at the window to spy on the former Imola Butterfield Fetters, who is wearing "no brassiere and not much else" underneath a "red-flowered dress" that had once been a "window curtain or a tablecloth."

Mrs. Rotunda is puzzled by Imola's love life, for in her estimation LeRoy Fetters, the registered pharmacist who was Imola's first husband, was a model spouse—so devoted that he even used to wash his wife's long black hair. Mrs. Rotunda also claims that she saw "black-and-blue spots the size of quarters" on Imola's arms, proof that the "Mexican manhandles" her.

Mrs. Phillips possesses inside information about the pair because they live near her "in one of those three-room shacks that the water company furnishes its Mexican workers." She tells the girls that Imola and Manuel do a lot "of sporting around together, in and out of the water" and "so far's washing is concerned," Imola is the one that does the washing now—"and not just his hair." This disclosure produces a flurry of excited commentary: "A Butterfield washing a Mexican! Sunk that low!" Ruby Graves says: "I expect he's pretty dark-skinned?" Mrs. Phillips explains that it's difficult to "tell the two of them apart" because they lie around sun-tanning after they "finish swimming or washing . . . And all the while, Imola is [n]aked as a jay bird."

The girls watch excitedly as Imola's lover approaches her in the street and Imola pulls a huge bunch of purple grapes from her bag and begins to pop them "alternately into her own mouth and into that of the Mexican." Then they kiss. "Poor Imola!" Mrs. Tetford sighs. "Where is her pride?" Emily Cooper, the story's narrator surprises herself by exclaiming "Pride? . . . pride doesn't enter in. She loves him." This comment is met by a long silence broken only when Mrs. Rotunda repeats:

"Love?" as if this were something infinitely alien and then, suddenly businesslike, orders the girls into marching position "hands on shoulders . . . an arm's length apart."[32]

Unlike the Pocahontas girls' husbands, who are entirely occupied with and identified by their professions, Manuel has neither a regular job nor regular hours. His energies are put to work solely in the service of life—to fight, to make love, to eat grapes, to bathe, and to serenade his lover. His vitality is infectious. By consorting with Manuel, Imola becomes indistinguishable from him. His otherness is carried by touch and by kiss. It is both a positive attribute and a communicable one.

West's story captures the underlying assumptions of *The New Yorker*'s writing about the life-giving properties of ethnic culture and the moribund nature of white bourgeois society. The girls march in strict formation while Imola "runs the gamut" with her Latin lover, going "from feast to famine." Black and blue marks notwithstanding, Imola seems a happy woman. The mild racism of the Pocahontas girls marks them as prisoners of the relentless uniformity of bourgeois life and blinds them to Manuel's enlivening powers. At a more unconscious level, however, the text of "Love, Death and the Ladies Drill Team," like that of "In the Reeds by the River," reveals a double standard concerning ethnics and their interplay with members of the dominant society. It would be impossible, for example, to find a story in the postwar *New Yorker* that would sympathetically portray a fifty-year-old WASP man making love to a fifteen-year-old girl, as Mr. deRocca does in "In the Reeds by the River." Nor would one find an appreciation of the erotic aspects of WASP wife beating. Ethnicity was the variable here. While Anglos marched in formation, ethnics obeyed a different drummer. The bereaved child in middle America, and the woman drying up in the arms of a registered pharmacist in Los Robles, California, were rescued by the life-giving kisses of Portofiro and Mr. deRocca and Manuel Ramos. By breaking (or being ignorant of) the strict rules of bourgeois society, these dusky saviors infuse its victims with hope and promise. They rescue them from emotional death. The behaviors that were tolerated in the name of this higher purpose would not, could not, be tolerated from their WASP opposite numbers.

The capacity to breathe life into a moribund culture was only the most grandiose of the claims made for ethnic others in *The New Yorker*. They were also generous in spite of their poverty, humbler, more philosophical, and less grasping than their white observers. This idea of the link between internal goodness and external hardship is intimately connected with a converse idea that seems to trouble *New Yorker* writers: that money is the root of internal corruption. This assumption runs through much of what is written about dark-skinned ethnics in the magazine and suggests some slippage in the smooth *New Yorker* terrain—in which affluence and social rectitude were presumed to be two sides of the cosmopolitan coin.

This sense of the naturally good "native" compared invidiously with his more complex and somewhat more venal Euro-American opposite number is the central subject of "Mr. Mookerjhee," a 1949 story by Robert Clurman about an inept Indian clerk at the United Press office in Calcutta. The narrator of the story, a journalist who has been sent to streamline the news bureau along Western lines, finds that Mr. Mookerjhee, sweet though he is, can neither type nor efficiently edit cables. Because the new bureau chief is touched by the incompetent clerk's timid gentility, it takes him some time to summon the nerve to fire him. When he finally calls Mr.Mookerjhee into his office, the little clerk sits with his hands neatly folded in his lap, and nods in sympathy as he is told just how inept he is. "His dark, liquid eyes forgave everything. He realized he was no good . . . The agency had been foolish to keep him as long as it had."[33]

In the name of efficiency another, more accomplished clerk, Mr. Bannerjhee, is hired to take his place, and Mr. Mookerjhee agrees to stay on for two weeks to train him. The two clerks establish an immediate rapport. Soon the two are having lunch together every day, and the bureau chief thinks as he watches them crossing the street holding hands (a commonplace amongst male Indian friends) that "something was going wrong."

Mr. Mookerjhee, on what is meant to be his last day at the office, arrives wearing his best clothes and begins collecting his things. The items in his desk have an archeological significance to the narrator. They are the simple effects of the strange small life of the other: "a cake of soap, a small blue towel, a comb, a bottle of sesamum, a pocket English dictionary, and several back copies of American news magazines, which he must have rescued from the wastebasket."

Mr. Bannerjhee, however, has a plan. He brings a news story to the bureau chief, claiming that Mr. Mookerjhee has copied it by himself. "Mr. Mookerjhee is very happy here," he explains. We "have become very good friends . . . I can't take Mr. Mookerjhee's job." At this moment, Mr. Mookerjhee enters the office and gives his compatriot a look of "benign reproach." He, of course, will not permit Mr. Bannerjhee to sacrifice his new job. "Mr. Mookerjhee's eyes were moist. Mr. Bannerjhee's eyes were moist." After two hours of talking, and much handshaking, the pair leave the chief's office "arm in arm, pausing long enough for Mr. Mookerjhee to put the soap, towel, and comb back in his desk."[34]

The bureau chief is rendered powerless in the face of the two men's philosophical refusal to compete with one another. His capitalistic priorities—efficiency, and modernity—crumble in the face of his employees' gentle antimaterialism. This is a story about someone who is enabled through contact with virtuous others to hear the beat of their drummer. In spite of this triumph of the meek, the story's tone suggests that the editor's capitulation is only a temporary lapse. The gentle lesson in decency delivered by the two clerks is tolerated rather than learned. The narrative voice in the story has a certain imperial flavor. The bureau chief gives in to the two men's fierce loyalty to one another with good nature and even a bit of admiration. Still, their behavior strikes him as a quaint cultural quirk, rather like the sight of two grown men holding hands.

This is just one of a number of *New Yorker* stories in which others were at once admired and patronized: Mr. Bannerjhee and Mr. Mookerjhee were seen both as exemplary and ridiculous. Their decency was attributed to the simplicity of their material world—a notion that undercut the sacrifice and nobility of Mr. Bannerjhee's gesture. They were guileless creatures, neither having nor needing much. Consequently, their lack of greed was not much of a stretch. They were at once more and less than the audience that was reading about them. While their purity was exalted, it was understood to be a product of their limitation. Neither empowered nor encumbered by the gifts of modern science and systematic reason, these innocent others were unfamiliar with the full-blown glories of capitalist accumulation. The bureau chief admired the unaffected virtue of the two clerks, but showed no inclination to emulate them. In the same vein, while European and American writers made use of the Noble Savage to criticize their society, they clearly had no intention of becoming savages themselves. Still, this veneration of the superior goodness of less privileged ethnics does suggest a nagging anxiety concerning the peaceful coexistence of affluence and virtue. The story of the simpler, purer other both exposed and appeased the self-doubt of those who told it. These romantic critiques of capitalistic materialism also constituted an indirect tribute to its seductive power.[35]

"Arab Editor," a 1946 short story by James Maxwell, is a virtual handbook of the ways in which the invention of the romanticized other served its inventors, both as an instrument of self-criticism and as a balm. The story focuses on a dinner conversation at the British Officers' club in Tripoli. The interlocutors are the American narrator, a former newspaperman who is there as an intelligence officer; Major Murdock, a British Arab Affairs officer; and Ahmed, the son of a wealthy Cairo merchant who edits a British-owned newspaper in Tripoli. Ahmed, the story's central character, straddles the Arab and European worlds. He wears "handsome, well-tailored suits . . . and [was] educated in Switzerland and England." The character belongs to the literary tradition of the tragic half-breed. The man beneath the tasteful worsteds is outraged by the postwar domination of his people, and is perfectly situated to see the central lie in all cultural hegemony. Ahmed characterizes the Americans and British who control his people as "hopeless sentimentalist[s]" who "ignore or emasculate" the real nature of the people they control.[36]

Major Murdock, the Arab Affairs Officer, represents the best of his type, a colonial British Arab hand, at once reverent and condescending toward the people he helps to rule. During the meal, the Major broods about the way that America has "turned its back on the philosophers and placed all its faith in the scientists. Your people, and ours, too, for that matter—could do far worse than study the Arabic philosophy," says the Major, as he sips pink gin. "I've known and studied these people for years, and their calm acceptance of life's fortunes never ceases to inspire me. The Arab is deeply contemplative. He searches his own soul for the truth that would be in all of us if we weren't diverted by materialism." The "tranquillity" of the Arab, he opines, "is far more valuable than the material wealth we enjoy." Ahmed rejects the Major's mythical Arab as a self-serving invention—a "balm for [his] conscience," the product of "a guilt complex."[37]

This story quite consciously provides *New Yorker* readers with an index of the uses and abuses of the noble other. Ahmed, straddling two worlds, can see through the idealization of his people by those who dominate them. He understands both the dehumanizing nature of the romance of the other and the way it functions to allay guilt. Ahmed points out that what the Major assumes to be "contemplation is often hunger . . . You credit us with high spiritual values so you needn't concern yourself with our physical needs." Turning to the narrator, Ahmed adds, "I think you once told me there's a phrase about Negroes used in your country—'They want to live like that.'" The Major then accuses Ahmed of having become "entirely too Europeanized" and materialistic.[38]

The New Yorker's uses of ethnicity can furnish us with a chart of some of the preoccupations of a significant faction of postwar American society. The magazine's stories tended to lionize Hispanics, Arabs, Native Americans, and Asians for their simplicity, their virtue, and their poverty, while concurrently patronizing them for these very attributes. These idealized representations functioned as an indirect way to criticize the smug affluence and gracelessness of postwar middle-class America. The emphasis on the purity and antimaterialism of others, their authenticity and their life-giving capacity, point to values which *New Yorker* contributors found lacking in themselves. Guilt, self-doubt, a sense of

THE WORLD THROUGH A MONOCLE

being out-of-joint with the natural world, and a fear of having lost or misplaced some essential piece of their own humanity were all implicit in the writers' perceptions of others. This suggests that while members of the *New Yorker* village clung tenaciously to the benefits of civilization, they could not help but wonder at its discontents.

7

MANAGING WITH SERVANTS

The New Yorker used the soft and romanticizing lens of distance for Fiji Islanders in weird headdresses, flamboyant black boxing champs, Native American orphans, and pure-spirited Indian clerks. The magazine's portraits of domestic servants, by comparison, were close-ups—descriptions of a relatively habitual intimacy between upper-middle-class families and the workers who entered their homes as indispensable familiars, yet strangers.

In the decade that followed the end of World War II, a significant portion of *New Yorker* fiction, poetry, and cartoons was devoted to the consolations and complications of living with help. On the magazine's pages serious fiction and journalism by important writers coexisted with countless stories, cartoons, and casual pieces concerning the troubling presence of servants in the household. Although many of these pieces about domestic help were less than distinguished literary efforts, they offer what is perhaps the best index of *The New Yorker*'s assumptions about social class.

The nature of the intimate relationship between employer and servant allows us to see deeply into what was perhaps the most profound peculiarity of the postwar liberal elite—its attempt both to claim privilege and disclaim its undemocratic nature. The profound ambivalence of the postwar liberal intelligentsia toward the entire notion of social class was deeply rooted in what Gunnar Myrdal has called the American Creed, with its emphasis upon the fundamental equality of all people. Postwar affluence too, with its almost universal availability of mass-produced goods for all, perpetuated a vision of an ideal democracy in which barriers of class were obfuscated. This alleged classlessness, however, gave rise to a desire among members of the upper middle class to distinguish themselves from the middle class by demonstrating a taste for goods and services that were not available to the others, while concurrently maintaining a commitment to egalitarian principle.[1]

Household help was a tried and true way to telegraph elite social status. However, while having servants demonstrated one aspect of sophistication, upholding egalitarian principle constituted another important component of postwar cosmopolitanism. There was no other arena in which a conflict between the two sides of the equation was more likely to take place than in the day-to-day relations between upper-middle-class cosmopolitans and their domestic servants. While transatlantic crossings, foreign films, and cocktail parties were all avenues of sophisticated living that could be pursued with relative ease, the maintenance of household help was fraught with difficulty because, by its very nature, this practice clashed with the ideals of a democratic society that were the chapter and verse of liberal doctrine. Thus this powerful cohort made itself blind to some class differences as it remained keenly aware of others.

While domestic help was assumed to be a necessary prop of civilized social life, the presence of servants inevitably raised issues about disparities between classes and races that many liberal intellectuals preferred to ignore. Because the denial of its own entitlement was a salient part of the ethos of the *New Yorker* village, quite often the fact of having help was dispatched with jaunty irony, as if the act of laughing at privilege somehow democratized it. A 1946 "Talk of the Town," for example, reported that a child at a progressive school (purportedly the child of an acquaintance of the anonymous "Talk" writer) had turned in a composition about a "very poor family," in which "The mother was poor, the father was poor, the daughter was poor, the cook was poor, and the butler was poor."[2]

The delicate etiquette of postwar race relations had the effect of suppressing virtually any comedic writing about black servants and their white employers. Although the majority of the actual household help employed in postwar Manhattan was still African-American, in most *New Yorker* pieces concerning domestic help in the North, the servants were white. The Negro family retainer remained a commonplace only in the magazine's writing about the American South. Just as the magazine relocated stereotyped images of black people into jungle milieus, postwar depictions of comical or incompetent household help were transferred to a population of dopey white servants. The magazine's "Maids Say the Darndest Things" genre (my title, not theirs), a series of humorous offerings describing servants' foolishness, illiteracy, bad grammar, and inability to decode the upper-middle-class text, entirely excluded black servants from its sizable canon.

Writing (especially humor writing) always takes place within some completely concrete cultural situation which readers will be able to "get." The very existence of a genre entirely devoted to detailing the eccentricity and obtuseness of white household help suggests both a sensitivity to racial stereotyping and a certain discomfort concerning class standing. A month rarely passed without the magazine printing at least one funny note from the maid/cleaning lady/house painter/handyman. These pieces inevitably included a clear signal of the employer's class status: "The hostess at a holiday buffet"; "A matron" in "the East Eighties"; "A well-certified young lady"; "A professional lady."[3]

A typical offering in the genre from an October 1948 issue concerned a tired businesswoman returning home to find the electricity off in her apartment and a note from her cleaning woman propped up against a candle placed in the kitchen sink. The note explained with misspelled formality that a string from the mop had become caught in an electrical cord "and cause a short circuit and it burned and at the same time it bleu the flues . . . If I could regret it I would. Lovingly, Ethel"[4]

The alleged humor in this piece derived from the slapstick vignette summoned up by the description the maid gave of the mop and the short circuit, the "lovingly, Ethel" that closed the letter, and the misuse of the word "regret." In a casual from 1946, inexplicably entitled "Aristocratic," Hilda, a maid who was "unaccountably devoting a two-week vacation to a tour of the middle west," wrote to her employers: "Haveing a fine time. Stopt in Cincinati 14 hrs. The Union terminal there, blt ten years ago, is the most exclucive in the world. Yrs."[5]

Hilda's postcard enhanced readers' sense of the distance between their world and that of their domestics. Although this maid has made an end run into elite territory by touring, sending postcards, and sightseeing, she is blind to the conventions of upper-middle-class vacationing. Her attempt to emulate the ways of her employers exposed her as a buffoon.

A doorman at a hospital was sent to search for a staff surgeon's lost Phi Beta Kappa key. Returning empty-handed, he shook his head sadly and said: "Gee, I hope he isn't locked out." A hostess at "a holiday buffet dinner decorated her table with a cornucopia centerpiece from which a mass of fruit poured forth in the classic tradition, and went upstairs . . . to fix her hair." Her maid regarded the cornucopia critically, "emptied it, stood it upright, propped it with some oranges, and had barely finished stuffing the last of the fruit into the horn when the first guest rang the bell."[6]

What is interesting about these anecdotes is the amount of class nuance embedded in them. Most striking, in light of the presumed enlightened liberalism of *The New Yorker*'s readers, is how much paternalism and class negotiation they contained. They also pointed to an employer class that was jealous of its turf and anxious to protect its symbols from being borrowed or understood by its servants. Yet although these pieces were fueled by an interest in class distinction, class itself was never mentioned. The discrepancies between employer and servant were attributed to differences in social style rather than differences in social caste.

In these casual pieces, white domestics were cast in the sort of minstrel show roles previously the purview of African Americans. These daffy white people broke things, committed malapropisms, and attempted to emulate their bosses—an effort which only served to highlight their inability to replicate the innuendoes of their employers' densely coded reality. Just beneath the surface of this paternalistic fun-poking lay a immovable heap of class dogma.

Clearly, given the frequency with which they appeared, there was something about these humorous tidbits that appealed to the magazine's readers. The "Maids Say the Darndest Things" motif emerged at a particular historical moment within a particular cultural institution. It is impossible, for example, to imagine the leading mass market magazines of this period, such as *Saturday Evening Post, Look, Life,* or *The Reader's Digest* publishing humorous articles about household help, largely because most of their readers did not employ domestic workers. Conversely, although *Vogue* and *Town and Country,* magazines with no democratic pretensions, were certainly presumed to be aimed at people who either had servants or liked to read about the sorts of people who had servants, the outlandish behavior of domestic help was rarely invoked. This distinction is revealing. The domestics in the high-end glossy monthlies moved silently through that world, fluffing pillows, serving tea, sporting livery, and opening limousine doors. In other words, they served; *New Yorker* domestics *interacted.* The comic representations of household help that appeared with such regularity in the postwar magazine seemed to suggest both a discomfort with servants and a certain reticence about managing them. In *The New Yorker* the line that sepa rated maid from mistress was often either unseen or ignored by many domestics. For their part, employers saw the line but were often reluctant to protect it. The delicate negotiations that took place across it suggested some tentativeness amongst upper-middle-class professionals about their class prerogatives. In some cases this uncertainty was the product of a certain egalitarian resistance to the enjoyment of privileged status. In other cases it was derived from the very recent acquisition of this status. Certainly it is possible that some *New Yorker* readers and contributors felt genuine befuddlement about how to manage these strangers who came into their homes and into their lives. When *New Yorker* servants intervened—made suggestions, sent postcards, rearranged centerpieces, and called their bosses "honey"—employers took note. They retaliated against this microinvasion, not by firing or reproaching their helpers, but rather by infantilizing them and translating their behavior into farce—a transformation that assuaged both the reluctance to claim privilege and the lack of confidence about how to make such claims.

Peter De Vries, a frequent contributor to the magazine, often wrote about the intricate class dynamics of the household peculiar to this cultural community. "Pygmalion," published in the magazine in 1952, documented the ongoing struggle for symbolic turf waged between master and servant. "Young and impressionable" Susan Kearns works for Mrs. Lovett, mistress not only of Susan but of a colorful idiom that resonates with the cadences of women of her class. "You were an absolute dove . . . I was sort of looking around the room for you when suddenly there was this creature in this sort of old-rose job, with her hair skun in a bun . . . chewed my ear off about gardens and things. Anyhoo." Susan, who has a "quick ear for the niceties of urban speech," is impressed by Mrs. Lovett's social patois and imitates her brilliantly. She practices her newly acquired lingo on her friends, refusing to go to a restaurant because it is "tearoomy," suggesting instead "a little steak place I know on Third Avenue. Sort of divey, but good."

One evening Mrs. Lovett returns home and finds Susan talking on the telephone. "Just wanted to make sure you got home after our little do," Susan croons, "and to say I enjoyed same. I've got a foul headache

. . . Anyhoo, you get married and have babies and things, so we don't *both* end up little old ladies who sort of carry umbrellas when it snows and give mulled-claret parties." Unnerved, both by the inflections and the words, Mrs. Lovett feels a "sensation a little like that of having caught an unintentional glimpse of herself in a glass."[7]

What is most interesting about the story is what it reveals about the precariousness of Mrs. Lovett's sense of herself. She assumes she is being caricatured rather than emulated, and accuses Susan, her keenest admirer, of thinking she is a "boob" and aping her in order to "keep [her] friends in stitches." "Do you do this sort of thing often . . . Give these impressions?" Confused by her employer's question, Susan responds: "I honestly think I try to give a good impression at *all* times and to do my part." Ahhh. Readers could breathe a sigh of relief. Susan may have been adept at imitating the idiom of their domain, but she still didn't know what an "impression" was.

These pieces are comedic snapshots of a world covertly ruled by class distinctions—a world presumably recognizable to *New Yorker* readers. The comedy in these pieces was dependent on the ability of the reader to identify with the employer and take pleasure in locating him or herself in some humorous detail of a larger map charting the vast social distance between employee and employer. The recurrence of this kind of humor week after week suggested a reader who could nod knowingly at Hilda's bad spelling, her use of tatty words like "exclusive," and the tastelessness of her vacation. The hapless servant who upended a cornucopia and the doorman who thought Phi Beta keys unlocked things (don't they?) were immediately recognized as people who did not understand class stanchions, failures that would mark them as clearly as if they had mistaken a finger bowl for a cup of soup.

These comic items functioned as quizzes. By getting the joke, readers of the magazine could authenticate their status and assure themselves that *they* would certainly have left the cornucopia on its side! These slightly mean-spirited offerings provide us with a sense of the fragility and the complexity of the maintenance of upper-middle-class status for the followers of the *New Yorker*. For many readers whose parents or grandparents had been immigrants or farmers or small-town residents in the South and Middle West, the social distance between servant and employer may have felt perilously insignificant. It may well have been the very narrowness of that strait and the ease with which domestics could navigate it that made these items so gratifying to *New Yorker* readers. The magazine represented these forays of domestics into their bosses' terrain as comedic examples of the childish inability of the servant class to play by the rules of the haute bourgeoisie game. By bathing these incidents in the benign light of farce, and employing the well-worn literary convention of the lower-class buffoon, the magazine defuses any potential class conflict and assures employers that their servants know not what they do; they, the employers, have the last laugh.

Although these anecdotal pieces imply that there is something troubling about the permeability of the boundary between employer and employee, they also make it clear that there is not much to be done about it. For people who did not like to insist upon class distinctions, having household help created real discomforts. On the one hand, it forced employers into a kind of unwanted intimacy with members of a lower class. But for a number of reasons—whether because of their own modest backgrounds, their egalitarian inclinations, or both—it was distasteful for them to formalize these relationships by reverting to rigid etiquette of class.

Unwilling as they were to pull rank with their employees, they were very amenable to ridiculing their various idiocies. In his short story "They Also Sit," Peter De Vries described his troubles with various hired babysitters, who seemed universally reluctant to maintain a respectful distance. First there was "a tall, colloquial sort from the Middle West, named Hoffman," who marched into the living room and proclaimed: "Pew, it smells like Whiting, Indiana, in here." She also pointed out that they had "holes under [the] sink big enough to fall through . . . rats and God knows what else can come up through the wall."

The "second sitter," Mrs. Balch, called De Vries "Mr. Debris," and also surveyed the house with mild contempt. The "last sitter," Mrs. La

Plante, whose politics De Vries described as "rabid moderate," was by far the most troubling. Her most memorable traits were "a hearty interest in controversial questions" and a desire "to share her belief in an obscure sect which holds that human welfare depends on some nervous identification with the Infinite, that a happy human being is like a radio tuned to the right vibrations, and that this is in some way bound up with diet." Had this sitter's opining been confined to business hours, it might have been less unsavory. But the fact that it assumed the form of unwanted social intercourse—weird pamphlets in the mail and unsolicited telephone calls—suggested a disturbing blurring of class lines.

What all of these helpers—the sitters, day workers, handymen—shared was autonomy from their employers, whose households and habits they regarded with some disdain. At least some of the difficulties that fictional *New Yorker* employers had with their employees apparently derived from their own lack of status, which was not, it seems, sufficiently upper-class to check the lower-class conduct of their help. The more time a servant spent with the employer the less likely he or she was to write a hortatory note or comment on the holes under the sink. While full-time live-in help hired by the very wealthy understood the etiquette of class relations, surrendered some independence, and often became socialized into their employers' world, part-time help remained disengaged, un-housebroken, less interested in cracking the code.[8]

In *New Yorker* fiction the maid who lived on her own or had, a husband, held political opinions or another job, was a disturbing entity. This kind of autonomy was seen as something threatening to the narrators in these pieces, who often revealed a degree of insecurity both about the hierarchical nature of master-servant relations and their own plausibility as members of the elite employer class. When the maid, the cook, or the cleaning lady maintained enough detachment from the household she had entered to make judgments about it, employers often were plagued by the disconcerting sense of exposing their furniture, their apartments, and their private lives to people who, whatever their social status, were capable of seeing through their employers' thin patina of class prerogative.

A frequent motif in the magazine's fiction on the subject of domestic help was the issue of confusing class origins. Stories and casual pieces describing interactions between employers and servants who weren't really servants, or didn't use to be servants, or who failed to act like servants, reflected the keen status anxiety of the new middle class. The presence of a hired "other" who knew more than the master of the house about setting a banquet table, or horseback riding, or manners in general was more than confusing for employers—it made them susceptible to an outsider's criticism of their style and taste, areas of particular vulnerability. It also had the effect of dislodging traditional servant/employer etiquette and creating for employers the uncomfortable necessity of conforming to some new and baffling array of practices.

In a 1949 "Talk of the Town" piece, "a Beverly Hills housewife" who had been looking for a cook finds a note from her maid explaining that Pauline "called about the cook job. She has worked for Richard Dix and Louis B. Mayer. If you'd like to see her, call her daughter's number, as she is booking all Pauline's interviews."[9]

The "mistress of a modest Westchester household" claimed to have made it through a most "trying experience" with "flying colors." The trying experience arose when "an applicant for the position of cook" showed up in a riding habit and "announced that the pay, accommodations, size of the family, etc., suited her fine, but that she had a horse that would have to be accommodated too." The matron, defined as "stableless but plucky," established the horse in a barn down the road and "the last we heard" the cook was "in the kitchen, happily baking a souffle." Presumably, the fact that the employer's household was a "modest" one contributed greatly to the "tryingness" of the experience. Had she been mistress of a large estate, or had the applicant showed up in a shabby coat or an apron, she could have dispatched the entire situation with ease.[10]

"Rudi," a memory piece written by Elizabeth McConaughy, the wife of the President of Wesleyan University, concerned an Austrian couple who came to work for her in 1938. When Rudi applied for the position, he explained to Jim McConaughy: "my wife and I wish to learn all sides of American life. We wish to learn to please all kinds of people. Someday I shall have my own hotel. Already Marie and I know the rich. In your home we shall learn to know the intelligent." Rudi keeps copies of Emily Post and the New York *Social Register* next to his cookbooks in the kitchen. He tries "tactfully to educate the professors and their wives" in various matters of taste, and frowns at them when they request cream in their afterdinner coffee. "He'll make a lady of me yet," the narrator exclaims to her husband.

The employers in this story—liberal intellectuals with enough money to have servants but with little or no interest in the more recherché aspects of etiquette—were typical of fictional *New Yorker* employers. While the McConaughys are certain that Rudi finds their household sadly lacking in upper-class accoutrements and savoir faire, they express their mastery over the situation by patronizing him, chuckling over his interest in social hierarchy, and indulging his taste for heel clicking, white uniforms, and high formality. Rudi becomes a family joke, a quaint figure in their own comic opera.[11]

While the *New Yorker*'s insecure employers displayed a certain discomfort with class distinctions and felt uneasy about their own claims to elite status, another significant body of writing concerning domestic help focused specifically on the pain of awakening to class differences. This genre dealt with the bittersweet topic of nanny love, and nanny love lost. These coming-of-age stories by author/narrators focused on the servants who had ruled over their seamless childhood worlds—worlds in which the notion of class has not yet reared its ugly head. The tragic dénouement in these pieces was the moment at which a child or young adult was forced to confront the fact of a family retainer's humanity, and concurrently the existence of social class. Through this recognition the narrator experienced something deeper—the loss of innocence that came with the knowledge of a cardinal fact: nanny is not one of us. It was at the moment that the narrator was exposed to nanny's otherness—her tawdry little flat, her sick mother, her sordid secret life—that childhood ended.[12]

Perhaps the archetypal example of this genre was Ludovic Kennedy's

"Grace Arrowhead," a story of a young man's class epiphany. The narrator has grown up with "Nanny," a woman whose "whole life seemed to be dedicated" to him. He could not "picture [her] as existing in any other environment" than his childhood home. For years he did not even know her real name, and when he eventually learned that it was "Grace Arrowhead," he found it "somehow unlikely and rather indelicate."[13]

John, the narrator, now a man of thirty, is paying a visit to his family's estate before taking an extended trip abroad. During his stay, Nanny falls on the ice and fractures her leg, an incident that forces him to measure a distance he has never before computed—the vast social space separating him from this woman whose love formed the nucleus of his childhood. Called upon to deal with the accident, John finds his old nurse moaning in pain. "Profoundly shocked" by the sight of her "frail body lying on the bright chintz of the sofa and the gaily colored cushions that emphasize[d] the drabness of her dress," he finds her suffering terrible and "grotesque." He is "curiously distressed" by the sight of a "little bundle of her things—a nightdress, bedroom slippers, a hairbrush, and a washing bag" that have been gathered together for her to take to the hospital.

"For thirty years," the narrator explains, "I had accepted her not as a being with hopes and desires and emotions of her own . . . not as one capable of suffering herself but as one who relieved the suffering of others." Faced with the reality of an "old, tired, sick woman," John is made painfully aware of the purposeful blindness of people of his kind to the human reality of those who serve them—a blindness which concurrently obscures uncomfortable inequities of class. "Never in all the time I had known her had I been conscious of any social distinction between us. We had never been rich, or Nanny, I think, very poor."

The sight of Nanny's suffering, her little bundle of belongings, her threadbare frock are visual cues that open John's eyes to Nanny's class origin. But he is destined to experience this truth at a deeper level. In the ambulance on the way to the hospital, his once docile, classless Nanny suddenly turns fierce and vulgar. She gives "a terrible cry" and accuses the ambulance attendants of being after her money. "Well, you won't get it. I've hidden it, see . . . You buggers!" Soon the ambulance is "drenched in a flow of [her] invective and abuse . . . fouler than anything" John has ever heard. "Like the steady discharge from a burst sewer pipe the stream gushed: memories from a childhood that froze the imagination; things observed and experienced . . . in nearly a century of living."

The horror of recognizing through the vehicle of language the coarse realities that the angel of his nursery must have encountered in her life away from him is at once illuminating and devastating for John. When he returns home months later, he is afraid that Nanny will remember the incident and that this shameful knowledge will make it impossible for them to return comfortably to their former roles. Boldly, he gazes into her eyes, looking "for the black shadow of recognition, for the evil thing [he] prayed [he] might not see." But there was only the same "kindness and gentleness and love" that he had long depended on. "Come and sit down, dear boy . . . I've got some crumpets for your tea. You always did like crumpets, didn't you?"[14]

The author has conflated two shattering ruptures which are indeed related: the recognition of the social fissure between servant and master, and the metamorphosis of the servant into a stranger for whom the narrator is no longer the center of attention. This moment represents an irreparable crack in the universe of privileged youth—a crack followed by the awareness that he has lost an Eden. Although the story was set in a wealthy English setting where nannies and butlers were presumably a commonplace, it speaks to the way in which living with servants forced employers (and their children) into conversations with "others." Unlike the precariously upper-middle-class households discussed earlier, in which anxious employers watched servants flagrantly trespass class lines, the upper-class domestic setting represented in this story conferred a kind of honorary aristocratic status on servants—a status that had the effect of repressing their social origins. Children growing up in such households were exposed to faux peers: butlers, nannies, and governesses who appeared to share in the ethos of those who employed them. The peculiarly democratic social space inhabited by small children and their caretakers, who ate together in the kitchen and slept in adjacent rooms would not withstand the test of time. Inevitably, the children had to outgrow this classless society and take their places in the larger and more hierarchical world.[15]

The moment in which the mask of classlessness was torn from the faces of these domestics was a terrible one. It had a transformative power, rather like the first kiss, the first drink, or the first death. Knowledge of class differentiation was a kind of awareness that could not, once it was introduced, be disavowed. And it was one source of the tension members of *The New Yorker* readership experienced on the subject of household help. While their desire to live in a democratic society was genuine, the preeminent need to be served and to demonstrate elite status drew them into hierarchical relationships with domestics in which the existence of class distinction could not be denied. An important component of upper-middle-class maturation in *The New Yorker*'s cosmology was the ability to tolerate or suppress this particular crack in the universe. Part of the cost of privilege, it seems, was the guilty knowledge of social inequity.

Peter Taylor's "What You Hear from 'Em?" told the story of the ruptured idyll between children and their domestic caretakers from the perspective of Aunt Munsie, an ancient black nanny who can recollect "helping about the big house when freedom came" and has raised the children of the Tolliver family for several generations. Just as the child narrators of stories about lost nanny love remained fixated on those sunlit interludes in which they were offered perfect love by a substitute parent, so too was Aunt Munsie obsessed with the consummate moment in her life when the "Mizziz" died and "her word had become law in the Tolliver household. Without being able to book-read or even to make numbers, she had finished raising the whole pack of towheaded Tollivers just as the [late] Mizziz would have wanted it done."[16]

Aunt Munsie's two favorite Tolliver children, Thad and Will, have long since left the small town of their birth and become rich men. But for the old woman they have left behind there is only one burning question, "What you hear from 'em?" This query is misheard by people who had never been "quality" as "What you have for mom?" and misunderstood by the people who were not even "has-been quality" (Aunt Munsie's terms) as a request for the latest news of the "boys," their families, and their fabulously successful business ventures. But what Aunt Munsie wants "to hear from *them* was when they were coming back for good," and she knew that their Christmas letters and half-hour visits during their rare trips home "never told her that."[17]

Aunt Munsie's strongest allegiance was to the white children she had raised. Her own daughter, Lucrecie, was, in Munsie's view, "shiftless" and liked "shiftless white people . . . In her heart, Aunt Munsie knew that even Lucrecie didn't matter to her the way a daughter might." Conversely, Lucrecie talked about her mother "as she would have any lonely, eccentric, harmless neighbor." Whenever Mr. Will or Mr. Thad would come to visit Aunt Munsie, Lucrecie "would come out to the fence and say, "Mama, some of your chillun's out front."

Surrogacy—the alignment of servant and child alike with an alternative family—lay at the heart of such stories. It is the ultimate rupture of this alternative family that accounts for their bitter sadness. The dénouement of this story, for example, comes when Aunt Munsie is forced to acknowledge that Mr. Thad and Mr. Will "ain't never comin' back." This realization drives her into a tantrum during which she attacks her own dogs and chickens with an axe. "'Why don't I go down to Memphis or up to Nashville and see 'em sometime like *you* does?' Aunt Munsie asked the collie. 'I tell you why. Becaze I ain't nothin' to 'em in Memphis, and they ain't nothin' to me in Nashville. *You* can go! . . . A collie dog's a collie dog anywhar. But Aunt Munsie, she's just their Aunt Munsie here in Thornton. I got sense enough to see *that.*'"

Munsie is commenting on something profound here: the evanescent nature of the alternative family. Pain, illness, adulthood, a change of venue could ineluctably alter the nature of these deep but tenuous relationships. While Mr. Thad and Mr. Will faithfully visited Munsie and brought their children to meet her, she has lost her power over them. Class, and in this case race, have intervened. She cannot draw them back to Thornton with her love and it is only in Thornton that she is their "aunt." She is left behind like a childhood toy or a pet and by losing her claim on their hearts, loses that part of herself that she values most.[18]

Munsie's race was, to be sure, a critical component of this story. The fact of her blackness, even more than her lower class stature, lent pathos to Munsie's idea of herself as the Tolliver boys' surrogate mother. The troubling undercurrent of the race problem lent a tragic dimension to *New Yorker* fiction about the impermanence of the intimacies that arose between African Americans and the families they served. And as caricatures of ample, kerchiefed Mammies vanished from the magazine's pages, they were replaced by another stereotype, the all-seeing black housekeeper. Wise to their bones, these natural pillars of strength ruled the lives of the white Southern matrons who employed them and were often their only genuine friends.

In his famous pejorative essay on *The New Yorker* of 1965, Tom Wolfe addressed the degree to which the journal had become a women's magazine—"a great lily-of-the-valley vat full of what Lenin called 'bourgeois sentimentality.'" *The New Yorker,* he explained, published "an incredible streak of stories about women in curious rural-bourgeois settings. Usually the stories are by women, and they recall their childhoods or domestic animals they have owned."[19]

They also recalled the profound intimacy they had shared with their maids. While most of these stories took place in Southern exurbs, they presumably had some resonance for Northern women trapped in postwar suburbs. In much writing about suburban households in this period, the husband was a shadow, hovering faintly at the edge of domestic life. The children too were often absent—away at Andover or Exeter, at Princeton, or married and living in California. The wife and mother was left with a fairly empty plate, which she attempted to fill with book and gardening clubs and menial household chores.[20]

These women often found that the central figure in their domestic landscape, the keeper of their secrets and witness to the emptiness of their lives, was a black servant. Although white servants abounded in the postwar *New Yorker* because of the magazine's wish to avoid cartoonish portrayals of American blacks, they did not have the same social function as servants of color. The conceit of the nurturing, observant domestic applied particularly to African Americans, who were supposedly endowed with the qualities of natural wisdom, patience, and nobility that were so often attributed to dark-skinned others in the magazine. Although domestic and employer were separated by enormous barriers of class, race, and education, they occupied the same social space and were condemned to the same line of work. While race determined the social trajectory of the domestics in these pieces, gender was what determined the social reality of their upper-middle-class employers. The decisive fact of their lives was that they were women.

In spite of their privileges, these suburban wives often had more in common with their black domestics than with anyone else in their lives. What lent an additional poignancy to these stories was the fact that at night and on weekends the servants maintained other lives. They may have had adoring daughters, delinquent sons, wildly jealous boyfriends who drank, doting husbands who waited patiently outside the back door to drive their wives home or sat companionably in the kitchen while their wives fixed dinner for their white employers. And the lonely matrons who employed them probably envied these lively and passionate family connections.

Frances Grey Patton—a frequent *New Yorker* contributor in those years—often focused her attention on the relationships between black employees and white employers. The narrator of her 1947 short story "The Falling Leaves" is Harriet Blake, a New Yorker who has been transplanted to suburban South Carolina. Harriet is discouraged by the South's lack of sophistication and the bleakness of the Southern November. The husband who has transported her there is little more than an offstage presence, and Harriet spends her days struggling with her "colored" maid Pearlie, whom she sees as hopelessly intractable. "Harriet knew how to train servants, for she had often observed her mother breaking in a new maid . . . Harriet had explained to Pearlie that vegetables could, and should be cooked without grease, though she knew that the moment her back was turned bits of fat back would be slipped into the boiling spinach. 'Just a morsel, to make it fittin' t'eat.'"

Harriet, who is "sorry for all colored people," bemoans the fact that Pearlie is both untrainable and illiterate. "Her duties seemed to come to her fresh each day, and she received them always with fresh surprise. 'You wants me to bresh up the sittin' room *this* mornin'?'" Pearlie would ask, "beaming." Not content to let Pearlie remain an unreconstructed "Southern Darky," Harriet sets out to make her into a dusky version of herself—to "wash glasses first in very hot water, then the silver, piece by piece," to read and write, to avoid putting grease in vegetables, and to stop saying "sho' ain't."[21]

"How many times have I told you how to answer the phone?" Harriet shouts. "Don't stand there like a kangaroo." The wily Pearlie retaliates in a style designed to pluck at Harriet's liberal Northern heartstrings, explaining that she "don't keep count good," that she hasn't had any "schoolin'. In Gatlin County, where I was raised, white folks is mean to colored folks." Harriet retorts that Abraham Lincoln didn't have any schooling either, and that he should be an inspiration for her race because he was willing to walk "five miles barefoot to school every day . . . I daresay if you'd been willing to do that you might have learned something . . . And if they were mean to you in Gatlin County . . . perhaps they had some provocation. Did you ever consider that?"

Once she has vented her fury, Harriet is filled with remorse. "I *couldn't* have said a thing like that," she thinks, imagining how her mother might have reacted had she "been there, her face shocked, as it always was by violence or injustice." Now contrite, Harriet becomes certain that Pearlie will leave her—will simply "put on her good street shoes—the high-heeled pumps that cramped her feet" and depart. Harriet is flooded with relief when the phone rings and Pearlie answers: "Yas, Ma'am. She sho' is home. But she's layin' down. She don't feel s' good. This here's homesick weather."[22]

Patton fashioned this piece to reveal Pearlie not as the victimized "colored" person of Harriet's imagination, but rather as an astute primitive, naturally more attuned and savvy than her employer. The happy ending of "The Falling Leaves" has Harriet making her peace with the facts of her adult married life by making her peace with the black woman who shares her home and her daylight hours. Once Harriet abandons her futile attempts to transform Pearlie, the maid can reassert her authority as an artful original with a comforting ability to cut to the heart of the matter. She cannot read books but she knows which way the wind is blowing. Pearlie recognizes "homesick weather" when she sees it.

Peter Taylor was *The New Yorker* writer who observed most acutely the meeting place between white employer and black servant. "Middle Age" is a story of a marriage gone sour, in which Taylor dexterously juggles race, class, and gender. In this deceptively simple vignette, a middle-aged suburban housewife with an errant doctor husband and an empty nest serves her husband a special dinner in a doomed attempt to please him. The meal is cooked and served with the help of Cookie, the housekeeper, a "brown, buxom negress perhaps a few years older than her mistress." Throughout the piece Cookie (the only person in the story with a name) and the wife are shuffled back and forth like interchangeable pieces on a playing board. Together they serve, cook, and cater to the "boss-man." The wife twitters over every detail of the evening meal as if by feeding her husband perfectly she can make the silences between them less strained and restore their love. "Do you think we would like a little more light?" she asks, implying that if *he* would like more light *she* too would like it. "We might. We might," he answers. Moments later Cookie enters the room, asking "Y'all want all iss light?" Her question shatters the forced serenity in the small dining room. By turning down the lights Cookie illuminated the reality of her mistress's vacuous life—her absent children, her negligent husband, her tasks all busy work.

The interplay between the threesome demonstrates the sad redundancy of two women ministering to one man who wishes he were elsewhere. The husband keeps up a rather mindless prattle in which he alternately praises his wife and Cookie. He compliments his wife as he inhales the fragrance of the string beans, saying: "You are too good to me." Cookie gets credit for the roast and the cold-water cornbread. "What's this? A roast? You're outdoing yourself tonight, Cookie." When the pie is served the doctor turns to Cookie saying: "This is where she can beat you, Cookie."

Taylor used the husband's racist paternalism to adumbrate his venality. While the mistress allies herself with Cookie and identifies with her, the "boss-man" displays a detached jocularity toward the servant that mirrors his disengagement from his wife. "Cookie," he teases, "'I've been wantin' to ask you how your "corporosity" is . . . And, furthermore, I understand from various people around that you have ancestors.' He winked at his wife."

Puzzled by these questions, Cookie asks, "What's he mean, Mizz?" "Just some of his foolishness, Cookie," she replies. The "boss-man" thinks "to himself that his wife was too good to tease even a Negro. 'She doesn't realize that they really eat it up.'"

Cookie and her mistress are a team, protecting one another and sharing the empty task of filling a barren household with food, light, and comfort. But for the husband, this home is little more than an impediment—a locale of duty. It is he, not Cookie who is the stranger here. "Two nights a week he *had* to be home for supper, and some weeks when his conscience was especially uneasy, he turned up three or four times."

The turning point of the story comes when Cookie, pushed too far by the "boss-man's" mocking interrogations, slyly confronts him about rumors she has heard about his affairs with some of "them ladies from the sandbanks." Here Cookie has taken her alliance with the "Mizz" outside of its conventional bounds. She is doing for her mistress what the timid matron will not do for herself: confronting her philandering husband. But the Mizz, clinging to her denial, rebukes Cookie tearfully, for having "forgotten [her] place for the first time, after all these years . . . I'm disappointed in you, Cookie. Go to the kitchen." Her husband assures her that Cookie's behavior is "only old-nigger uppitiness," but the distraught wife in a stunning display of false consciousness condemns Cookie and allies herself with her husband. Yet when the husband suggests that Cookie should perhaps be fired, the wife takes a position of her own for the first time in the story. "No, no . . . I can't fire Cookie. I'll speak to her tonight. It'll never happen again."

Within moments the doctor is out the door to make some "housecalls." He can still hear the "senseless voices" of his wife and Cookie emanating from the house. He leaves the two women alone together once again and makes his way with "light, sure steps" to the driveway where his "car, bright and new and luxurious, was waiting for him."[23]

Peter Taylor's 1949 "A Wife of Nashville" covered some of the same turf as "Middle Age"—the absent husband and the lonely matron with a domestic as her sole ally—but it seriously addressed the painful irreconcilability of the gap between servant and employer, between white and black. On its surface, the story is a simple account of four maids who entered and exited the lives of the Lovells, an affluent Southern family. But while this piece appears to be about a stream of servants in much the same way as Peter De Vries's "They Also Sit," Taylor's story touches upon the way in which the attempt to acquire the perfect servant is, in part, a search for love and solace—a search that is doomed to fail because of the unbearable intractability of distinctions of class and race.

Each of the maids who passes through the Lovells' household forms a close bond with her mistress, for whom each departure is a painful rupture. Every succeeding maid is better at providing the glue that holds the Lovells' life together and better at offering Helen Ruth, the story's protagonist, genuine intimacy. The bonds that exist between servant and mistress are forged out of proximity and a gendered understanding of the world beneath appearances—a world that is categorically inaccessible to men. Like "Middle Age," this story places gender above race as a determinant of consciousness. The author seems to say that the distance between men and women may be greater even than the distance between black and white, servant and mistress.

Before Jess McGehee came to work for the Lovells, Helen Ruth Lovell has had what her husband liked to call "earlier affairs" with three domestics. Jane Blakemore, the maid the Lovells had when they were first married, consistently violated the line between servant and employer and was altogether too plainspoken. She was also Helen Ruth's only companion in the early days of her marriage, when John R., her husband, was on the road all the time, and the two women were "shut up together in that apartment at the Vaux Hall."

Jane Blakemore was followed by Carrie, whose "curiosity and . . . gossiping were especially trying for Helen Ruth." There is a potent moment in the story that illuminates the degree to which Mrs. Lovell's life is affected by the scrutinizing presence of the black domestics—the only witnesses to her interior life. One day, during a particularly difficult period when she was separated from her husband, she happened to see Carrie and Jane Blakemore together. "She tried to imagine exactly what things the black Jane and the brown Carrie were talking about, or, rather, *how* and in what terms they were talking about the things they must be talking about." The hour her maid and her former maid spent together seemed to Helen Ruth "the most terrible hour of her" separation. At the end of it "there was no longer any doubt in [her] mind that she would return to her husband, and return without any complaints or stipulations." The complicity between the two dark-skinned women feels like a betrayal to Helen Ruth, reminding her of the enormous social distance that lies between "a wife of Nashville" and a black servant. It is presumably the desolation born of that recognition that drives Helen Ruth back to her husband.

Carrie quit to become an undertaker and was replaced by old Sarah, who stayed with the Lovells six years and had a weakness for bad men. Although Helen Ruth is impressed by Sarah's "religious convictions" and her "kindness with the children," she is horrified to learn that the maid's ex-husband killed her only child by rolling over on it when he was drunk. Ruth Helen is so distressed by this piece of biographical information that she begins to feel a real "hatred toward any and all the men who came to take Sarah home at night." Four months later Sarah quits abruptly, explaining that she "was going to get married to a man named Racecar and they were leaving for Chicago in the morning." The incident shows what impact the domestic's personal, more intense private life has upon the daytime family formed by maid and mistress. It is often the black man at the back door who shatters the mistress's delusion that she has succeeded in socializing her servant into her world.

Jess McGehee, who follows Sarah, is a vessel of perfect love. She manages the Lovells domestic life flawlessly and is utterly absorbed with her surrogate family. In fact, Mrs. Lovell worries that Jess "had no life of her own," and the "way she idealized" them was a favorite subject of the family's "negro jokes."Jess had snapshots of each member of the family, "taken with her own Brownie," tacked up above the washstand in her room. She kept a scrapbook containing the boys' school grades, their compositions, which she copied painstakingly in longhand, and every old photograph "that Helen Ruth would part with." Sometimes Mrs. Lovell would send Jess to her relations in Brownsville, but she was always back in a few days, claiming that "she didn't care for" her kinfolks.[24]

However, like Aunt Munsie's transitory familial relationship with the Tolliver boys, Jess's adoption of the Lovells as her family is an illusion that is smashed by the maturation of the children. As this surrogacy is sundered, Jess finds a new friend, "the Mary who works for Mrs. Dunbar," with whom she eventually flees to California. This defection, marked by lies and deception on Jess's part—deceptions of which Mrs. Lovell is fully aware—is the moment of reckoning in the story. For in protecting Jess and allowing her to slip away, Mrs. Lovell is offering the ultimate acknowledgment both of the gulf between them and the bond: a bond that is built upon their womanhood. After Jess leaves, Helen Ruth reflects on the inability of her husband and sons to "recognize her loneliness or Jess's or their own . . . it was strange to see that they were still thinking in the most personal and particular terms of how they had been deceived by a servant, the ignorant granddaughter of an ignorant slave." Trying to make them see what she and Jess have always known, that "everything that happened in life only reflected the loneliness of people," Helen Ruth also acknowledges the distance between the races: "My dears, don't you see how it was for Jess? How can they tell us anything when there is such a gulf?"[25]

When *New Yorker* contributors wrote about domestics, they were separated from their subjects by vast differences of caste and/or race. In the very act of describing members of another culture, these writers offer us transparent revelations about how they and their readers perceived the world. For it is most often through the hiring and employment of domestic helpers that the kind of people who read the *New Yorker* came in contact with people who were less privileged than they were. While the postwar magazine occasionally depicted a lower-class waitress or a low-life drunk and was sprinkled with portraits of bookies, chorus girls, fight promoters, and underclass heroin addicts, these were generally picturesque fictions seen from a distance. When one of these outsiders became a domestic servant, however, this distance shrank. It was in this guise that the "other" could become an intimate of the *New Yorker* family.

It is certainly significant that the problem of having and taming household help was pandemic enough in the *New Yorker* reading world to warrant an entire genre of its own. However, these pieces tell us little or nothing about the interior lives of the servants themselves. Instead, they are packed with the assumptions about class, race, and gender that were the underpinnings of the *New Yorker* world. The "Maids Say the Darndest Things" genre provides a window into the insecurity of middle-class professionals concerning class prerogatives and barriers. So too is the *New Yorker* genre that focused on maids who were equestrians and butlers who were really hoteliers. Tales of haughty or highly autonomous household help express the tenuous hold that some citizens of the *New Yorker* village had upon their elite status. The rather mean-spirited snobbery of the magazine's offerings concerning the foibles of household help does not jibe at all with either its general tone or its social concerns. Suggestive of a regnant class that was standing on shaky ground, these pieces reveal the size of some of the fault lines with which the *New Yorker* terrain was riven.

The empty plate of the suburban housewife was the true subtext of *New Yorker* fiction detailing the fused lives of African-American maids and the women who employed them. Stories about the relationships of black domestics and white matrons illuminate the sterility of suburban homelife and the meager possibilities offered to upper-middle-class wives, left to care for large empty houses in bedroom communities, with black domestics as their only witnesses. These stories have a disturbing subtext: these white women are also lonely domestic workers, not all that different in their social function from their poorer black counter-parts—the women who enter their homes each day to provide comfort and company.

Although *New Yorker* stories about the antics of day-workers, baby-sitters, and doormen bristle with snide humor, there is a pathos in many of the other fictional pieces about servants that suggests something of the difficulty of maintaining both a clear social conscience and material ease. The number of stories in the magazine adumbrating the painful moment in which children recognized that the nanny or maid who ruled their childhoods was not "like" them implies that the existence of class was disturbing to *New Yorker* readers and contributors. Social class was an adult secret, and its discovery augured the end of innocence. These fictional descriptions of the moment in which class differences are first recognized dispel the sustaining liberal myth that class doesn't matter. When a domestic steps into a *New Yorker* household and be-comes an intimate stranger there, entitlement, identification, compassion, paternalism, and love are all curiously intermingled.

THE WAR BETWEEN MEN AND WOMEN

A cartoon of a bosomy young woman on a leash collecting coins in a tin cup for a hurdy-gurdy man, and a "Profile" of Dorothy Day, the founder of the Catholic Worker movement, a woman sometimes described as the conscience of the Catholic Church—these images occupy the opposite ends of the postwar *New Yorker*'s spectrum of depictions of women. The distance from monkey-substitute to quasi-saint is considerable, and it was populated by an array of housewives, showgirls, debutantes, compulsive shoppers, nags, spinsterish entrepreneurs, and sex objects.[1]

The wide variety of feminine types featured in the magazine certainly illuminates its ability to offer readers a locale in which the disturbing inconsistencies of a world in flux could coexist. What is more interesting, however, about this curious cast of female characters is what it can tell us about upper-middle-class assumptions concerning men, women, and domestic life in general. Just as the magazine's images of servants helped to expose the disjunctures between the external social conscience of its readers and their unconscious needs and anxieties, this peculiar double standard is even more starkly revealed in its pejorative representations of women. Although the magazine's editorial voice was unerringly egalitarian and democratic, its short stories and cartoons detailing upper-middle-class domestic life were charged with a snarling contempt for women and a unequivocal disinterest in equality. In *The New Yorker*'s geography, it seems, the closer one got to home, the farther one veered from democratic principle.

The aftermath of World War II was a tense period for relations between the sexes. Alleged natural distinctions between men and women had been exacerbated by their very different experiences during the war. And yet at this moment of acute estrangement men and women were marrying, having children, and moving to the suburbs together in record numbers. Some scholars have seen the headlong leap into domesticity as a reaction to the uncertainties and anxieties of the immediate postwar period. Fears of Soviet Communism, atomic attack, or another Depression were rife. Social science professionals—psychologists, doctors, and social workers—argued that the confusions of the postwar world threatened to destabilize the family and promote a sexual free-for-all. These experts, along with the mass-market magazines, harped on the necessity of early marriage for a healthy family life and a healthy nation. Pamphlets and guidebooks with titles like *Win Your Man and Keep Him* insisted that twenty-one was the healthy age for marriage, and that women who did not use their wiles to get married were somehow failing themselves and the nation. Because "scientific" advice was so highly valued in the postwar years, this call by experts for the revitalization of the family was heard across the land. Backlash against women's increased independence during the war combined with the shadow of nuclear holocaust to foster a burgeoning family ideology among middle-class Americans and to promote the idea that domestic life could provide an antidote to the terrors of the atomic age. This created an unprecedented pressure to rush into marriage.

But at the very moment that men and women were most pressured to couple, they were also tempted by other prospects. For example, despite expectations to the contrary, the size of the female labor force increased after the war, and more women also entered colleges and universities. In aid of sexual freedom, contraceptives were more readily available than ever before. Thus women had a number of alternatives to early marriage, yet at the same time record numbers of them were choosing to marry young and produce multiple offspring. The disparity between the opportunities available to middle-class women and the options they chose was the backdrop upon which *The New Yorker*'s depiction of the relationship between the sexes was drawn.

For their part, many young men had relished the masculine rigor of military life and were often loathe to submit to the feminized constraints of early domesticity. The war had offered bourgeois men an opportunity "for moral and physical testing" that was not available within the mundane routines of corporate life, and had given them the chance to escape or delay the demands of middle-class domesticity. Whatever their personal doubts concerning the prospects of domestic bliss, young postwar men and women were ultimately convinced that it was perhaps better to marry than to burn.[2]

The New Yorker's refusal to glorify the nuclear family distinguished it from all other general-interest magazines in this period. The magazines for married women, *Redbook, McCall's,* and *Ladies Home Journal* certainly aggrandized the delights of home and family. The newer, more democratic fashion magazines, *Charm, Glamour,* and *Mademoiselle,* offered unmarried women, many of whom were college-educated career girls, tips on how to lure and hold a man. *The New Yorker,* which had more women readers than men and was thought by some to have actually become a women's magazine in this period, did nothing to promote domesticity, extol the charms of marriage, or present a coherent womanly ideal.[3]

The magazine portrayed women variously, now as gold-digging party girls, now as middle-aged children or parasitic housewives, but also as independent career women who infused their enterprises with a special brand of feminine instinct. The magazine's unremitting subversion of the domestic ideal was consistent with its cosmopolitanism and its rejection of the Cold War fight against domestic Communism. From the baroque domesticity of the Addams family, to the legions of nagging wives in its short stories and cartoons, to its insistence that married men and women essentially inhabited antithetical cultures, *The New Yorker* sabotaged postwar notions of the family as either a haven of serenity or a hedge against Communism. However, what is most astonishing about the magazine's depictions of the domesticated female of the species is its hostility. The impossibility of achieving a harmonious union between the sexes—a failure that was blamed largely on women—was simply a fact of life in the pages of the postwar *New Yorker*. But it had not ever been thus.

Certainly two prior decades of *New Yorker* tradition played an important role in shaping its postwar depictions of women. Comic conventions, once entrenched, were difficult to depose. The large-breasted fortune hunters and matronly clubwomen who had been the stock of prewar cartoons continued to take their place in the magazine's panoply of feminine stereotypes well into the mid-fifties.

The most persistent of these prewar types was cartoonist Helen Hokinson's ample-bottomed clubwoman. Hokinson was a product of the Middle West, and her mother had introduced her to the milieu of the "club ladies of Mendota, Illinois." Since her first appearance in a July 1925 *New Yorker,* the Hokinson woman has become a part of America's cultural vocabulary. A stereotype built out of the genuine article, the portly lady in bold print dress and tiny hat came to Broadway matinees and took lunch at Schrafft's. Helen Hokinson often received fan letters from women who saw themselves in her cartoons: "My husband thinks you must have seen me trying on hats." Or "Oh, you were drawing me two months ago, all right, even if you never laid eyes on me. But not now! I've taken off 20 pounds."[4]

Hokinson's girls were, however, more than plump and idle housewives with silly hats. They were also enthusiasts, eagerly trying new recipes, wandering through art museums, studying sculpture and Japanese flower arranging, burying their heads in tony romantic fiction, and swooning over Haywood Hale Broun's visits to their book clubs. They were, in fact, far less square than their husbands, businessmen who generally found their wives' arty passions puzzling or irksome. What is endearing about Hokinson's girls is that they just wanted to have fun. They were not defeated by their excess weight or their husband's censure. Part of their charm was their buoyancy, the fact that they seemed so happy and so uncomplicated. Readers found them hilarious but Hokinson's girls were not in on the joke.

"Of course," a large woman explains to her dressmaker, "you understand these measurements are only temporary." A Hokinson lady tells her milliner, without a hint of irony or self-reproach: "My husband has very definite ideas. He doesn't want me to look like a mushroom or a rabbit." In a double-page spread, Hokinson's favorite subjects are featured in one of their primary habitats, the New York Flower Show. As they enter the show, one matron says to another: "If we get separated look for me in Cyclamens." Two women survey a rather stark floral arrangement. One asks the other: "Do you really think it's playing fair to shellac a pussy willow?"[5]

Hokinson's bouncy matrons appeared in a variety of settings on the magazine's covers, proving that in spite of their sheltered lives, they were not strangers to adventure. A Hokinson woman might be found on the back of a mule cart in Bermuda, attempting to smuggle a small dog onto a commuter train, or consulting a gypsy fortune teller. She tried on hats; played charades; and worried about the proportions in a new mixed cocktail. Perhaps the archetypal Hokinson cover painting was one that was printed posthumously: A stout woman in a white suit and large pink and white hat stands at the counter of an art supply store in a setting that resembles Provincetown or Nantucket. Gaily oblivious to an arty couple in berets and striped fishermen's shirts who observe her with open disdain, she clutches a list in her white-gloved hand as the salesman helps her to purchase oil paints, brushes, and canvases. It is her innocent belief that she can easily join the ranks of artists, her lack of self-consciousness, that made her far more than a fat buffoon. Hokinson girls were hope incarnate.[6]

In part because of the accident of Hokinson's death in 1949, and in part because of the larger historical accidents of the postwar world, by 1950 the truly affectionate portrayal of girlish upper-crust housewives began to vanish from the magazine. Unable to withstand the slings and arrows of postwar gender relations, Hokinson's women, like gendered dinosaurs, very slowly became extinct, coexisting briefly with the hard-edged portraits of the leaner, meaner suburban housewives who took their place.

Like the Hokinson woman, the comic figure of the sexually attractive gold-digger was a holdover from the twenties and thirties. Popularized by Peter Arno, perhaps the most widely known artist of the Ross era, these cartoons derived their humor from the idea of sex as a capital asset. Arno's favorite subjects were the lecherous older men and avaricious younger women who formed one another's prey base.

The basic assumption of this comic convention was that men's pursuit of women was animated almost entirely by a desire for sex—a commodity that was most easily procured by purchasing it outright. In these cartoons, physically attractive women were represented as entrepreneurs who capitalized on their sexual assets. Men were eager customers, willing to purchase love using the frank currency of mink coats, pearl necklaces, designer gowns, and penthouse apartments. There was a certain frankness in these exchanges. The men put their pearls and furs right out on the table while the women made no bones about taking them. Arno's girls were neither victims nor were they the evil exploiters so popularized by the femmes fatales of postwar film noir. The look of open delight on their faces as they homed in on their kill denied them the status of dangerous women.

In a 1948 Arno cartoon, for example, a woman in a tight-fitting dressing gown opens her front door to greet a man entirely obscured by a stack of large gift-wrapped boxes. Grinning ecstatically she says: "Come in, come in, whoever you are." As another beautiful young girl admires her new pearl necklace, its donor, a man three times her age, leers at her, saying: "And now, Miss Evans, I wonder if I could take a small liberty?" An anxious looking middle-aged man has just given a beautiful young blonde a small valise full of currency. She gazes at it rapturously, one hand lightly on the man's shoulder, as he says "Of course you realize this washes me up at the bank."[7]

The idea that women, whether they were trying to turn a man into a husband or a sugar-daddy, were essentially mercenary, not only persisted but flourished in the postwar years. In fact, the animosity that was a notable aspect of gender relations in this period brought renewed vitality to these stereotypes. One shapely cartoon glamour girl confides to another: "I want a normal woman's life—husbands, children." A 1947 cartoon barracuda confides in a girlfriend: "All I want is what every woman wants—full title to the house, the furniture, custody of the children, half of the personal property, and plenty of alimony." In the background of a 1947 Robert Day cartoon, two goldminers who have just struck gold cavort about in a mountain river, waving their mining pans joyously above their heads. In the foreground two comely young women on horseback (gold-diggers once removed) survey the pair. One says to the other: "Oh, look! Let's ride over and introduce ourselves." A chorus girl seated at her dressing table tells another: "If I had to choose between a man with brains and a man with brawn, I'd pick the one with the most money."[8]

Over time, these glamorous mercenaries and Hokinson's good-natured housewives seemed to morph into another, less cheerful, less sexual stereotype, that of the upper-middle-class suburban wife whose financial profligacies forced her husband—born for better things—to remain trapped in the rat-race.

The magazine that often portrayed the relationship between the sexes as a pitched battle was produced by both women and men. The personnel shortages of World War Two made it necessary for Ross to hire women not only as contributors and top editors (which had been a long-standing practice), but in numerous other positions long the purview of men. John Cheever, Irwin Shaw, E. J. Kahn, Jr., Gardner Botsford, Edward Newhouse, St. Clair McKelway, all either enlisted or were drafted. Women were working as "Talk" writers, fact checkers, and editorial assistants. In spite of Ross's grumbling about "lady editorial assistants," he adapted to wartime exigencies brilliantly, rehiring Katherine Angell White and hiring various women who made an enormous impact on both the tone and the content of the magazine.[9]

Hence it is impossible to make claims for the postwar *New Yorker* as a tight-knit old-boys' network or an enclave of nineteenth-century gender attitudes. Although Ross married three times and had rather troubled romantic liaisons, his working relationships with women were productive and congenial. His biographer describes him as a man with Victorian notions about gender roles, sex, and virtue. "Yet," he adds, "at a still-impressionable age [Ross] tumbled into Jazz Age New York, a time and place where those traditional attitudes and roles were being pitched out like so much bathtub gin. The man who emerged could appreciate the modern woman, all right, but more so intellectually than emotionally." Although Ross might have had difficulty maintaining romantic unions with the new breed of modern, independent women, he profited greatly from their entrance into the workplace. His veneration of Katherine Angell; his productive though troubled partnership with his first wife, Jane Grant, a zealous feminist who helped him found the magazine; and his longstanding reliance upon women editors and writers were more than lucky accidents. Ross hired, published, and nurtured a number of powerful women editors and writers including Andy Logan, Lillian Ross, Emily Hahn, Janet Flanner, Angelica Gibbs, Mollie Panter-Downes, Jean Stafford, Kay Boyle, and Mary McCarthy. The presence of these women on the magazine's editorial staff and amongst its contributors had far-reaching consequences both for *The New Yorker* and American journalism in general.[10]

However, *The New Yorker* was far more a feminist endeavor than it was a venue for feminist discourse. The women who edited and wrote for the magazine were, by the standards of any period, liberated. Their style of liberation, however, resembled that of the adventuresses of the twenties and thirties, women like Amelia Earhart, who led emancipated lives but did not engage in feminist rhetoric. The magazine's feminism was rooted in the conditions of its production rather than anything it *said* about women. For although *The New Yorker* ran many "Profiles" concerning distinguished women, published fiction and poetry by women, and had women reporters filing from all over the globe, it virtually ignored underlying questions about the inequality that undergirded middle-class gender relations.[11]

Although *The New Yorker* disavowed the domestic ideal, this subversion was largely accomplished at the expense of women, by depicting domesticity as a feminine plot designed to emasculate men. For the most part, pieces in the magazine detailing the achievements of distinguished women bypassed the domestic ethos by focusing on widows, divorcees, or maiden ladies. When the subjects of *New Yorker* "Profiles" were married, they were often women who had made businesses out of traditional women's activities such as gardening, cooking, and childrearing. These married careerists tended to present themselves as subservient in the home. In fact, the credibility of married, high-profile working women in this period sometimes depended on their willingness to leave the domestic ideal unchallenged. Married career women walked a tightrope suspended between family and work, authority and deference. Although they may have shattered male hegemony in the workplace, they generally continued to honor it at home.[12]

The ideal public woman in the postwar *New Yorker* was someone who existed outside the constraints of domesticity and gender altogether. Eleanor Roosevelt exemplified this ideal. In a 1948 "Profile," E. J. Kahn described the widowed former First Lady as "the most popular living American of either sex," and "the personification of the American conscience." Phillip Hamburger, in a review of a fledgling weekly television show in which Mrs. Roosevelt presided over a televised tea party, described the party as less a "high tea" than "an interstellar one." The topic was atomic energy, and her guest list included David Lillienthal, Robert

Oppenheimer, Sen. Brian McMahon (the chairman of the Congressional Joint Committee on Atomic Energy), and Albert Einstein. The fact that no other women were there escaped comment. Although Hamburger professed "unlimited respect" for Mrs. Roosevelt, he found the tea-party format somewhat inadequate for solving the world's problems. He did add, however, that "of all the people now turning up on television," Mrs. Roosevelt was certainly "in a position to do the thing right."[13]

While the magazine designated Eleanor Roosevelt as the nation's conscience, Dorothy Day, one of the founders of the Catholic Worker movement, was given the tough job of being the moral conscience of the Catholic Church. "Many people," Dwight Macdonald wrote at the beginning of his "Profile" of Day entitled "The Foolish Things of the World," think that she "is a saint and that she will someday be canonized." Agreeing that sainthood could well be her destiny, Macdonald diminished the heft of Day's earthly power somewhat by describing her as looking, in her "sensible shoes and drab, well-worn clothes," like an "elderly school teacher or librarian" who incorporated "the typical air of mild authority and of being no longer surprised at anything that children or book-borrowers do." This description of Day, the latter-day-saint, as a sexless spinster (she was only fifty-five when Macdonald wrote this) was a recurrent theme in pieces about female icons. Mrs. Roosevelt and Miss Day, at the high end of the magazine's spectrum of women leaders and entrepreneurs, occupied a place only a little below the angels. They were both exempt from "The Foolish Things of the World" and existed in a stellar dimension outside sexuality, domestic chores, or even marriage. Kahn's "Profile" of the widowed Mrs. Roosevelt, for example, was significantly titled "The Years Alone." Dorothy Day's marital status was a bit more muddled. As a young woman living in Greenwich Village she had fallen in love with an atheistic biology instructor and entered into a common-law-marriage with him until her only daughter was born. This event so overwhelmed her with gratitude that she felt compelled to join the Catholic Church. This "step meant either living in mortal sin or renouncing the child's father who . . . spurned the idea of marriage, and she reluctantly chose the latter."

Removed by principle or destiny from the demands of ordinary womanhood, these icons became something more (or less) than women. Mrs. Roosevelt might play hostess at a traditionally feminine ritual, the tea party, but this event was in fact a summit conference in garden-party clothing. These "Profiles," which appeared to ascribe to their subjects an uncommon level of mastery, really depicted these women's triumph over gender, their ascendance to the status of honorary men.[14]

While many of the other notable women profiled in the postwar magazine existed on a more mundane plane than Mrs. Roosevelt or Dorothy Day, they too were often widowed, divorced, or spinsters. In fact, the working women who were presented in the most idealized way in *New Yorker* "Profiles" were often "maiden ladies" who lived and worked outside of the perimeters of the conventional domestic ideal. Several of these pieces, illustrated with line drawings showing mannish-looking women with cropped hair and business suits, contained broad hints that their subjects were either gay or very much like men.[15]

Janet Flanner's "Profile" of Cheryl Crawford, the Broadway producer credited with the success of "Porgy and Bess" and "Brigadoon," was accompanied by a line drawing of Crawford, emphasizing her masculine mien and a description of her as a "scholarly Middle Westerner of austerely chiseled character and countenance who likes serious books, can recite all of Keats' odes from memory, and talks as little as possible." In spite of her emphasis on Crawford's mannishness, Flanner stressed her subject's gender—the fact that she was "a woman in the house" (note the author's playful insertion of the theatrical use of "house" into the domestic cliché of "woman in the house"). Using the argument of female exceptionalism, Flanner insisted that Crawford's record of box-office triumphs was so impressive that on Broadway "she is almost superstitiously credited with having some special feminine formula" for success. In the case of "Brigadoon," for example, "the feminine formula she used . . . included the elimination of a lot of customary, costly, masculine waste." She achieved these economies "like millions of women . . . merely by cutting things down with a paring knife and by keeping her eye fixed on every dollar."[16]

Berton Roueche's 1948 reportage, "A Cup of Lemon Verbena," concerned a pair of women described as "two sociable spinsters" who owned an herb farm together. With their shared joy in work, their gentle way of teasing one another, and their mutual enthusiasm for herbs, this twosome formed an unconventional version of the domestic ideal. Miss Arnold, who credited Miss Thomas with turning her into a professional herb farmer, explained that around the time the pair became friends, Miss Thomas had "lost her apartment. She didn't have any place to live, so I asked her to move in with me. We've been together ever since . . . It was a lucky day when we met."[17]

The successes of these women were portrayed not as feminist triumphs but rather as individual victories. On the infrequent occasions when the magazine did engage in feminist discourse, it used the language of a fledgling women's movement in which women members of the liberal intelligentsia regarded oppressed women as "other." Virtually no attention was given to the possibility of upper-middle-class men oppressing women of their own ilk. By and large, in *The New Yorker* the oppression of women was seen not as consequence of gender differences but rather as a class syndrome, something that happened to lower- and middle-class women who had neither the economic nor intellectual means of defending themselves.[18]

These examples of a nascent feminism concerned the degradation of lower-middle-class women by those who capitalized on their passivity and ignorance. Although most of these short stories and journalistic pieces were written by women, their narrators seemed exempt from the kind of problems that plagued their subjects. These pieces tended to sidestep the enormity of the power differential between men and women, blaming the problem on class, economic institutions, or on the women themselves.

In fact, in *The New Yorker* the oppressors of women were often other women. "One Sweet Little Business," a 1948 "Profile" of Mrs. Veronica Dengel, is very critical of the power-driven forty-seven-year-old woman who claimed to have invented the beauty "make-over." More Mildred Pierce than Eleanor Roosevelt, Dengel refers to herself "as a personalysist and a beauty engineer." Although Angela Gibbs, the Profile's author, emphasized the shrewdness and vulgarity of her subject, she reserved most of her rancor for the beauty business itself, which she indicted for its economic exploitation of lower-middle-class women who had neither the self-esteem nor the intellectual rigor to resist its cheap enticements. Dengel, she argued, preyed upon women "who have had it dinned into them by advertisers that they are thoroughly repulsive."

As ultimate proof of the spuriousness of Mrs. Dengel's claims, Gibbs pointed out that the "personalysist" conflates beauty and anti-Communism. "We are safe from Communism and all other 'isms,'" Dengel proclaims, "as long as our women can wear lipstick like a badge of courage. Take the lipstick off every American woman today, let them remain without any cosmetics for three days and three nights, and we would find ourselves a dispirited, despondent nation." By linking feminine grooming with the future of democracy, Mrs. Dengel placed herself at the heart of the domestic containment camp in which national security was linked to the security of the family. It was the women's job to *hold* onto her man (and her children) in order to provide the emotional ballast both for the family and for the nation. Mrs. Dengel, whose second book was *Hold Your Man!*, liked to emphasize her own "essential domesticity" and often peppered her lectures with references to her daughter, "Snookerpoo," and her son, Eddie.[19]

Just as Gibbs condemned the beauty business for its exploitation of women, Lillian Ross's critique of the Miss America Pageant, "Symbol of All We Possess" (1949), condemned the exploitation inherent in that enterprise. Ross thoroughly undermined the legitimacy of the contest in her first few sentences, when she pointed out that there were thirteen million women in the United States between the ages of eighteen and twenty-eight, and that *all* of them were eligible to compete for the title of Miss America if they had graduated from high school and were "not negroes."

The focus of Ross's essay is Miss New York State, Wanda Nalepa, a twenty-year-old registered nurse from the Bronx. Setting out to illustrate the sexual objectification of women that was the mainstay of the Miss America Pageant, Ross described the salacious ramblings of the male spectators, judges, and participants. An elderly man in "a green-and-purple checked jacket" asks, "They got any tall ones?" Earl Wilson, the gossip columnist, tells the folks at the press table that he likes " 'em big."

Ross is a tricky journalist. A direct predecessor of Tom Wolfe and the "new journalists" of the late sixties and early seventies, she allowed her subjects plenty of rope with which to hang themselves. Avoiding interpretation, she commandeered the language and the ambience of the contest, turning it back on itself. The piece is sprinkled with vital statistics, bust sizes, thigh measurements, hair and eye colors, and shoes sizes. The contest's M.C., for example, tells the judges to make sure that the girls' thighs and calves "meet at the right place."

Ross's critique of the Miss America Pageant, which was meant as an attack on an institution that insulted women, succeeded, in part, by replicating this degradation. Ross presented the contestants, the officials, and the audience as lower-class, lower-brow people with bad values and worse taste. Wanda Nalepa, Miss Ross's subject, was characterized as a passive, thin, uncertain girl whose chiropractor boyfriend raved about her "perfect back." Wanda had no talent to display in the contest, so she planned to just get dressed up in her nurse's uniform and make "a little speech." Other entrants in the pageant's talent contest were Miss Alabama, who sang "'Neath a Southern Moon"; Miss Nevada, whose talent was "raising purebred Herefords" ("she had wanted to bring one of her cows [on stage] . . . but the officials wouldn't let her"); and Miss Florida, who sang "Put Your Shoes On, Lucy," which was announced in a release to the press as "Put Your Shoes on Lucy."[20]

It is difficult to separate Ross's contempt for the Miss America Pageant from her contempt for the contestants themselves. Although she expressed compassion for the entrants, whose lives were so shabby that participation in a beauty contest was an aspiration, hers was the compassion of the privileged outsider. Ross did not identify with her subjects—women whose victimization seemed to have more to do with class than gender. The message here was that the oppression of women was something that happened to proletarian girls who were just too credulous or too passive to resist it.[21]

The idea that the victimization of women was something that took place in other climes and among other classes was also at the heart of a short story by Wilma Shore published by the magazine in 1949. Shore situated her micro-tragedy of sexual politics amongst working-class people in a vague Southern California exurb. This piece, consciously concerned with the issue of women as property, was populated by characters who would never read *The New Yorker*.

The subject of Shore's doleful "The Moon Belongs to Everyone" was the blurry line between marriage and indentured servitude. In this story, a man is left with two small children after the sudden death of his wife. For months after the funeral he muddles along miserably with the help of various housekeepers. Eventually he solves his housekeeping problems by marrying Louise, an orphaned college girl who has been working for him during her summer holiday. On their wedding night, when Herbert tells Louise that he loves her, she says: "I love you, too . . . And I'm going to be a good wife for you, Herbert. I'm going to take good care of you and the kids." She adds with a smile, "and you don't even need to pay me any more." Herbert draws back in dismay. What a "terrible thing to say," he exclaims, insisting that he married her because he loved her. "'And I did,' he thought. 'I know I did.' But for a moment it seemed to him as though he could never know for sure."[22]

What is sad about these people is their paucity of options. The two central characters slide inevitably into circumstance, because they are neither imaginative nor willful enough to create alternatives for themselves. They are both in search of family and connection and, Shore seems to be saying, this makeshift arrangement is the best that they can do. The young woman will forego a college education and become an unpaid housekeeper. For his part, the widower is willing to live in a marriage built upon the shaky foundation of necessity. He is not a venal exploiter, nor is she a cunning opportunist. In Shore's melancholy world, men and women are caught up in conventional structures over which they have very little control. And it is because they are ordinary, neither terribly smart, nor terribly ambitious, that they are so thoroughly entrapped. The victims of sexism in Shore's story, as in Lillian Ross's attack on Miss America and Angela Gibb's assault on Veronica Dengel, are people doomed to live in an unsatisfying and sexist world because they lack consciousness. Their names, their language, their environments all suggest that these are the little people who know not what they do. These pieces are artifacts of a feminism of advocacy, of pity. They inevitably contain a tacit understanding that more enlightened people with wider horizons would do, could do, better.

The New Yorker's enlightened people did indeed reject the view that women were the property of men. They replaced this idea with the notion that men were controlled and dominated by women. This was perhaps the central assumption of the magazine's postwar depictions of upper-middle-class domestic life. The sense of an irreconcilable disjuncture between the sexes was the magazine's chief comic conceit in those years. The impossibility of harmonious cohabitation between the male and female of the human species was simply a commonplace. While The New Yorker's images of women ran the gamut from mannish entrepreneurs to fortune-hunting chorus girls, they all fit an overarching cultural pattern of "hostile symbiosis" between the sexes in postwar America.[23]

New Yorker men and women were at odds about everything: where to live, how to live, money, sex, marriage, decorating, and the affairs of the world. There was a war at home. While the larger society promoted the idea of happy housewifery and suburban affluence for all, the magazine's text bellowed a resounding NO! In its gender wars women shopped, nagged, and tried to dominate their husbands. Men, for their part, withdrew, tuned-out, and ignored their wives. To the late twentieth-century reader, these representations of sexual dissonance appear extravagant in their degree of rancor. In a magazine generally characterized by a tone of gentle detachment, the level of animosity reached by the battle of the sexes is striking. Particularly its cartoons, which were the magazine's most unconscious element, reveal an intense preoccupation with gender differences. The cartoon's perpetual subtext was that even when men and women were the products of the same social class, they inhabited antagonistic cultures.

Marriage was perceived as a feminine construct—a trick played by women upon men who feared and despised the institution but were no match for the feminine will and wiles. "I'll be glad when Bill and I are married," one nattily dressed young *New Yorker* cartoon woman tells another, "and I can stop pretending I don't know anything about baseball." "*Now* are you satisfied?" an angry bridegroom in a 1949 cartoon asks his dismayed bride, as they walk arm-in-arm from the chapel. A marooned couple watch as a minister, bible in hand, wades onto the shore of their tiny island. The woman is elated, the man terrified. A Charles Addams cartoon shows a pair of newlyweds in their honeymoon suite. While the groom innocently unpacks his pajamas, the bride, a triumphant smile upon her face, heats up a branding iron in the sitting room fire, preparing to mark her property.[24]

In postwar domestic ideology, the home was portrayed as women's proper sphere. This relegation of female power brought with it the fear of a rogue version of the ideal homemaker. The preoccupation with a monstrous mom who threatened to engulf and devour the family was a phenomenon contemporary psychologists called "momism," a name coined by febrile patriot and anti-Communist, Phillip Wylie, in his bestselling book *Generation of Vipers*. In this aberrant variation of exemplary housewifery, sexually frustrated women smothered their husbands and children (especially their sons) and made them into passive pantywaists who would be unable to defend their nation in the face of a possible Communist takeover. The more power a woman wielded over a man's destiny, the more she threatened the natural order of things. Fear of momism crested just as the domestic ideal was about to vanish. By the early fifties, when the ideology of domestic containment seemed most infrangible, its days were numbered.[25]

It is not difficult to understand why *The New Yorker*, with its tradition of urban cosmopolitanism, would consistently subvert the postwar suburban domestic ideal. What is far less easily understood is why it did so by subscribing to "momist" notions of the man-eating housewife—woman as soul-devouring fiend.

The woman-dominated male was a well-represented cartoon stereotype. Wives harangued their silent, brooding husbands at every opportunity—in gondolas, on life rafts, on rooftops surrounded by floodwaters, in bed, and out. "If *I'm* stupid, what about you?" a fat woman seated at a dressing table shouts at her husband. "You married me, didn't you?" A prisoner in a striped uniform is lectured by his hatchet-faced wife in the visiting room. Surveying this disagreeable domestic tableau, one of the guards remarks to the other: "That explains why Hagen wasn't in on last week's [jail] break." A very large woman and a very tiny man enter the Audex hearing-aid store in silence. When they emerge, the man is wearing a hearing aid and the woman is nagging him. A man and woman are seated in a bumper car ride at an amusement park. The man steers while the woman shouts: "Look out! For goodness sake, can't you keep your mind on your driving? Turn left! Slow down!" A man in pajamas sits silently on the edge of the bed as his enraged wife simultaneously prepares for bed and shouts at him. She places her hair in a net, creams her face, and then puts on a neck strap that holds her mouth shut. In the cartoon's last panel, the man, sensing his advantage, stands over his infuriated but muted wife and shouts back.[26]

These domineering wives drove their husbands into a manly underground where they hid from women's relentless demands. The husband interrupted at some male pursuit, whether it was newspaper reading or bill paying, was an omnipresent motif in the hostile climate of *The New Yorker*'s cartoon households, giving the lie to Tolstoy's notion that all unhappy families are miserable in their own special ways. Clearly, the safest haven for a hen-pecked *New Yorker* cartoon husband was behind the newspaper—the chief locale to which married men repaired to avoid the shrill ministrations of their wives. For their part, nagging cartoon wives loved nothing better than to interrupt husbands at this pastime.

A scowling cartoon husband keeps his eyes on his newspaper as his wife, dish towel in hand, scolds him: "If my nagging upsets you so much, why don't you just do as I say?" A man is seated in his easy chair trying to read with his dog at his feet. His wife is seated uncomfortably in the chair facing him, a sorrowful expression on her plump face. She has, apparently been trying to engage him in conversation. The husband looks up from his book and snarls: "What do you mean, am I happy? Are you trying to start another argument?"[27]

The man behind the newspaper became such standard cartoon fare in this period that the concept itself became a joke, generating comic variations on a theme: A minister and his wife are seated at breakfast. She glowers; he peruses his bible. A high-ranking military officer studies a globe placed in the center of the breakfast table; his wife stares disconsolately into her coffee cup. Male and female archaeologists eat breakfast at a makeshift table near a digging site. She glares across the table at him as he studies an ancient stone tablet. A six-year-old girl scowls at a six-year-old boy who is ruining her tea party by reading his newspaper at the table. Perhaps the most telling version of the man-buried-behind-his-newspaper motif is a cartoon depicting a large hotel dining room in which a number of middle-aged couples are having breakfast. The husbands are all absorbed in their newspapers, while their wives gaze out into the distance or focus glumly on their meals. Only one man dines alone. He is without newspaper and gazes tranquilly into space, enjoying his solitary repast.[28]

A peculiarly pitched domestic sketch by James Reid Parker juggles several of the more idiosyncratic elements of *The New Yorker*'s presentation of normal domestic relations. In a story entitled "Westchester Igloo," Mr. Talbot, a suburban husband, grumpily takes up a book his wife has brought him from the Browse-Awhile lending library. Talbot likes murder mysteries and finds this intervention into his leisure time deplorable—even more deplorable than the "eggplant fiasco" his wife had given him for dinner. The book is *Inuk*—a French priest's anthropological study of an Eskimo tribe. After a silent half hour, during which Mrs. Talbot reads a romantic novel, Mr. Talbot declares *Inuk* "darned interesting." He is especially delighted to learn that Eskimos have little use for women. "Listen to this," Talbot says brightly: "The Eskimos are a race of men. Their opinion of women is not high. Only a few women are permitted to live, and these few carry no weight whatever in Eskimo society." The enraptured Mr. Talbot reads on: "He, the man, will build the igloo; she, the woman, will tend it. He will kill the seal; she will cut out the blubber and keep the lamp filled with oil . . . To him the rifle, the knife, the dogs, the whip, and the right to give orders. To her the lamp, the cooking, the sewing." Mrs. Talbot begins to regret bringing the book home. "I guess they *are* awfully primitive," she offers lamely. Her husband responds by claiming that the Eskimo division of labor seems to "work out pretty well," and reads her a particularly brutal sequence about the forced extermination of female babies.

After Mr. Talbot reads his wife several more horrifying facts of Eskimo life, he casually mentions that he is still hungry—an allusion to her unfortunate effort to substitute eggplant for meat at the evening meal. She nervously begins to wonder "what there might be in the refrigerator" that might make up for that disastrous dinner. Mr. Talbot, for his part, gleefully informs her that Eskimo men often swap spouses for the night "without consulting the wives." This piece of information sends Mrs. Talbot scurrying towards the kitchen to throw a piece of bacon—"blubber"—into the frying pan. Wiping a tear from her eyes she gratefully notes that she is "under no compulsion whatever to use the fat that was oozing out of it as a filling for lamps." The story's conscious intention is formulaic. A cagey husband tricks his wife into submission. Mrs. Talbot may be little more than a privileged servant to her husband, but at least she wasn't murdered at birth. The piece is offered up as situation comedy, but for the modern reader it has a sadistic resonance.[29]

In *New Yorker* cartoons the cold war between men and women often heated up to the point of homicide. As a sightseeing couple examines the Roman Coliseum, an imaginary scene plays in a balloon over the husband's head in which his toga-clad wife attempts to flee from three snarling lions. In another cartoon, a husband sleeps in a hammock while his wife, noting the storm clouds overhead, attaches him to the lightning rod on their roof and waits for the inevitable. A smiling middle-aged woman, seated in an armchair, holds a smoking snub-nosed revolver as she talks on the phone. "Nothing much, Agnes," she says. "What's new with you?" Barely visible in the corner of the cartoon is her husband's supine body. An Angostura Bitters advertisement that ran in the magazine during this period shows an enraged man standing at a broken skyscraper window with glass shards and a cocktail glass littering the floor. The silhouette of the woman he has just flung out the window is visible in the shattered glass. He screams at the street below: "And don't come back without the Angostura." In a three-panel cartoon, a man comes home with a stuffed moose head he wants to mount over the fireplace. In the first panel his wife greets him, arms akimbo, saying: "Over my dead body." In panel two the husband removes a revolver from his jacket, and in panel three he is seated comfortably in front of the fire, smoking his pipe. His dead wife lies on the floor behind him. The moose head is on the wall.[30]

Most of these cartoons of spousal murder were the work of Charles Addams. His most famous creation, the Addams family, was a group of black-clad creeps who lived a vampire's bohemian version of the haut-bourgeois life. In a Gothic suburb, abounding with bats and spider webs, the Addamses maintained a romantic marriage and doted upon their weird children. They functioned cheerfully together as macabre outsiders. Charles Addams's spousal murderers, by contrast, lived externally conventional lives. These homicidal men and women were portly, middle-aged inhabitants of New York apartments, summer cottages, and suburban ranch houses. They reclined in hammocks, sat on slipcovered chairs, read current novels, and wore Peck and Peck and Brooks Brothers clothes. Always adept at undercutting the thrust of upper-middle-class culture, Addams seemed to suggest that the horror of bourgeois marriage required no Gothic trappings. While the Addams clan offered a blithe crypto-bohemian antidote to the increasingly uniform suburban world of *New Yorker* readers, his chronicles of murder depicted a far darker fantasy of escape: violence.

Given that any one of the cultural differences between men and women might be grounds for homicide, taste and consumption were a particularly dangerous bone of contention between the sexes. Daniel

Alain's 1947 cartoon of adjoining men's and women's shoe stores was meant to illustrate the differences in the way the sexes approach shopping. On the women's side of the store, sweating, harried salesmen thread their way through mounds of shoe boxes to wait on bossy, irate women. On the men's side, order prevails. Only a few shoe boxes litter the floor. Serene salesmen help smiling male customers. Women are presented here as driven and demanding consumers; men as good-natured and off-hand about the acquisition of goods. A powerful emotional connection to shopping was assumed to be a feminine characteristic. For women, shopping was a critical part of their social function—something that lent meaning to their lives. It was, however, an urge that could easily slip out of control and become a pathology. In this view of the world of shopping, a man entering a retail store was rather like a nonalcoholic entering a skid-row bar. He might order a drink, but he just doesn't get it. "Are *men* allowed to exchange things?" a parcel-laden man asks a department store floorwalker in a 1946 Whitney Darrow cartoon.[31]

There may be no inherent contradiction between seeking goodness and the quest for goods. But the idea that these two components of postwar cosmopolitanism somehow conflicted was strongly suggested by the fact that the pursuit of goods was attributed solely and disapprovingly to women. While *New Yorker* men hid behind their newspapers, their feminine counterparts were inevitably laden with parcels. To be sure, advertisers had been targeting women as the family's primary consumers since early in the century. What was significant about the magazine's feminized depiction of the accumulation of possessions was its extreme malignity. Desiring goods, nagging to get goods, and relentlessly pursuing goods were women's blameworthy preoccupations. A Hokinson woman in an elegant department store asks the floorwalker: "Where is whatever is reduced fifty per cent?" In a 1948 cartoon a woman holds a wallpaper sample against a wall and asks her husband, who is buried in his newspaper: "How do you think this one would look, dear, with a rug of the same silver green and slipcovers of a mildly contrasting shade of lemon yellow, maybe bound in russet." A Dutch woman scowls at the clogmaker as she tries on an endless succession of

THE WORLD THROUGH A MONOCLE

wooden shoes; an Eskimo woman tries on pair after pair of snow shoes. A woman surrounded by shoe boxes smiles conspiratorially as the salesman promises: "No exchanges, and no refunds—you'll have your husband over a barrel." Women's ceaseless avarice for goods was seen as something that could put a husband over something larger than a barrel. This female obsession with getting and spending was seen, at its worst, as an agent of male emasculation. By forcing men to meet constantly accelerating standards of family consumption, women pressured them to remain in the rat race and abandon their youthful dreams. At the same time that politicians and economists lauded the marvels of a growth economy, the women who purchased the abundance of goods flooding the marketplace were vilified as shallow and parasitical. If there was a conflict between a belief in social justice and a desire to accumulate luxury goods, *New Yorker* men had seized the untainted moral high ground way above the teeming marketplace in which women acted out their unquenchable need for more.[32]

Perhaps the primary object of the postwar *New Yorker* wife's desire was a house in the country or the suburbs. And it was inevitably women who were held accountable for the forced march of urban families into the provincial wilds. Apartment shortages, government policies, highway development, and the baby boom converged to produce the explosion in the construction of suburban single-family residential housing. Although these new "bedroom communities" promised domestic security and offered a solution to many of the spatial and economic problems facing the sprawling new families, they also generated a significant amount of gender strife. And the suburban tract home, promoted in American mass culture as the centerpiece of family "togetherness," was criticized by others as the embodiment of the creeping conformity and emotional alienation of American society. The blight of exurbia provided an ideal subject for some social commentators, because it enabled them to focus on questions of taste rather than those of power and to skirt any assault upon the larger framework of the society. They depicted the fledgling tracts as nightmarish rows of identical houses ruled by overbearing housewives, whose absent husbands and over-indulged children drove them to the brink of nervous breakdowns. While magazines like *House and Garden, House Beautiful,* and *Sunset* depicted suburban living as a kind of Eden-with-a-bar-b-que, cultural critics saw it as nothing less than a sterile purgatory.[33]

The move to the suburbs did not necessarily condemn its participants to life in an air-conditioned nightmare, but it did create geographical and emotional fissures within the family. Husbands worked long hours far from the locus of family life and were consequently alienated from its daily realities. Suburban life also separated educated men and women from the urban cultural and intellectual communities that had sustained them. Women were isolated at home, often with young children. And children, especially adolescents, felt at times like prisoners of the new communities that provided safety and security, but little in the way of street life or excitement.

Although the many discontents of suburban life were experienced by all members of the family, women perhaps felt them most keenly. Yet within the *New Yorker* village it was assumed that a house in the country or the suburbs was every woman's dream and every man's nightmare. A cartoon from the spring of 1952 showed a man and a woman gazing happily at a ramshackle house with a "For Sale" sign on its overgrown front lawn. In the fantasy-balloon over the man's head, the house is still a shambles, and he is peacefully supine in a hammock beside it, drinking wine and loafing. In the balloon over the woman's head, the house is in perfect repair, she is tending a neat garden, and the man is grumpily pushing a lawnmower.[34]

This assumption of female culpability for suburban life emanated from a group of people Barbara Ehrenreich has dubbed the "gray-flannel dissidents." This would be a man who had always lived by the rules, had married, had children, and found an appropriate white-collar job that enabled him to move to the suburbs. He bought a house and then perhaps a bigger house and settled comfortably into the role of mature, well-adjusted breadwinner. He was, in fact, just like his neighbors, "except for some slight transcendence that distinguished him," such as "an appreciation for Modigliani or an investment in psychoanalysis."

Part of what made him different was an abiding sense of his own superior virtue, coupled with a suspicion that something was wrong with the society he lived in. Clearly, the problem was neither political nor material, because ideology had been declared dead and these bourgeois dissidents had attained a level of affluence that exceeded their wildest dreams. What was wrong was conformity, which Ehrenreich calls the "code word for male discontent."[35]

By the mid-fifties, academicians (sociologists in particular) had ossified these male grievances into a body of official wisdom. David Riesman's construct, the "outer-directed man," reinforced the average gray-flannel rebel's gnawing perception that "conformity . . . meant a kind of emasculation." In *The Organization Man,* William F. Whyte bemoaned the passage of the virile individualism of earlier forms of capitalism, arguing that the corporation had crushed the creativity of its white-collar workers by rewarding conformity above all things.[36]

If social critics blamed the blandness and moral flabbiness of postwar America on the corporation, gray-flannel dissidents saw another snake in the grass—women. Amidst cries of "momism," many upper-middle-class men blamed their wives for forcing them to forsake their dreams and keep their miserable noses to the corporate grindstone. Although the corporation may have crushed male initiative, it became men's ally in the struggle against the tyranny of women. Men "stayed late at the office" to avoid wives who waited at home armed with rolling pins.[37]

By forcing men into domestic servitude, women robbed them of their individuality, their freedom, and ultimately their masculinity. Male urban exiles trapped by "the commuting train, and the Republican Party and the barbecue pit" did not take responsibility for their removal from the city. It was not their choice. Their lives, they claimed, were run by women. This mild insurgence against conformity and against women fit within *The New Yorker*'s perimeters of permissible social criticism. It was a wistful, passive form of rebellion which ignored much larger issues, such as the profound dissatisfaction of many suburban women and the extent to which men determined the shape of family life. The blindness of gray-flannel rebels to the grave imbalance of power between bourgeois men and women produced a strain of dissent that was never "more than a lament," yet stooped at its nadir to a "nasty reprise against women."[38]

By the late forties, the typical milieu of the magazine's fiction was no longer the carefree bohemia of New York cafe society in which *The New Yorker* was born. The party-going, hard-drinking cosmopolitans of an earlier era had been replaced by people who talked about trellis repairs, golf, and wisteria. In Nathaniel Benchley's short story about the fate of urbanites who move to the country, "The Castaways," he commented that "all dames want to move to the country." Thus Jim Burrage, the central character, has moved to Connecticut at his wife's urging. The setting is a suburban Saturday-night party, during which an incestuous crowd of local exurbanites assembles and gets drunk. Something is missing from the evening. "That's what we need out here," a male guest laments, "a good saloon. Lord, how I miss them." Burrage warns his city friends about the horrors of life in Connecticut. You would "go nuts . . . It's like living on a desert island with the same people around you all the time." This diatribe is interrupted when his wife reminds him that it is his turn to drive the Sunday-School carpool the next morning. He groans miserably and shuffles off to bed.[39]

Many *New Yorker* short stories concerning suburban married life simply assumed that men's capitulation to a feminized existence was a natural feature of adulthood. These stories were often written in the arch self-loathing tone that might be used by a housebroken dog in explaining such training to a fellow canine. Men who had once pondered great thoughts were reduced to worrying about crabgrass and leaky roofs. How the mighty had fallen!

Peter De Vries's suburban oeuvre poked fun at his male comrades as they tried to adjust to living in the "wild." Beneath the light irony of these pieces, however, the melancholy rumble of compromised masculinity could be heard. In "Household Words," De Vries's narrator struggles with the vocabulary of home-owning domesticity. While he is trying to relax on a Saturday morning, his wife hands him a list of things to buy, among them a credenza and some toggle bolts. "You know what toggle bolts are, don't you?" she asks. "Bolts to hang toggles on?" he asks hopefully, adding that some of "this stuff is hard to get even in translation. Last week you wanted me to rabbet a splat." Here the failure of men and women to communicate is not metaphorical but literal. They speak different tongues. The move to the suburbs has only widened the cultural gap between them. The wife in this story has "gone native," establishing residence in the suburbs and becoming well-versed in the jargon. Her husband, on the other hand, is little more than a weekend visitor who struggles with the rudiments of the vocabulary. He is more at his ease in the workplace—a congenial clime where he is fluent in the vernacular.[40]

Although men blamed women for the vague afflictions of suburban life, women were often were the family members most painfully affected by it. Various *New Yorker* pieces on suburban women confirm, albeit covertly, that Betty Friedan was not breaking new ground in the early 1960s when she addressed the "problem without a name." In "Operation Housewife," published in the magazine in 1946, Phyllis McGinley wrote: "She often says she might have been a painter, / Or maybe a writer; but she married young. / She diets. And with Contract she delays / The encroaching desolation of her days." The invocation of the "encroaching desolation" of a suburban wife's days was assumed to require no elaboration.[41]

However, the blame for the emptiness at the center of suburban women's lives was placed (often by women writers) on women themselves. Their indolence, materialism, and lack of imagination were the culprits here. *The New Yorker* tended to portray these functionless women as predatory rather than desolate. Purposelessness and disappointment, the twin blades of suburban women's lives, cut away all of their soft edges. In this sterile, self-created Eden, women lost their innocence. The fact that many of them had servants further degraded their function. Often these women acted only as overseers of the women's work that was accomplished in their homes.

Two 1949 stories written by women illuminate the notion of the housewife as both depressed and mean-spirited. Decla Dunning's "Wait for the Dial Tone" centers on Marian, a suburban housewife with a telephone party line. She spends her mornings chain-smoking and gossiping on the phone with her sister-in-law, who complains that her maid hasn't polished the silver for two months. A stack of unwashed dishes awaits Marian in her kitchen, Bootsie the cat wants to be fed, and the laundry needs to be done. Still Marian lies on her bed, smoking and talking.

Then, to her horror, she discovers that the phone is dead. She considers using the neighbor's phone to call the telephone company, but she is still in her housecoat and that would require getting dressed. Cut off from her life line, Marian listlessly turns to her housework. She wonders if the other woman on her party line might summon the energy to report the dead phone, then thinks that perhaps she, too, "would find it too difficult and complicated to make a move." As she makes the beds, Marian has "a thought, idle and lightly humorous," that nearby in a house very like hers, "with a family that could well be much the same as hers," there was "a woman who, like herself, was defenselessly facing the day ahead."[42]

Esther Evarts's "Just Depressed" takes place at a luncheon reunion between two upper-middle-class housewives and Frances Mabee, a friend of theirs who has just been released from a mental hospital. After her husband's death, Frances had a mental breakdown and was sent to a tony sanitarium described as "just like a hotel." When Millie learns that her friend Madge has invited Frances to join them for lunch she says: "You *couldn't* have . . . She's out of her head, but completely." Madge insists that Frances was never crazy, "just depressed," and Millie retorts tartly that she herself has often been depressed: "[I]n fact, I am depressed most of the time, if the truth were known."

Millie is worried that Frances will start "acting funny," but when she arrives at the restaurant she is stunned by Frances's unembarrassed greeting, her serene composure, her perfect clothes, and the scent of her expensive perfume. Frances gaily declines a martini, explaining that the smell reminds her of the paraldehyde she had to take at the hospital. Then she recounts an incident in which she attacked the woman in charge of occupational therapy with an ashtray, explaining that she "objected to the stags on the woman's sweater . . . [T]he things I did: Or so they tell me. Six stitches in her arm."

When Frances asks what Millie has been doing that's exciting, the only incident she can dredge up is that her husband, Harry, had gone to Chicago unexpectedly on the very night she had managed to get "Kiss Me Kate" tickets.[43] In the course of the conversation Millie, who has described herself as depressed "most of the time," finds herself envying her friend's wild excursion outside the boundaries of bourgeois domestic life. In this story, aberration offers a passport out of the mundane. The narrowness of Millie's compassion, the fact, for example, that she did not want to lunch with a friend who had been a patient at a sanitarium, matches the narrowness of her domestic life. While Frances actually acted out her rage, the most Millie can boast of is that she "could have" killed her husband for making her attend "Kiss Me Kate" without him. The lack of incident in Millie's life has made her small and resentful. Ultimately, she would rather be Frances than be herself.[44]

This troubled world in which men blamed women and women blamed themselves offered one untroubled vantage point from which to survey the battle of the sexes: the safe world of the cartoon fantasy balloon. In this imaginary locale men could lust after women without having to marry them or buy them mink coats; women could imagine men draping them in mink and pearls without having to repay them either with sex or the unpaid servitude of housewifery. Considering the predominance of images of betrayal and overt rancor that characterized married sexual relations in the magazine, the postwar proliferation of a long-standing cartoon genre featuring male and female fantasies about the opposite sex is significant. In this imaginary realm, no one can talk back. The bubble (literally) cannot burst.

Informed by an enthusiasm for Freud and notions about the unconscious, this comic convention is rooted in the assumption that when a man sees a woman he finds attractive, he undresses her in his mind. For these fantasy cartoons to be funny, they had to tap a vein of associations shared by artist and reader alike. The following examples suggest a number of these shared assumptions: In a Sam Cobean cartoon, a young blonde woman meets a portly older man at a party. He appears in a balloon over her head, naked except for his pince-nez, his wallet, and a pocket full of cash. In a chic nightclub, a scantily clad showgirl approaches the table of a flush-looking patron in dinner clothes. In the balloon over his head, she is naked. In the balloon over her head, she is wearing a mink coat. A woman sees a handsome priest in the street and imagines him in laymen's clothes. A manly looking bulldog sees a French poodle wearing a little plaid coat. In the balloon over the bulldog's head, the poodle is coatless. An emir and his eunuch pass a veiled woman in the street. In the balloon over the emir's head the woman is naked. The eunuch's balloon is empty. This absence of erotic fantasy is unnatural, something that could only happen to a neuter.[45]

The New Yorker's female cast did not mature into a unified feminine type in the years following World War Two. As Hokinson's happy matrons, Arno's big-eyed show girls, and Mary Petty's frankly anachronistic Gilded Age Park Avenue dowagers headed for the cartoon boneyard, they were not replaced. An examination of the magazine's covers for 1952, for example, gives us no real sense of who its woman reader was. Was she a suburban housewife, a Park Avenue dowager with a lorgnette, an arty bohemian sporting a smock and a beret, or a cigarette-smoking career girl? Just as sensitivity about ethnic stereotyping eradicated many images of African Americans from the magazine in this period, confusion about what sort of women populated the *New Yorker* reader's world had the effect of diminishing their presence in cover art. Old portrayals were inappropriate, new portrayals were still undeveloped. Only thirteen of the fifty-one covers from 1952 depicted women at all. Men, children, and distant landscapes abounded. Two covers portrayed women in their earlier club-woman form: a mink-coated woman and her prize-winning French poodle pose for photographers at a dog show; a wife hopefully models a mink coat for her distraught husband who studies the price tag. There is a bride, a bobby-soxer, an old New York style dowager at dinner with her son, and one career girl.[46]

Yet *The New Yorker* counted numerous women among its editors, illustrators and writers. This contradiction is compounded when one examines its readership. By 1947 the majority of the magazine's new readers lived outside of New York City, many in suburbs of less than ten thousand. Many of these new readers were women. By 1949, women represented 45% of the readership. By 1954, women readers had out-stripped men, constituting about 54% of the readership. Market studies also suggest that although men were often listed as the subscriber of record (as Head of Household), women readers were likely to read more of the magazine, especially the fiction. For these upper-middle-class women, most of whom had some college education, the magazine func-tioned as a surrogate intellectual community, reconnecting them with the cosmopolitan world from which they had been separated by mar-riage, child bearing, and geography.[47]

In an essay published in the *New York Herald Tribune* in 1965, Tom Wolfe addressed the degree to which *The New Yorker* had become an organ of the suburban woman's life—in essence, a woman's magazine. "Since the war," Wolfe noted, the suburbs of "America's large cities have been filling up with educated women with large homes and solid hub-bies and the taste to . . . *buy expensive things. The New Yorker* was the magazine . . . they heard their professors mention in a . . . good cultural way. And now here they are out in the good green world of Larchmont, Dedham, Grosse Point, Bryn Mawr, Chevy Chase, and they find that this magazine . . . is speaking right to them—their language—cultural and everything."

It is certainly true that by 1950 *The New Yorker* had come to possess a certain cachet for upper-middle-class women. But what Wolfe fails to note, in claiming for the magazine "the status of a totem" that touched "a little corner in the suburban-bourgeois woman's heart," was the peculiar hostility of its representations of women and the chilling per-spective of much of its fiction on the nature of bourgeois domestic life.[48]

The question then suggests itself: why would women, the majority of the readers, tolerate representations of women that were largely pejora-tive or anachronistic? Whether it was self-loathing or false conscious-ness that allowed them to embrace these malign portraits of their own sex cannot be truly known. It is certain, however, that at the jagged intersection of these two facts of *New Yorker* history—its popularity with women and its degradation of them—one can retrieve some of the contradictions that abided in the world of the women for whom *The New Yorker* was more than just a magazine.

The feminine types featured in *The New Yorker* have much to tell us about a significant segment of postwar American society. Too cosmopolitan to wholeheartedly embrace the jejune niceties of domestic ideology, yet too conventional to resist its comforts, the men and women who read and wrote for *The New Yorker* took their rightful places in the domestic tableau without seriously questioning its assumptions about gender relations—assumptions that were about to be addressed explosively in American society. The married women in *New Yorker* fiction and cartoons did not work outside the home. Indeed many of them did not work *inside* the home. Often their sole avenue of worldly authority was the power to consume. Even the women with notable careers portrayed in the "Profiles" spoke of having to ask their husbands before they could consent to an interview. It was the inability of *The New Yorker,* generally a socially conscious magazine, to scrutinize the central fact of male hegemony that gave rise to its wax museum of nags, bitches, courtesans, and dimwits. Its overall hostile presentation of women suggests a kind of huffy bewilderment. On the eve of a revolution in gender relations, *The New Yorker* darted uncomfortably among disparate images of women without resolving its own contradictions, and still insistently proclaimed against all evidence to the contrary that it was women, wily, instinctive, seductive, and materialistic, who held the winning hand.[49]

GOODS AND GOODNESS

Writing in 1954, the cultural critic Joseph Krutch described *The New Yorker* as a magazine "whose scene is a bar—especially a bar which is either very elegant or very low." High or low, there is perhaps no better roadmap of the magazine's complex *Zeitgeist* than the one conveyed in its conflicting portrayals of the social meaning of alcohol. In the *New Yorker* world there was one thing that chorus girls, dissatisfied suburban husbands, cafe society roués, military officers, overstuffed clubwomen, and nuclear physicists all had in common: they drank!

In 1925, the magazine was born into a bibulous world—a place in which hard drinking in defiance of Prohibition was a sign of social acumen. Robert Ripley, the alcoholic journalist who created "Ripley's Believe It or Not" in the 1920s, often reminded his readers that New Yorkers were destined to drink hard and that, in fact, the word "Manhattan" meant "place of drunkenness" in the dialect of the Indians who had been its original denizens. Hence knowledge of the whereabouts of speakeasies, the possession of bootleg whiskey, and the ability to throw a cocktail party were signs of savoir-faire that were highly prized by the professional middle class in its struggle for social status. The Prohibition Era's view of drinking as an act both elegant and rebellious continued to inform *New Yorker* depictions of drink well into the 1950s.[1]

Although the magazine's memories of Prohibition's delights remained sharp, the idea of alcoholism as a disease slowly began to penetrate its editorial consciousness. This caused *The New Yorker* to fluctuate between the earlier tendency to romanticize alcohol and the more contemporary medicalization of excessive drinking, and produced an unreconciled array of bleak Third Avenue barflies, happy inebriates in top hats, gentlemen advertising fine imported spirits, problem alcoholics, and unruly cocktail party guests.

In the magazine's perception of intelligent postwar cosmopolitanism, to be sophisticated was to demonstrate one's distinction through the tasteful enjoyment of goods and services that were not consumed by the masses. In those years, upper-middle-class professionals embraced trans-Atlantic crossings, foreign films, cocktail parties, imported spirits, and monogrammed luggage as necessary props of civilized adult social life. There was, however, a dawning awareness that while elite consumerism represented one aspect of sophistication, the demonstration of intellectual enlightenment was an equally important measure of one's worldliness. The members of the *New Yorker* community (readers, editors, contributors) seemed to be powerfully attracted to both sides of this equation. *New Yorker* readers became adept at translating possessions such as the right wine or an imported Scotch into proofs of their successful relationship to the world of goods. They were, concurrently, genuinely engaged with questions about the condition of the world and believed that watching over it was part of their responsibility as an affluent elite. In the same way, one needed to be enlightened both about the finer points of drinking and serving spirits, and the dangers of alcoholism.

Where alcohol was concerned, *The New Yorker* thus seemed to cover all possible bases. Clubby gentlemen drinkers competed for page space with high-rolling remorseful alcoholics and low-life drunks. A cartoon depicting alcoholic hallucinations (cheerful elephants that looked "pink" even in a black and white cartoon, waiting patiently outside an Alcoholics Anonymous meeting for their owners) could appear beside an advertisement for King's Ransom Scotch that displayed whiskey bottles nestled amongst leather-bound books such as Burke's *Peerage, Baronetage, and Knightage,* and a caption reading: "Distinguished Members of the Aristocracy."[2]

Overlapping and even conflicting views were characteristic of the postwar *New Yorker*'s representations of alcohol. Advertisements for spirits presented drinking as an aristocratic pastime, while cartoons and casuals ridiculed these claims. In much of the magazine's fiction and many of its cartoons, alcohol was portrayed as the chief lubricant of a civilized social life—a lubricant whose dangers the magazine both acknowledged and scorned. Drink was commonplace, drink was fraught, drink was debonair.

Without question, the people who wrote, edited, and read the magazine regarded drinking as an integral part of social life. Even a cursory examination of the biographies, memoirs, and institutional histories of the magazine and its contributors makes it clear that heavy drinking was a fact of *New Yorker* life. Harold Ross was a legendary hard drinker, until his ulcers forced him to climb reluctantly onto the wagon. John McNulty, the magazine's Third Avenue correspondent who reported (sober) on the action in the low-life bars that littered that Avenue, had to stop drinking in the late thirties. Dorothy Parker and Robert Benchley's alcoholism is well-documented. John Cheever wrote copiously about his own struggles with drink. James Thurber was a mean drunk who was described by acquaintances as the nicest guy in the world until after five o'clock. Ring Lardner, John O'Hara, Edmund Wilson, and Franklin P.

Adams all struggled with alcoholism, and some of them lived tragically short lives. "This was the generation," Ann Douglas explains in *Terrible Honesty*, her study of Manhattan culture the 1920s, "that made the terms 'alcoholic' and 'writer' synonyms."[3]

The post-World War II generation of *New Yorker* writers were the heirs to this hard-drinking legacy. E. B. White once explained: "Before I start to write, I always treat myself to a nice dry martini. Just one to give me the courage to get started. After that I am on my own." Describing his own morning regimen during his early hard-drinking years on the magazine, E. J. Kahn explained: "I get out of bed and throw up and take a shower and shave and have breakfast." Brendan Gill, a bit shocked by this admission, asked: "You throw up?" "Of course," Kahn replied, "doesn't everyone?"[4]

The children in *New Yorker* stories of the late forties could still observe drinking as a natural and particularly congenial element of adult life. Deborah, the golden-haired three-year-old in John Cheever's "Sutton Place Story," was "a city child" who "knew about cocktails and hangovers." She saw her parents most often at the cocktail hour, when she would be brought in to say goodnight to them while they drank with their friends. Sometimes she would be invited to pass the hors d'oeuvres and "she naturally assumed that cocktails were the axis of the adult world." Deborah had been known to "make martinis in the sand pile," and she thought that "all the illustrations of cups, goblets, and glasses in her nursery books were filled with Manhattans."[5]

Throughout the 1950s, over 80% of all *New Yorker* households polled drank or served alcoholic beverages. This statistic suggests the importance of alcohol in the social lives of the readers of a magazine that reviewed the movie "The Lost Weekend" as that "prize-winning temperance lecture." Because of its affluent cosmopolitan readers, its dependence on liquor advertising for revenue, and its long association with sophisticated cafe society, *The New Yorker*, despite its frequent lip service warnings about the perils of pathological drinking, demonstrated a certain resistance to the pious argot of sobriety.[6]

In city apartments and suburban ranch houses alike, the drunken

THE WORLD THROUGH A MONOCLE

party continued to be the hub of fictional *New Yorker* social life. "Deck the Halls," Nathaniel Benchley's Christmas offering for 1948, was a near-anthropological study of the *homo New Yorkus* c. late forties and his party-giving mores. Nathaniel Benchley was the son of the humorist Robert Benchley, a man noted both for his wit and his alcoholism, who had been Dorothy Parker's dearest friend. In this story, a sophisticates' tree-trimming party turns psychedelic when the guests get drunk before the champagne punch is served, inhale the helium from the balloons, and talk in high chipmunk voices. It is the sort of party at which people say things like: "Phooey on Picasso. . . . How about Botticelli?" and George Curtis who "can be pretty funny" is enlisted to give a humorous "medical lecture" using an anatomical chart—"Tiny Tim Travels Through the Thorax." Two depressed writers stand by the helium tank and agree that if they don't each write a great book by the following year, their careers will be over. A woman cries, a drunk sleeps it off in a chair, someone demonstrates the Mexican Hat Dance, and two men discuss naval tactics on the floor, using forks and knives as submarines. The story's effect was derived, in part, from its power to elicit knowing nods from readers. Midcentury *New Yorker* fiction that focused positively on alcohol as the axis of sophisticated social life also served as a counter-point to the blandness of many depictions of postwar suburban life. The party drinkers in stories whose subplot was the life-enhancing effects of alcohol did not conform to mainstream stereotypes of married, upper-middle-class professionals—fathers who wore hats and neckties to pic-nics, or mothers with neatly set hair, aprons, and high heels who made soup for lunch—although these more conservative corporate types cer-tainly did their share of drinking in this period. In these *New Yorker* stories alcohol allowed middle-class professionals to transcend the limi-tations of proper behavior by doing the Mexican Hat Dance, inhaling helium, or extemporizing on Picasso. They were gray-flannel rebels, more free-spirited than their neighbors and co-workers. They inhabited a bourgeois bohemia in which alcohol was the chief sacrament, function-ing as a transformative agent—a ladder out of the dreary homogeneity of postwar upper-middle-class adulthood.[7]

In the cartoons, the jaunty portrait of the devil-may-care drunkard lived on well into the 1950s. These depictions of upper-class sots drinking themselves into unconsciousness relied on familiarity for their humor. They were minutely nuanced repetitions of a conventional comic genre, in which liquored-up gentlemen in tuxedos were ejected from bars, private parties, nightclubs, and restaurants:

A white-jacketed butler, his face a mask of gentility, pushes a cocktail cart bearing an unconscious partygoer; under the elegant awning of the Club Macao, an inebriated man and woman in evening dress are carried from the club by dinner-jacketed waiters, while a stiffly formal doorman summons a cab. In a multi-part cartoon, a drunk is hurled from a chic cocktail lounge. In subsequent panels his belongings are hurled out after him: his homburg, his topcoat, his cane, his gloves and in the final panel, his female companion, depicted here as an additional piece of personal property. Especially interesting in these images was the way in which, in spite of the drunkenness of the central figure, the setting as well as the servants who bore the weight of the genteel drunks remained static, expressionless, unrumpled. Drinking in these instances did not interrupt the operation of business as usual or effectively spoil anything. Drinking to the point of unconsciousness was (if a man did it) still funny. A 1950 Peter Arno cartoon, which is indistinguishable from an Arno cartoon in the thirties, portrays a tuxedo-clad gentleman passed out on a couch with a whiskey tumbler on the floor by his feet. The comatose guest is surrounded by men and women in evening dress who regard his supine body in a notably sanguine fashion. "Oh, you just missed it!" a woman says, "Mr. Casey's been absolutely *scintillating.*"[8]

The scintillating upper-class drunk did not, however, have a monopoly on drinking as a good man's vice. Well into the late forties, *The New Yorker* continued to publish writing that romanticized masculine lower-class drinking. The idealization of the demi-monde—with its seedy bars, bookies, pimps, bar-girls, and punch-drunk former boxers—was a remnant of a cultural tendency prevalent in the twenties and thirties. This fringe milieu, described by A. J. Liebling's biographer as a "windowless antiworld of swarming tricksters," held great allure for intellectuals and journalists. Although the romance with this saloon culture was clearly on its way to extinction after the war, it continued to be a theme in many of the magazine's cartoons, John McNulty's "Third Avenue Correspondent" pieces, "Talk of the Town" casuals, and occasional "Notes and Comment" items.[9]

By then, however, *The New Yorker* too was showing clear signs of the decade-long alteration in the way the American middle class understood alcohol. Some of the romance went out of heavy drinking after a number of coinciding historical events, among them Repeal, the Depression, the founding of Alcoholics Anonymous in 1935, and World War II. It was no accident that Alcoholics Anonymous emerged in a decade shaped both by the end of Prohibition and the Great Depression—a period in which material conditions were such that middle-class people could easily become desperate enough to seek help.[10]

The social prudence of the postwar years also played a part in altering attitudes toward alcohol. The idea of heavy drinking as a pathology requiring a cure was consistent with the new emphasis on maturity promoted by the war and its aftermath, which had heightened Americans' awareness of the sheer dangerousness of human history. The awakening from the naive and sentimental political illusions of the prewar period to a more wary and adult understanding of the world was often expressed in the Freudian idiom of maturity—a maturity in which the happy prewar childhood was replaced by cautious restraint. The sense of precariousness that tainted the peace, the new affluence, and even the sanctity of the family hearth certainly had an impact on perceptions of the social meaning of drink.[11]

Thus by the time the film version of Charles Jackson's novel about a middle-class alcoholic, "The Lost Weekend," was released in 1945, many respectable Americans had come to see alcohol as a threat to themselves and their peers. Affluence, it seemed, offered no protection against the problem of alcoholism. In fact, the abuse of alcohol held special dangers for members of a class in which membership could not be inherited. If hard work, self control, and willingness to delay gratification were attributes critical to middle-class professionals who wished to maintain or increase their status, then alcohol held myriad dangers for them.[12]

By the late forties, then, problem-drinking began to cast a shadow over *New Yorker* fiction, stories in which children watched their drunk parents make fools of themselves, husbands kissed other men's wives, cafe society drunks tried to sober up in fancy drying-out hospitals, alcoholic guests ruined social gatherings, and nights of festive drinking were more and more frequently punctuated by days of hangovers and bitter remorse.

James Thurber's "Six for the Road" was a story about the same boozy subculture depicted in "Deck the Halls," but while Benchley's story was a reverie, its night of drunken revel cast in the warm glow of fond memory, Thurber's story made fun of a pair of *problem* drinkers, the Spencers, who just didn't know when to go home. This tiny comedy of manners was focused on the delicate line between acceptable and unacceptable drinking behavior.[13]

The narrator of "Six for the Road" explains that Emily Post's advice on the problem of guests who overstay their welcome simply cannot be applied to Mr. and Mrs. Harry Spencer, a pair of out-of-control alcoholics, "and *their* circle." For the Bloodgoods, the luckless hosts of a party attended by the drunken duo, the trouble begins when Harry Spencer's recitation of the Gettysburg Address in imitation-Negro pronunciation ("All men are cremated eagles," and so on) drives John Greenleaf Hanty, a former editor of the *Old Masses,* from the party in a huff. The Spencers' behavior exacerbates their host's stomach rash and eventually forces the other guests to leave too. Undaunted, the Spencers continue to drink and perform their "talking-horse routine" and their tour-de-force—the Apache dance, which they interpret "as it would be done by a Supreme court justice and his wife, then by an arthritic psychiatrist and his amorous patient, and finally by a slain dowager and her butler, the slayer."

Readers presumably recognized both the familiar milieu and the familiar stereotypes—Hanty of the *Old Masses;* Jim Bloodgood and his great publishing failure, *"They Ain't Nobody Here but Us Chickens*—a merry account by a young woman of six months spent on a poultry farm with her city-bred French poodle, Franchot," and the obsessive drinkers whose overindulgence spoiled things for everyone.[14]

While a more sober view of alcoholism infiltrated the magazine somewhat haltingly, by the late forties it had penetrated deeply enough to produce a small assortment of pieces focusing on alcoholism as a problem. Although the vestigial assumption that drinking—upper-class, lower-class, social, problem, heavy or otherwise—was an acceptable good man's vice remained shakily in place, the innocence of this position had been appreciably eroded by darker notions about alcoholism. The new knowledge had the effect of energizing *New Yorker* portrayals of working-class barroom drinking. For while it had become increasingly problematic to aestheticize gentlemen drunks, it was still possible to depict the lower-class inebriate as charming—and drinking as the quaint though problematic custom of a primitive culture. John McNulty, who wrote for *The New Yorker* from 1937 until 1955, was the poet laureate of the Third Avenue bar. While the romance of drink was always present in his work, after 1945 it became tinged with an increasing sense of the terrible toll that daily drinkers paid for their habit. "One heard [about McNulty] that he had once been well known for his drinking, but [by the late thirties] he had long been careful not to drink at all." This explains the important role he played as *The New Yorker* writer who most bridged the gap between the older paeans to drink and the newer, more cautionary tales of lives derailed by alcohol.

With an unerring ear for the vernacular and a compassionate eye, McNulty brought alcohol's tragic dimension to the magazine. He recreated the truncated possibilities of single men like Paddy Ferrarty, the night bartender in a Third Avenue saloon, who "lives in a furnished room" where he "sleeps daytimes and reads westerns." Or Grady, the tough cabby who makes a living following drunks from gin-mill to gin-mill and driving them home. His patrons are, in the voice of a bartender narrator, "fellahs that have good enough jobs to keep them in liquor money, works regular but mostly devotes themselves to drinking and singing and arguing. Not rum-dumbs, but warming up to be rum-dumbs."[15]

McNulty's "This Lady Was a Bostonian They Call Them" clearly demonstrated his role as a broker between the competing meanings of alcohol. Here the author stands outside the story's frame, directing the readers' attention to the social distance between the quaint low-lifes they observed from a distance in *New Yorker* stories and the well-upholstered comfort of their own world. He also seems to be drawing attention to his role as a translator of the cadences of one culture for the amusement of another. In this piece, the narrator is Little Marty, a cabman who has "a way of talking that he can pronounce capital letters." Late one night Marty picks up a woman in his cab, "she's a Bostonian they call them," and she is in New York for the dog show. Marty's powers of observation are keen: "She got clothes look thicker than the clothes they wear here . . . I got to say I was surprised she had a husband—somehow I got the idea from the thick clothes she wouldn't have a husband." The Bostonian asks Marty to have a drink with her at a bar, a request that distresses him. "I got no shave and I don't look good—how can I look good wearing this cap?" He chooses a Third "Avenyuh" place where he has known one of the bartenders "since kids." Here, playing upon the identity of the assumed reader, the author commented sagely on the class voyeurism of his own art: "In front of the bartender knew me for years," Marty explains with some bitterness, "this Lady Bostonian kept saying, 'This is quite a picturesque scene, isn't it?' . . . How could it be a picturesque scene me with no shave, three o'clock in the morning, sitting up at a bar with a Lady I never seen before?"[16]

McNulty's chilling "Third Avenue Medicine" was an examination of a kind of "medical observation" practiced by Third Avenue bartenders. This entire diagnostic technique can be summed up in two phrases: "The snake is out," and "the elevens are up." The snake is out is a reference to the vein that runs along the "left temple of a man's head," which is invisible until a drinking man gets into his fifties, when it "gets to acting up." If the bartender tells him to "take it easy . . . that only gets him sore." Not until the bartender tells him that "the snake is out" will a man slow down on his drinking; this phrase will do it when "no amount of lecturing" could. The other phrase, "the elevens are up," is something of a death knell for old drinkers and is not said "to a man to his face at all." The "elevens" are the two cords on the back of the neck, which, on an elderly alcoholic, stick out like two ones "making the number 11." The bartender says: "The elevens are up . . . quietly and sadly, like a priest or a judge," because the elevens denote fatal illness and "there's not much more time." In tragicomic strokes McNulty sketched an entire culture with its own language, its own wisdom, and its own set of rules. (Old-fashioned glasses are bad to throw, "reciters are one of the terrors of tending bar," and the Irish, well, "they brood easy.")[17]

Eventually, McNulty turned his attention also to the painful interior monologues of upper-middle-class alcoholics who were trying *not* to drink. In "Eleven Dollars a Day," a high-rolling alcoholic who lights his cigarettes with Pipers Club matches is trying to sober up in a "pretty fancy hospital," while in "Slightly Crocked" a man sits on the veranda of his beach club and congratulates himself for perfectly balancing rye whiskey with ocean swims and in this way canceling "out the harm of the whiskey and (keep) the fun of it. For a man who tended to go overboard on drinking, that was the ideal seldom achieved."[18]

Although McNulty did touch upon the plight of upper-middle-class drinkers, it was for John O'Hara to become the Boswell of the powerful, affluent alcoholics whose dismal half-lives were played out on the beaches of Malibu, East Hampton, and the supper clubs of Manhattan and Beverly Hills. His characters were often internally defeated—either people on their way down from dazzling heights of fame and success, or those whose inner anguish was so profound that worldly success could not comfort them.

In O'Hara's stories alcohol dissolved class distinctions. His characters were often "picture" people like Dan Schecter, the principal character in "Everything's Satisfactory." Once a Hollywood high-flyer, he has become a sad fixture at the Klub Kilocycle, often called "the little club without charm." Schecter's drinking has progressed to the point where he is at the mercy of his social inferiors—headwaiters and bartenders who knew him in better days at better clubs. These underlings make sure that "one of the boys" drives him home so that when he wakes up he will be alone in his own bed with his car "in the driveway, intact." His lawyer is tired of squaring his "motoring lapses," and the woman he is carrying a torch for has decided to stay with her husband. Although Schecter's decline is obvious to everyone in the story and to the reader, his alcoholic grandiosity keeps him from experiencing himself as he really is.[19]

For Leda Pentleigh, the aging movie queen in O'Hara's "Drawing Room B," alcohol enables her to continue living in denial of her decline. Leda, the occupant of compartment B on the train to Los Angeles, is a "striking, stunning, chic, glamorous, sophisticated woman, who had spent most of the past week in New York City, wishing she were dead." This coupling of natural gifts with unnatural despair was O'Hara's forte. Leda experiences the pain of her own descent as a series of affronts: "the wrong tables at restaurants and the inconveniently timed appointments at hairdressers and the night of sitting alone in her hotel room while a forty-dollar pair of theater tickets went to waste . . . The standup by . . . the aging architect . . . The ruined Sophie dress and the lost earring at that South American's apartment." O'Hara relays an elaborate story of personal declension in a shorthand that was presumably entirely legible to his readers. The low point of the tale comes when Leda, assuming that courtship is what has brought a handsome New York stage actor to seek her out, discovers that he wants to ask advice about getting an agent in Hollywood. A nasty skirmish ensues in which she accuses him of patronizing her and of being a "swish." Shaken by her own loss of control, Leda pulls a bottle of bourbon from her bag and pours "herself a few drinks." She rings for the porter and gives him ten dollars to find the actor and "tell 'im that I'd like to see 'im, please." Like Dan Schecter, Leda is forced to entrust herself to the care of underlings who bear mute witness to the vast disparity between who she thinks she is and who she has become.[20]

Alcoholism was not the *cause* of the internal defeat experienced by O'Hara's men and women, people who, despite the obvious bounty of their lives, were awash in bitterness, self-pity, and a hunger for a larger share of love and favor than it was their destiny to possess. Their common trait was a tendency to see themselves as blameless victims of a world in which the too scarce resources of affluence, beauty, and passion had been meted out unfairly. Although they were often told by others that their drinking was a problem, O'Hara's alcoholic subjects saw drinking as a solution. His view of alcoholism, while it was clearly informed by the disease concept, skirted the issue of the powerlessness of the alcoholic over whether or not to drink. For O'Hara alcoholic drinking was not so much a compulsion as a last resort. In the face of defeat and dwindling options, alcohol provided his fictional protagonists with a brief respite from the grave disappointment of life near the top.

The power of O'Hara's work derived from his ability to write from inside the bourgeois alcoholic subject. Alcoholism was not a class problem confined to the quaint denizens of Third Avenue watering holes and could not, therefore, be dismissed as just a sad product of lower-class existence. It was, quite simply, a precondition. From the vantage point of O'Hara's protagonists, compulsive drinking seemed like a rational solution to a critical dilemma—the sense that try as one might, a piece of the puzzle of human happiness was always missing, and getting what one wanted did little to slake one's thirst for more.[21]

In a journal as concerned with class (and drinking) as was *The New Yorker,* the notion of alcoholism as a democratic disease, as likely to strike a movie star as a cab driver, carried considerable punch. Over time, the idea of the corrosive power of drink disqualified both the magazine's devil-may-care high-society drunk and his rum-dumb lower-class counterpart as objects for humor or light fiction. What was left in their wake was a body of work delineating alcohol's bleaker aspects, along with a bounty of upscale advertising emphasizing its aristocratic charms, and a significant number of derisive cartoons and casuals contradicting the content of these upscale promotions.

"One of the odd things about advertising," E. B. White wrote in 1946, "(and there are many odd things about it) is that the public rather counts on it." Offering a self-conscious apology for the *New Yorker* advertising/editorial mix, he explained that advertising not only "pays the bills" but also has a peculiar capacity to "complement reading matter." There is in advertising, White contended, "an unreality, a rhinestone brilliance, an unworldliness, and a promise. The ads are the reader's dream life, the reading matter his waking hour. We suspect he loves them both. After a column of pure thought, a half page of crunchy goodness."[22]

The New Yorker's representations of alcohol served both the waking and the dreaming hours of its readers. The presence of the copious liquor advertising next to its satirical editorial responses to it displays one of the magazine's essential contradictions. Here upper-class aspirations vied with contempt for snobbery; keen social consciousness challenged an equally keen nose for upscale commodities.

The editorial department's long-standing distaste for the magazine's own marketing campaigns was very much driven by Harold Ross's biases. It galled him when, in *The New Yorker*'s early days, he had to accept deceitful and unsavory advertising just to keep the magazine alive. He saw advertising as an inherently dishonest enterprise, and even after the magazine became successful and contained advertisements from "purveyors of premium goods like so many strings of pearls," Ross rankled at his dependency on them.[23]

Although advertisers were willing to pay premiums to reach the magazine's affluent audience, and it was these revenues that kept the magazine afloat, Ross was determined to establish the autonomy of the editorial side. As early as 1934, for example, he published a spoof of a Camel cigarette campaign featuring testimonials from attractive housewives, which was inadvertently run right next to one of the Camel ads. By running parodies of advertisements that were appearing in the magazine, Ross could subtly pretend that the left hand of editorial didn't know what the right hand of marketing was doing. By promoting and mocking elite consumption at the same time, the magazine enabled readers to simultaneously respond to ads and see through them, thus satisfying two critical prerequisites of knowingness, two sets of longings.[24]

The separation of *The New Yorker*'s advertising department from its editorial side ultimately played a part in making *The New Yorker* a superlative marketplace for expensive consumer goods. While the split between the two sides of the magazine reflected a genuine antipathy toward the whole enterprise of advertising on the part of the editorial staff, this division (and readers' awareness of it) enabled *The New Yorker* to provide its readers with editorial positions that seemed untainted by the crass vernacular of advertising. This disassociative sleight-of-hand served to increase the legitimacy of the magazine's editorial content and, ironically, its advertising content as well. As the magazine increased its credibility with a class of consumers who scorned the vulgarities of the mass market, it increased its appeal as a showcase for expensive, hand-crafted, and imported goods. An ad for a Cartier cigarette case or a pleasure cruise gained a certain heft when it ran side by side with a "Profile" of the U.N. Secretary General or a John Cheever short story.[25]

Postwar liquor advertisers promoted their products as metaphorical keys to the kingdom of distinction and manipulated the readers' quest for distinction by highlighting the cultural legitimacy of their products. The advertising tactic of presenting products in high-status contexts was not new in 1945. Since the 1920s, advertising had been constructed out of the yearnings and aspirations of Americans rather than out of their reality. Historians of advertising have shown that in the advertisements of the 1920s and 1930s all kinds of products—starch, cigarettes, chewing gum, and laundry soap—were placed in upscale settings to give them a "class image." Advertisers created a virtual art form, a kind of "capitalist realism" which was built upon the assumption that people didn't want advertising to replicate their actual lives or social relationships. One would, for example, be hard pressed in an examination of the ads of the twenties and thirties to find "even fleeting glimpses of such common scenes as religious services, factory workers on the job, sports fans . . . or working class families at home."[26]

In the postwar *New Yorker,* the products that advertisers displayed in swanky settings—ocean cruises, liver paté, gold scatter pins shaped like Scotty dogs, and expensive brandy—*belonged* in these settings. And although many of the magazine's readers could only aspire to possess such items, a significant number could and did buy these luxury goods. Advertisers paid high premiums for lineage and hailed the potency of *The New Yorker* as a market for expensive products, a development that suggests both the success of their marketing strategies and the enormous buying power of the magazine's readers. *New Yorker* advertising campaigns were often specifically aimed at a target audience of intelligent, middle-class people who had enough disposable income to purchase an embossed silver Tiffany cigarette case, but had probably not inherited such an item. These affluent, middle-class professionals constituted a nonetheless insecure and anxious elite.[27]

The magazine's advertisers offered, indirectly, to guide this status-conscious audience through the marketplace by suggesting that their choices could set them above the common herd (the rest of the middle class), who bought poorly made, cheap, and tasteless objects. Playing upon the insecurities of these consumers, advertisers anticipated social anxieties and proffered insiders' tips. For example, 21 Brands, a liquor distributor, offered a chart of "a few of the really outstanding wines" along with "indications as to their proper usage." Korbel Champagne, the ad instructed, was "for weddings, certainly," while Wente Bros. Sauvignon Blanc was touted as a "crustacean companion." A 1948 Drambuie ad illustrated with a elderly gent in white tie and tails suggested "a dram of Drambuie" after dinner. At the bottom of the ad there was a definition: "Dram. A small drink. When used in reference to Drambuie, a luxurious after-dinner adventure." Insisting that "SOME JOBS CALL FOR A *SPECIALIST!*" Prof. Hugh Bline, Heublin's "barman in a bottle," explained in rhyme that when a man needed a haircut he would turn to "A specialist, the barber!" But "when the average male must serve / A Daiquiri or such, / He mixes it himself—although / He lacks the master touch!"

The ad featured a cartoon of a businessman wearing a coat, a tie, and a woman's apron who fruitlessly attempted to prepare a mixed drink while a cool-looking chap in white tie and tails observed him with frank pity. This ad alerted the consumer to the likelihood of his or her own social ineptitude and then offered to solve it—a kind of one-two punch—at once perpetuating status anxiety and providing the means to allay it. In this way the magazine's advertisers portrayed the proper consumption of alcohol as an agent of social transformation, which could, if used properly, place the drinker on the same rung of the social ladder as the polo players, hostesses, and clubmen who shared their excellent taste in wine, champagne, and after-dinner drinks.[28]

"To possess things from the past," Pierre Bourdieu has argued, "accumulated, crystallized history, aristocratic names and titles, chateaux or 'stately homes' . . . vintage wines and antique furniture, is to master time, through all those thing whose common feature is that they can only be acquired in the course of time." By consuming alcohol in a discerning manner *New Yorker* readers could, some ads implied, turn back the clock in the uncertain postwar world. Some liquor advertisers made claims for their product's capacity to satisfy readers' longings for tradition, antiquity, immutability, and rarity—all presumably antidotes to the tasteless homogeneity of a mass market that provided middle-class Americans with styrofoam cups, deep frozen vegetables, tract homes, and the first MacDonald's hamburgers.[29]

In part, liquor advertisers' emphasis on historical continuity sought to assure American consumers that in spite of the war, their product had remained unchanged and was once again available. An ad for Benedictine, "La Grande Liqueur Française," described it as "A gracious custom four centuries old . . . a subtle, golden elixir still made in the old abbey." "Imported Once Again" was the caption of a 1946 Cherry Heering ad which reminded readers that the famous Danish liqueur has been around since 1818. "Again France sends you her sovereign champagne," a Lanson Champagne ad proclaimed. "The world has seen many changes since Lanson Champagne first found favor two centuries ago at the court of Louis XV. But the quality of Lanson, its sparkling verve and magnificent flavor, remain unchanged, unmatched." An advertisement for Melrose Rye Whiskey frankly attempted to satisfy both snobbery and prudence concerning alcohol: "Pay a little more. Drink a little less." The small print under the headline was: "Unchanging in a Changing World." Haig and

Haig whiskey was sold with the headline: "1627 *First* Still . . . 1948 Still *First.*" Remy Martin cognac ads ran with the caption: "sipped with delight by seven generations."[30]

These claims had a deep resonance for *New Yorker* consumers, whose present was marked by explosive social change and haunted by the prospect of World War III in the future. Such ads offered not only an assurance that a certain liquor had remained unchanged, but also that by purchasing it one could actually participate in preserving the past. This idea informed many of the magazine's advertisements for other upscale goods and services such as perfume, jewelry, trans-Atlantic cruises, luggage, and resort hotels. Somehow, the ads seemed to declare, by solving the problem of what to consume, the buyer was indirectly addressing problems that were graver, grander, even global.[31]

While many middle-class Americans took unreserved delight in the postwar boom, hailing the democracy of goods as the centerpiece of the free world, followers of *The New Yorker,* despite their enormous buying power and penchant for elite goods, maintained a Thoreauvian distaste both for advertising and mass consumption. This resistance to the lure of advertising was in itself a demonstration of an aspect of sophistication—the capacity to see through advertiser's claims. The magazine frequently tweaked its advertisers in humorous pieces ridiculing the successful advertising campaigns that were its bread and butter. These sallies, dispensed as internal antidotes to the promotions for high-end goods that filled its pages, ministered to readers' ambivalence about the powerful hold that elite consumption had upon them.

The Lord Calvert's whiskey promotion, "Men of Distinction," and the magazine's satirical responses to it indulged both the dreaming and waking desires of the *New Yorker* reader. The campaign was a series of full-page photographic portraits of celebrities and wealthy businessmen wearing dinner clothes or tasteful tweeds and holding highballs. These ads attempted to present the consumption of alcohol as an aristocratic pastime on a par with polo playing or riding to hounds. The ironic responses to these ads in the magazine's cartoons and in "Notes and Comment" should be understood as one voice in a crypto-debate about the merits of elite consumption, the idiocy of advertising, and the value of knowingness amongst postwar cosmopolitans. While account executives calculated actual sales of whiskey and crowed about the amazing success of the "Men of Distinction" campaign, *New Yorker* contributors made fun of it.

In a 1947 "Notes and Comment" concerning the "Men of Distinction" campaign, E. B. White playfully addressed some of the chief contradictions of the intellectual community over which he presided as honorary mayor. He turned his attention to Mr. Stuart Cloete, a well-known critic of the advertising business, who had claimed in his book, *The Third Way*, that advertising made people dissatisfied with their lives and the way they looked, and was essentially nothing more than "*the art of making people discontented and unhappy in order to sell them a product* [Italics Mr. Cloete's]." Acknowledging that he was in wholehearted agreement with this sentiment, White opened the *New York Times* only to see a Calvert "Men of Distinction" ad "with Mr. Cloete in the starring role!" His entire demeanor, the "rich herringbone coat, contented grasp of highball, general air of wicker-chair, planterish leisure" would certainly "make most people dissatisfied with what they are (workaday clods) and how they look (undistinguished)." Beneath Mr. Cloete's aristocratic portrait the caption "describing his drink—'so *rare . . .* so *mellow* that it is produced only in limited quantities'" seemed designed to "stir up discontent in the multitudes for whom this nectar . . . must forever remain a bright, upper class chimera."[32]

The comment did more than ridicule the hapless Mr. Cloete: it addressed both the manipulative tactics used by Madison Avenue in its liquor advertising and the issue of class as it related to taste and consumption. By touching the sensitive spot at the intersection of class and taste, White was satirizing his own audience, which was clearly vulnerable to the appeals to snobbery that White was ridiculing. Yet the end result of this teasing was permissive. Readers could satisfy a desire to drink aristocratic brews and wear the tweed caps and driving gloves of whiskey-drinking clubmen, while their favorite *New Yorker* humorists helped them to laugh at this impulse.[33]

In a "Notes and Comment" item from the following year, White took another shot at the Lord Calvert's campaign. He noted that *PM* magazine had managed to track down a fellow named Henry Kopf at a sleazy bar in Union City, New Jersey. Kopf, it seems, was currently appearing in an advertisement for Calvert's, and *PM* had "made much of the fact that he was unshaven and seedy in appearance . . . apparently thinking it peculiar that a fellow like Kopf should be publicized as an endorser of Calvert's." This attitude, White argued, "strikes us as errant snobbery." "We" would just as soon "take Kopf's word on Whiskey as that of a more stylish authority, such as Adolph Menjou." Humorously saluting Calvert's as "an egalitarian company," White congratulated them for "doing things the 'American Way.'"[34]

Here, with his customary agility, White juggles the profoundly contradictory elements in the magazine's self-presentation without dropping a single ball. By introducing a former "man of distinction" reduced to unshaven alcoholic, presumably because he drank too much Calvert's whiskey, White manages to tip his hat to the more destructive aspects of drinking while concurrently conflating democratic principle with the right of a seedy guy to consume and represent an elite product. In making fun of the snobbery of Lord Calvert's marketing strategy, he succeeds both in suborning and expressing the ideal of the equality of goods as "The American Way."

In a 1946 "Notes and Comment" White directly took on the issue of distillers' "uneasiness" about selling alcohol as an elegant social prop in light of the new emphasis on the "disease" of alcoholism. The advertising business, he said, had reached a "new pinnacle" with the House of Seagram's placement of a six-column newspaper ad responding to the release of "The Lost Weekend," to "sound a solemn warning that *'some men should not drink.'* (They didn't actually name us, but we know who they meant.)" Seagram's is right, White opined, "we shouldn't drink," but "now we at least no longer need be in any doubt *what* whiskey we shouldn't drink. Henceforth, when not drinking, we shall be careful to not drink Seagram's."

White pointed out that liquor companies were "haunted by the specter of alcoholism" and the certain "knowledge that someone, some-where, is probably drinking the wonderful elixir too fast" and will soon "go out like a light." This knowledge, he explained, caused the distiller to "turn on his own child in a delirium of righteous anger." White ridiculed Seagram's, White Horse, and Calvert's alike, arguing that their liquor promotions merely proved that in advertising you can really say just about anything. Citing a pair of ads by White Horse and Calvert's, he pointed out that they were essentially "doing the same thing" in "different ways." The Calvert's ad promoted whiskey "by showing a man in the act of drinking some," while White Horse recommended it by "showing a horse letting the stuff alone. They seemed equally effec-tive to us, and we could hardly wait till five o'clock."[35]

White's disdain for the content of New Yorker liquor campaigns resonates with Northrop Frye's idea that our "reaction to advertising is really a form of literary criticism." If we are to defend ourselves against an absurd and frustrating world, Frye argued, we have to "detach our imaginations" from advertising in order to "see around it." Although we may approach advertising with the jaunty self-confidence of players in an "ironic game," it is a perilous contest, because our passivity in the face of the market "creates an illusion of detachment and mental superiority even when one is obeying its exhortations." Although we may know that advertising "says what it does not wholly mean," Frye explained, we become dependent on its "versions of reality." White's satiric pieces about the magazine's liquor advertisements certainly helped readers "see around" advertising that was meant to seduce them. By reading and agreeing with White's pieces, New Yorker readers could demonstrate their worldliness by succumbing to the blandishments of the market while resisting them intellectually.[36]

The "Man of Distinction" campaign was also a frequent target of the magazine's cartoonists. In a Charles Addams cartoon in the September 7, 1946 issue, a vacationer is posing for a portrait in a boardwalk photo booth. His head pokes through a hole in a backdrop depicting the body of a gentleman seated in a club chair, pipe in one hand, highball in the other. A banner over his head reads: "For Men of Distinction." Neither the man nor his plump wife, who watches from the sidelines in an ill-fitting bathing costume, look like legitimate candidates for distinction of any kind. The joke appears to be about the liquor industry's cynical encouragement of class aspirations and the naive faith of consumers in the possibility of altering one's social status through the act of consuming alcohol—a faith that advertisers were certain abided in the hearts of many *New Yorker* readers.[37]

A 1947 cartoon portrayed an aristocratic portrait gallery—a collection of paintings of gentlemen sporting mutton chop whiskers, wearing wigs and frock coats. The final portrait in the collection is instantly recognizable as a "man of distinction"—an effete modern chap wearing a tasteful herringboned sports coat and holding a highball. While the paintings from earlier eras showed gentlemen posing with sun dials and leather-bound volumes, the last man had only a drink. Thus the earmarks of aristocratic taste were no longer symbols of science or classical texts, but rather consumer goods that were available to anyone with enough money to purchase them—a premise upon which *New Yorker* advertisers based their appeals to the magazine's readers. What now passed for nobility was essentially indistinguishable from the crass appeals of commerce.[38]

If the skid row bum lay in the gutter at the low end of *The New Yorker*'s spectrum of representations of alcohol, certainly Lord Calvert's "Man of Distinction" occupied the high end. Sam Cobean brought the two together in a 1948 cartoon in which a down-and-out alcoholic stands before a Salvation Army band telling the story of his fall from grace to a small group of equally hapless drunks. He describes his modest upbringing by God-fearing parents and his exemplary university career. After he graduated from college he went to work in a large corporation and gave himself over entirely to his career:

> I neither drank nor smoked nor let pleasure deflect me from my objective . . . my devotion was rewarded . . . until finally I was elected Chairman of the Board . . . At the height of my career, I was invited to pose for an advertisement featuring men of out-

standing accomplishment. I accepted this honor. The photographer posed me before his camera and placed in my hand a glass of liquid. Out of curiosity, I took a sip—and then another sip.[39]

This cartoon caption described both the dream and the nightmare career trajectories of a postwar middle-class corporate executive and reflected one of the central dilemmas of the bourgeois condition. While membership in both the upper and lower classes tended to be inherited, for the middle class birth alone provided no guarantee of eventual class position. In order to maintain one's standing in the upper echelons of the middle class, one had to earn one's place through long years of education, self-control, and personal discipline.[40]

The "Man of Distinction" in Cobean's cartoon had been so masterful at controlling his impulses and desires that he was awarded the ultimate prize for a middle class professional: an opportunity to pose for an advertisement in which he would be portrayed as an aristocrat. However, the sheer exhilaration of crossing the line from hardworking, gratification-delaying Chairman of the Board to ersatz gentleman causes him to drop his guard, and he slips precipitously from the top of the middle class to the bottom of the heap. While this humorous cautionary tale was intended to ridicule the snobbery implicit in Lord Calvert's advertising campaign, it also reveals very particular assumptions about the relationship between corporate success and self-control as well as an awareness about the risks of alcoholism for upper-middle-class professionals.

Preoccupied with class differentiation, members of the upper echelons of the middle-class often relied upon consumption to establish status and distinguish themselves from others. To achieve this result, consumption had to provide the cues through which upper-middle-class people could recognize each other outside of the workplace. Discriminating consumption became a means of displaying personal identity and social authority, and the range varied according to the milieu. At the *New Yorker* level, lawyers, stockbrokers, advertising men, designers, publishers, editors, and their educated wives participated eagerly in the commercialism of American life, both shaping and profiting from it, but they expressed a marked resistance to the very culture that earned them their livings. These anticommercial consumers scorned mass-market goods. They shopped with an eye toward European aristocratic tradition, quality, and durability. Thus the act of choosing a commodity in the *New Yorker* marketplace took on great weight; as social relations could be objectified in the things one possessed, the act of buying was neither superficial nor merely practical.[41]

Advertisements promoting alcohol as an aristocratic social prop and an ongoing editorial chorus ridiculing these claims provide an archetypal example of the way *The New Yorker* served the powerful and conflicting aspirations of its audience to possess both elite consumer goods and a democratic sensibility. Its unique mix allowed socially conscious men and women to enjoy the pleasure of knowing and having only what was right.

CONCLUSION: FAULT LINES

At the end of World War II the United States had reason to exult. Fascism had been vanquished, the Depression was over, and this country had become the richest and most powerful nation on the planet. For the white middle class the postwar period ushered in a era of unprecedented prosperity, enabling it to experience the kind of privilege that had once been the preserve of the very rich. These postwar privileges were not, however, equally shared by all Americans. For most women, Hispanics, African Americans, Native Americans, and Asians the benefits of the "good war" were far more ambiguous, the truth of its democratic promise far less certain.

Cultural critics, themselves also the beneficiaries of postwar affluence, tended to underplay the social and economic ambiguity of the
war's legacy. Thus by the late 1940s and early 1950s, the preoccupation
with social justice that had characterized the ideology of intellectuals in
the 1930s was seen as less than respectable. Instead, the postwar intellectual bemoaned conformity, mediated questions of taste, and acted as
"a kind of high-grade consumer adviser." Feeling that American political institutions had grown too stable and too intimidating to offer
citizens the privileges of a true participatory democracy, these social
critics called for internal activism, a posture which presupposed the
futility of any assault on the larger framework of the society. This shift
from the broad-based social concerns that had characterized the serious
highbrow magazines in the 1930s turned out to dovetail neatly with *The
New Yorker* formula. The magazine, once anathema to writers on the
left, became a haven for them in the postwar years. In this period
cultural critics like Dwight Macdonald and Mary McCarthy, who had
once criticized the magazine for its "Park Avenue attitude," now wrote
for it and brooded about the "shapelessness" of modern American life.[1]

The New Yorker's tone and format were admirably suited to the constraints and ellipses of postwar discourse, and the magazine appealed to a
significant segment of the American public because it could resolve two
of its more powerful preoccupations: a desire for social distinction and a
genuine concern with egalitarian democratic principles. There was, however, a price to pay for reconciling such disparate sets of longings. To
achieve the desired balance, certain significant power inequities that existed within postwar American society—servant and employer, rich and
poor, white people and people of color, the Third World and the First,
and closest to home, men and women—were glossed over, inverted (as in
the case of gender relations), or transformed into matters of taste or mere
cultural preference.[2]

The magazine presented its readers with a diagram of the world that
was, like any partisan view, a highly stylized rendering. Its own geography was writ large, while other places and other peoples were pushed
out to the margins. This world view allowed for significant gaps in its

topography. Lost in some Bermuda Triangle, for example, was a sense of the social cost of privilege. While *The New Yorker* consistently demonstrated a concern with important social issues such as racism and inequality, it underrepresented the extent to which the maintenance of social privilege—the still water in which the magazine floated—was antithetical to these concerns.

There was, in fact, a shrill counterpoint to the "quietly liberal" voice of the postwar *New Yorker*. When the magazine treated large global matters such as war crimes, international peacekeeping, presidential politics, nuclear deterrence, or the HUAC investigations, a tone of justice and civility prevailed. On the other hand, when the subject matter was closer to home, more directly rooted in class and gender distinctions, a peculiar edge came into the *New Yorker* voice. In its representations of certain types—the worker who doesn't know his place, the shrew, the doofus doorman, the clueless maid, the avaricious matron at the shoestore or at the milliner's—there was a curious absence of the gentle good humor and worldly liberalism that were understood to be the bywords of *The New Yorker* text.[3]

Beneath the surface of the magazine's politically correct text, from which conscious examples of flagrant sexism, racism, and class consciousness had been conscientiously expurgated, lay a vital subtext in which these suppressed elements continued to flourish like mushrooms in the dark. This sub-rosa *New Yorker* content has something very important to tell us about the intellectual boundaries of the postwar liberal community and its requirements for membership.

E. B. White once alluded to *The New Yorker*'s mix as a "column of pure thought, a half a page of crunchy goodness; after a hard editorial, a brand new helicopter, easy to own and operate." This distinctive alchemical amalgam appeared capable of dissolving the profound cultural contradictions of postwar liberalism. Readers, for example, seemed largely untroubled by the coexistence of ads for upscale goods with editorial pieces that ridiculed the undemocratic nature of these ads. This was merely a first step toward accepting as natural a much wider array of conflicting representations. Feminism coexisted with sexism, an intense preoccupation with social class mingled with a commitment to equality, a contempt for racism and an unconscious strain of it stood cheek-by-jowl. The magazine bestowed its legitimacy upon a wide range of positions, stretching from the anachronistic to the cutting edge. And the pieces of this complicated puzzle fit together neatly enough to look like harmonious elements of a coherent value system. The magazine's capacity to blend vastly contradictory elements made it attractive to an ever wider circle of readers. Members of old New York society could enjoy the theater and opera reviews and ignore E. B. White's pleas for world federation. College professors could disregard the articles on polo playing and read about the Nuremberg trials and the rise of socialism in Italy. Doctors could chuckle over short fiction detailing the mild vicissitudes of suburban life and filter out the retrograde cartoons depicting gentlemen drunks being hurled out of chic supper clubs. The magazine's layout unconsciously schooled its audience in techniques for tolerating cognitive dissonance. While editorial content could be attended to selectively, it was clear that college professors, housewives, and Park Avenue dowagers alike saw the ads. This gave the magazine wide appeal and increased its persuasive power—both as an advertising medium and as an intellectual and cultural milieu.[4]

A *New Yorker* promotional pamphlet sent to advertisers in 1948 was headlined "It's Not the Size, It's the Ferocity," and was intended to alter the traditional tendency of advertisers to base per-line advertising costs on circulation figures. This promotion stressed that the actual number of *New Yorker* subscribers was disproportionate to their power to consume expensive goods and services. One *New Yorker* promotional piece cited the overwhelming response to an advertisement featuring Alfred of New York shirts, into which advertisers had slipped "a very tough little chess problem."

Within days the magazine had received thousands of responses to the chess problem—from "Bankers, Lawyers, Atomic Scientists, Business Executives, Government Officials, U.N. Delegates, Women, Teachers—in a word, from all kinds of bright people from all over the place." Not only were readers trying to solve the chess problem, they were also buying Alfred of New York shirts in record numbers as delighted retailers ordered and reordered. This is a striking example of the way the magazine served its readership by conflating discerning consumption and intellectual sophistication.[5]

By furnishing readers with a locale in which intellectual interests, materialism, and urbanity could coexist, *The New Yorker* functioned as a powerful cultural broker in the postwar years. This was not a role that it assumed consciously, nor was it some kind of plot either to silence the radical impulses of its readers or coerce them into the upscale market. Its cosmopolitan mix offered readers an opportunity to indulge in dynamic material consumption and in passive political spectatorship—a heady blend which could be experienced as a form of active citizenship in a sophisticated polity. The magazine performed for them the task of spanning the anxious chasm between goodness and acquisitiveness. This marriage of contradictory impulses occurred in a kind of journalistic global village—a place whose inhabitants shared affinities, were plagued by the same inner conflicts, and played by the same rules.[6]

In a poem expressing the ethos of the great *New Yorker* backyard at midcentury, "The Williamsons," Louise Owen describes her neighbors, with whom she shares a taste for Lucky Strike cigarettes, the *New York Times*, the *Atlantic Monthly*, the *Saturday Review*, and the Book-of-the-Month Club; Guinness Stout, Highland Cream, and oysters on the shell; shopping "at Altman's and the French Bazaar."

> The shows that we attend, the things we eat;
> Van Gogh, Cole Porter, aspirin, Shredded Wheat,
> The Lunts, Chanel, and travelling by air.
> I see new facets every time I pass
> Debris that shows, like bits of looking glass,
> Fragments of Williamsons, whose whole I seek,
> Dropped in their rubbish barrels week by week.[7]

In the rich debris of the postwar *New Yorker*, it is indeed possible to recover aspects of the Williamsons and other readers who saw the same Broadway shows and enjoyed "The Lunts, Chanel and travelling by air." But the magazine's lavish discursive detritus reveals far more than just a sense of the aesthetic and consumer preferences of the members of the *New Yorker* community. Also exposed are many of the less consciousness assumptions of the society in which the magazine flourished, its wishes, its lies, and its power relations. The members of the powerful cohort that read the postwar *New Yorker* were bound to one another by more than a keen appetite for commodities and culture. Beneath the bright surface of their analogous tastes and opinions, they shared another, darker commonality. Their unprecedented abundance was not without its discontents. They were riven by doubts about the conflict between an enjoyment of social privilege and the moral cost of such privilege—the fear that such privilege might weaken principle and erode character.

In October of 1957, *The New Yorker* published Eugene Kinkaid's "The Study of Something New in History," an examination of the troubling behavior of American POWs during the Korean War, in which "one out of every three Americans taken prisoner . . . collaborated with the Communists," and "two out of five died, many at the hands of their fellow Americans." According to Kinkaid and Army officials, the cause of this "wholesale breakdown of morale" was not solely Communist cruelty or brainwashing, but was rather "the entire cultural pattern which produced these young soldiers." The failure of American prisoners to attempt escape, to abet their fellows, or to withstand Communist indoctrination could be traced, Kinkaid argued, to deficiencies in our own culture—"home training of children, physical fitness, religious adherence, and the privilege of existing under the highest standard of living in the world." The "sinister and regrettable things" that transpired in the POW camps seemed to be the result of a kind of spiritual collapse. Prisoners consistently demonstrated an absence of the sorts of inner resources that would cause "a man to act, however dark the situation, as an ethical fearless human being." At its heart Kinkaid's piece was a portrait of the perils of prosperity. His indictment of the "moral tone" of the nation struck a chord with *New Yorker* readers, who wrote "from every part of the country" to say that they had been "contemplating and discussing the study's obvious messages and the responses that these aroused in them."[8]

Beset by the sense that something was wrong, these midcentury *New Yorker* readers wore the crown of privilege uneasily. They were worried about their good fortune, and they were worried about their world. Their sense of the problem was that affluence had an erosive effect upon integrity. This anxiety made them particularly eager to resolve the troubling conflict between privilege and principle—to find a way to fuse entitlement and human decency into a coherent value system. But the fact that the members of the most privileged middle class in American history did not entirely succeed in this enterprise is illuminated by their failure to convince their own children of its legitimacy. Some of these children acted out their disenchantment with the internal contradictions in their parents' value system in a fashion that had far-reaching consequences for American political and cultural life. While their parents fretted about the possibility that privilege had made them soft, their offspring saw a direct relationship between privilege and the perpetuation of social injustice.

"The Port Huron Statement" of 1962, the social manifesto of the Students for a Democratic Society (SDS), began with these words: "We are the people of this generation, bred in at least modest comfort, housed now in universities, looking uncomfortably to the world we inherit." Troubled by the failure of America to deliver on the values of "freedom and equality for each individual," the children of postwar plenty "began to see complicated and disturbing paradoxes" in their world. "The declaration 'all men are created equal . . .' rang hollow before the facts of Negro life in the South and the big cities of the North. The proclaimed peaceful intentions of the United States contradicted its economic and military investments in the Cold War status quo."[9]

Empowered by the very privilege they disparaged, and roused by the imprecations of the civil rights movement, the children of the *New Yorker* village went to Berkeley and Columbia and the University of Wisconsin, where they condemned their parents and the United States both for their avid materialism and their betrayal of the ideal of participatory democracy. As the children of middle-class liberals acted upon the democratic principles they had learned at their parents' knees, marching shoulder-to-shoulder with African Americans, manning the ramparts of an allusive revolution, burning their draft cards, "seizing" universities, and appropriating People's Park, the generation that had spawned them—people who saw themselves as decent, socially conscious citizens—often expressed mystification at both the venom and the stylistic excesses of their countercultural progeny. There is, in fact, a bittersweet twist to the bewilderment of these parents, who had certainly had their own doubts about the compatibility of democracy and privilege. Many of them had disregarded their own misgivings, moved to the suburbs, abandoned youthful bohemian dreams, risen in the corporate hierarchy, sacrificed to pay for piano lessons and private education. And they had done all of this in their supreme eagerness to provide perfect, secure lives for their offspring, who now nipped at the hands that had fed them so richly. It is possible that in addition to telling us a great deal about its readers and the myriad incongruities of their world, the postwar *New Yorker* can also help us to understand something about their legacy—the passionate social guilt of their children.[10]

NOTES / ACKNOWLEDGMENTS / INDEX

1 THE LAY OF THE LAND

1. Charles McGrath, "Life and Letters: The Ross Years," *TNY*, February 20 & 27, 1995, pp. 180–183. Ross was, in fact, the co-founder and co-owner along with Raoul Fleischmann, who financed the fledgling magazine. For a discussion of Fleischmann and his contribution see Thomas Kunkel, *Genius in Disguise: Harold Ross of the New Yorker* (New York: Random House, 1995), pp. 207–239.

2. Christopher P. Wilson, "The Rhetoric of Consumption: Mass-Market Magazines and the Demise of the Gentle Reader, 1880–1920," in *The Culture of Consumption*, ed. by Richard Wrightman Fox and T. J. Jackson Lears (New York: Pantheon Books, 1983), pp. 41, 45; George H. Douglas, *The Smart Magazines* (Hamden, Conn.: Archon Books, 1991), pp. 11–13.

3. Douglas, *Smart*, pp. 15–16; Wilson, "Mass-Market Magazines," pp. 48–52, 60; Edward Bok quoted in ibid., p. 55; Ellen Gruber Garvey, *The Adman in the Parlor: Magazines and the Gendering of Consumer Culture* (New York: Oxford University Press, 1996).

4. Douglas, *Smart*, p. 19. For an acute description of the New York in which *TNY* emerged see Ann Douglas, *Terrible Honesty: Mongrel Manhattan in the 1920s* (New York: Farrar, Straus and Giroux, 1995).

5. Peter Berger and Thomas Luckmann, "Social Mobility and Personal Identity," *Archives Européennes de Sociologie*, 5 (1964) pp. 331–343; Mary Douglass and Baron Isherwood, *The World of Goods* (New York: Basic Books, 1979) pp. 75–76; Sinclair Lewis, *Main Street* (New York: Harcourt, Brace & World, 1920), p. 265.

6. Douglas, *Smart*, pp. 10–11.

7. James T. Patterson, *Grand Expectations: The United States 1945–1974* (New

York: Oxford University Press, 1996), pp. 70–71; Clifford E. Clark, Jr., "Ranch-House Suburbia: Ideals and Realities," in *Recasting America: Culture and Politics in the Age of Cold War,* ed. by Lary May (Chicago: University of Chicago Press, 1989), pp. 171–172; Frederick Siegel, *Troubled Journey: From Pearl Harbor to Ronald Reagan* (New York: Hill and Wang, 1984), p. 93.

8. Patterson, *Expectations,* pp. 71, 76–79; Elaine Tyler May, *Homeward Bound: American Families in the Cold War Era* (New York: Basic Books, 1988), pp. 3–15; Elaine Tyler May, "Rosie the Riveter Gets Married," in *The War in American Culture,* ed. by Lewis Erenberg and Susan E. Hirsch (Chicago: University of Chicago Press, 1996), p. 137; Carl Abbott, *Urban America in the Modern Age: 1920 to the Present* (Chapel Hill: University of North Carolina Press, 1987), pp. 64, 66; Clark, Jr., "Ranch-House Suburbia," pp. 171–172.

9. Abbott, *Urban America,* pp. 66–67.

10. Thomas Bender, *New York Intellect* (Baltimore: Johns Hopkins University Press, 1987), p. 334. For a discussion of Manhattan in the 1920s, see Douglas, *Terrible Honesty,* pp. 3–72.

11. F-R Publishing Corporation, "The New Yorker: Editorial Policy and Purpose" (New York, 1946), p. 3; Publishers Information Bureau, "Retail Advertising Standings for 1947."

12. Dwight Macdonald, "Laugh and Lie Down," *Partisan Review* (1939), p. 53.

13. "*TNY:* Type and Character of Readers" (New York: F-R Publishing Corp., 1946); "*TNY:* Character of Readers" (New York: F-R Publishing Corp., 1949); "Character of Readers" (New York: Department of Market Research, *TNY* Magazine, 1959). Per capita income for 1950 from *U.S. Bureau of the Census Statistical Abstract of the United States,* 91st ed. (Washington D.C.: U.S. Department of Commerce, 1970), p. 312.

14. Publisher's Statement—Magazine Form, *The New Yorker* (Chicago: Audit Bureau of Circulations, 1925, 1939, 1949, 1959, 1970).

15. "Character of Readers" (1946, 1959); "Visits to the City of New York" (New York: *TNY* Magazine, 1960), pp. 5, 7, 13, 14.

16. Patterson, *Expectations,* pp. 68, 79.

17. Irving Howe, "The Treason of the Critics," *The New Republic,* June 12, 1989, p. 29; Louis Menand, *New York Review of Books,* March 23, 1995, p. 10.

18. Jason De Parle, "Spy Anxiety," *The Washington Monthly,* 21 no. 1 (February 1989), p. 12; Howe, "Treason," p. 29; Lionel Trilling, "Our Country and Our Culture," *Partisan Review,* 19 no. 3 (May–June 1952), pp. 319–320. See also James Sloan Allen, *The Romance of Commerce and Culture* (Chicago: University of Chicago Press, 1983); Jackson Lears, "A Matter of Taste," in *Recasting America: Culture and Politics in the Age of Cold War,* ed. by Lary May (Chicago: University of Chicago Press, 1989), pp. 48, 50.

19. Patricia Travis, "What We Talk about When We Talk about *The New Yorker:* Reading and Middle Class Identity at the Gentlest of Magazines," 1996, ms., pp. 2, 4.

20. Phillip Fisher, *Hard Facts: Setting and Form in the American Novel* (New York: Oxford University Press, 1985), pp. 133–134.
21. Letters to *TNY:* Barbara Von Treskow (Hamburg, Germany), January 4, 1952; Miss Julia Sohnlein (Monroe, Mich.), undated; Mrs. Harry E. F. Wright (Tucson, Ariz.), September 28, 1953. Box 952, Records of *TNY,* at the New York Public Library Rare Books, Manuscript Division, New York.
22. Kunkel, *Genius,* p. 6 ; Mary McCarthy, "Up the Ladder from *Charm* to *Vogue,*" in *On the Contrary, Articles of Belief* (New York: Farrar, Straus and Giroux, 1961) pp. 177, 183, 175–176; Lears, "A Matter of Taste," pp. 38–57; De Parle, "Anxiety," p. 12.
23. Letters to *TNY:* Hugh Gilchrist (Canberra, Australia), 27 July, 1954; Margaret Houston (Jackson, Mich.), 14 February, 1953; Leila Vannewitz (Vancouver, Canada), 9 January, 1954; Fred Graeser (Oakland, Calif.), 2 May, 1953; Dennis Winston (New South Wales), 23 May, 1955. Box 952, The Records of *TNY* at the New York Public Library Rare Books, Manuscript Division, New York.
24. Travis, "Reading," p. 34.
25. Letters to *TNY:* Mrs. Leslie Kendall (Evanston, Wy.), February 20, 1952; Richard McCarthy (Wyandotte, Mich.), May 26, 1954; Charles Ross (Washington D.C.), October 17, 1950. Box 952, The Records of *TNY* at the New York Public Library.
26. Contributions from readers in Box 951, The Records of *TNY* at the New York Public Library Rare Books, Manuscripts Division.
27. My formulation of the difficulties of using *TNY's* text as a mirror is inspired by Roland Marchand's discussion of using ads as historical documents in *Advertising the American Dream* (Berkeley: University of California Press, 1985), pp. xvi–xix.

2   BEYOND THE MANHATTAN SKYLINE

1. Dwight Macdonald, *Politics Past: Essays in Political Criticism,* (1945; rpt. New York: Viking, 1970), pp. 25–26, originally published in *Politics* (August 1945); Richard Pells, *The Liberal Mind in the Conservative Age* (New York: Harper & Row, 1985), pp. 44–45.
2. Kai Erikson, "A Final Accounting of Death and Destruction," *New York Times Book Review* (August 9, 1981), p. 24.
3. Phillip Swirbul, "David Lillienthal and the AEC," ms., 1987 ; Paul Boyer, *By the Bomb's Early Light* (New York: Pantheon, 1985), p. xvi; Gallup Poll, September 1945; "The *Fortune* Survey," *Fortune,* December 1945, p. 305; Leonard S. Cottrell, Jr., and Sylvia Elberhart, *American Opinion on World Affairs in the Atomic Age* (Princeton: Princeton University Press, 1948), p. 15.
4. Rob Paarlberg, "Forgetting about the Unthinkable," *Foreign Policy,* 10 (Spring 1973), p. 132; Anne O'Hare McCormick, "The Promethean Role of the United States," *New York Times,* August 8, 1945, p. 22.

5. Bruce Bliven, "The Bomb and the Future," *The New Republic,* August 20, 1945, pp. 210–212; T.R.B., "Washington Notes: Atomic Anxieties," *The New Republic,* August 20, 1945, p. 222; Macdonald, *Politics Past,* p. 169; Swirbul, "Lillienthal," pp. 1, 12; *The Journals of David E. Lillienthal,* vol. II: *The Atomic Energy Years, August 7, 1945* (New York: Harper & Row, 1964); Spencer R. Weart, *Nuclear Fear: A History of Images* (Cambridge: Harvard University Press, 1988), p. 104.

6. Charles McGrath, "Life and Letters: The Ross Years," *TNY,* February 20 & 27, 1995, pp. 188–189; James Thurber, *My Years with Ross* (Boston: Little, Brown, 1957), pp. 295. 171.

7. Brendan Gill, *Here at The New Yorker* (New York: Carroll & Graf Publishers, 1987), pp. 167–168. *The New Yorker Overseas Edition Armed Forces Weekly* (New York: F-R Publishing Corp.), dist. by Special Service Division, Army Service Forces, U.S. Army, 1943—1946; [E. B. White], "Notes and Comment," December 28, 1946, p. 15; Dale Kramer, *Ross and The New Yorker* (Garden City: Doubleday, 1951), pp. 265–266; Thomas Kunkel, *Genius in Disguise* (New York: Random House, 1995), p. 352; McGrath, "Ross Years," pp. 180, 188. *The New Yorker Book of War Pieces* (New York: Reynal and Hitchcock, 1947), passim.

8. Kunkel, *Genius,* p. 93.

9. [E. B. White], "Notes and Comment," September 1, 1945, p. 13, and August 18, 1945, p. 13.

10. Ibid., December 8, 1945, p. 25, and April 13, 1946, pp. 23–24.

11. Kunkel, *Genius,* p. 400; Russell Maloney, "Tilley the Toiler," *The Saturday Review,* August 30, 1947, p. 9.

12. [E. B. White], "Notes and Comment," August 18, 1945, pp. 13–14. White's account of the blind girl in Albuquerque is based on a report that appeared in a New Mexico newspaper about a blind girl in an automobile traveling directly in the direction of ground zero during a bomb test. The army claimed that the strange bright light she had seen was caused by the spontaneous combustion of an ammunition dump.

13. Maloney, "Tilley," pp. 8–10; *Commonweal,* March 10, 1950, "A More Meaningful Tree," p. 573; Robert Warshow, "E. B. White and *The New Yorker,*" in *The Immediate Experience: Movies, Comics, Theater and Other Aspects of Popular Culture* (Garden City: Doubleday, 1962), pp. 107–108; E. B. White, *The Wild Flag* (Boston: Houghton Mifflin, 1946), pp. 42, 62, 150–151.

14. "TOTT: Fateful Night," August 18, 1945, p. 15, and "TOTT: Gags Away," p. 16.

15. Karl Shapiro, "Homecoming," *TNY,* August 18, 1945, p. 28.

16. Robert Simpson, "The Infinitesimal and the Infinite," *TNY,* August 18, 1945, pp. 26–34.

17. Ernest Kroll, "In a Georgetown Garden," *TNY,* July 20, 1946, p. 24.

18. Weart, *Fear,* pp. 104–105; Frank Sullivan, "The Cliche Expert Testifies on the Atom," *TNY,* November 27, 1945, p. 27.

19. "Notes and Comment," June 15, 1946, p. 15; [E. B. White], "Notes and Comment," June 29, 1946, p. 13; "Notes and Comment," July 27, 1946, p. 11.
20. [E. B. White], "Notes and Comment," April 20, 1946, pp. 21–22, and March 9, 1946, p. 13. The magazine published many Bikini test cartoons. See Robert Day's cartoons of June 29, 1946, p. 27 and June 15, 1946, p. 17. For other *TNY* comments concerning Bikini Island see: "Notes and Comment," June 15, 1946, p. 15; [E. B. White], "Notes and Comment," June 29, 1946, p. 13; "Notes and Comment," July 27, 1946, p. 11; E. B. White, "Books: Journal of a Contaminated Man," *TNY*, December 4, 1948, pp. 171–177.
21. Roger Angell, "Some Pigs in Sailor Suits," *TNY*, April 13, 1946, pp. 32–33.
22. [E. B. White], "Notes and Comment," November 17, 1945, pp. 21–22; "Notes and Comment," December 1, 1945, p. 15; "Notes and Comment," June 8, 1946, p. 19; [E. B. White], "Notes and Comment," July 13, 1946, p. 15.
23. See Karl Shapiro, "The Convert," *TNY*, April 13, 1946, p. 28.
24. Geoffrey T. Hellman, "A Reporter at Large: The Contemporaneous Memorandum of Dr. Sachs," *TNY*, December 1, 1945, pp. 78–80. An interesting counterpoint to this article is Alva Johnston's reverential profile of Albert Einstein, "Scientist and Mob Idol," *TNY*, December 2, 1933, 23–36; December 9, 1933, pp. 29–32.
25. Daniel Lang, "A Reporter at Large: White Sands," *TNY*, July 24, 1948, pp. 40–46; "Our Far-Flung Correspondents: Blackjack and Flashes," *TNY*, September 20, 1952, pp. 100–111; "A Reporter at Large: The Long Island Atoms," *TNY*, December 20, 1947, pp. 33–43; "A Reporter at Large: The Center of Reality," *TNY*, March 20, 1948, pp. 62–77; "A Reporter at Large: A Romantic Urge," *TNY*, April 21, 1951, pp. 75–93; "A Reporter in New Mexico: Los Alamos," *TNY*, April 17, 1948, pp. 76–89. For a collection of Lang's early atomic bomb pieces, see Daniel Lang, *Early Tales of the Atomic Age* (Garden City: Doubleday, 1948.)
26. Lang, "White Sands," pp. 42–43.
27. Daniel Lang, "A Reporter at Large: A Fine Moral Point," *TNY*, June 8, 1946, pp. 62–76.
28. Daniel Lang, "Our Far-Flung Correspondents: The Atomic City," *TNY*, September 29, 1945, pp. 46–51.
29. Lang, "Blackjack and Flashes," p. 100.
30. Ibid., pp. 100–101.
31. Ibid., pp. 101–109.
32. John Hersey, "Hiroshima," *TNY*, August 31, 1946, pp. 15–76; Paul Boyer, *Bomb*, pp. 204–205; Kunkel, *Genius*, p. 374; Russell S. Hutchinson, "Hiroshima," *Christian Century*, September 25, 1946, p. 1151; Henry L. Stimson, "The Decision to Use the Atomic Bomb," *Harper's Magazine* (Feb. 1947), pp. 97–107. See also Martin J. Sherwin, *A World Destroyed: Hiroshima and the Origins of the Arms Race* (New York: Alfred A. Knopf, 1975); Martin J. Sherwin, "Hiroshima as Politics

and History," *Journal of American History,* 82 no. 3 (December 1995), pp. 1085–1093.

33. Kunkel, *Genius,* p. 402. For a commentary on the attitudes of the magazine's more conservative subscribers toward White's "heretical" one-world pieces, see Kunkel, *Genius,* p. 403.

34. Macdonald, "Laugh and Lie Down," pp. 50, 47; Warshow, "E. B. White and *The New Yorker,*" pp. 105, 107–108; Mary McCarthy, "A Letter to the Editor of *Politics,*" *Politics,* November, 1946, pp. 3–5.

3 RED HUNTING AND THE NEW YORKER VILLAGE

1. Bruce Bliven, "Franklin D. Roosevelt," *The New Republic,* April 23, 1945, p. 548; Dwight Macdonald, "The Death of F.D.R.," in *Politics Past: Essays in Political Criticism* (New York: Vintage, 1970), pp. 285–286.

2. Stephen Whitfield, *Culture of the Cold War* (Baltimore: Johns Hopkins University Press, 1991), pp. 2, 127–151; William H. Chafe and Harvard Sitkoff, ed., *A History of Our Time* (New York: Oxford University Press, 1983), pp. 49–63. See also Edwin Bayley, *Joe McCarthy and the Press* (Madison: University of Wisconsin Press, 1981); David Caute, *The Great Fear: The Anti-Communist Purge Under Truman and Eisenhower* (New York: Simon and Schuster, 1978); Whittaker Chambers, *Witness* (New York: Random House, 1952); Robert A. Divine, "The Cold War and the Election of 1948," *Journal of American History,* 59 (June 1972); Martin F. Herz, *Beginnings of the Cold War* (Bloomington: Indiana University Press, 1966); Walter La Feber, *America, Russia, and the Cold War, 1945–1971,* 2nd ed. (New York: John Wiley & Sons, 1972); Allen J. Matusow, ed., *Joseph R. McCarthy* (Englewood Cliffs: Prentice-Hall, 1970); Victor Navasky, *Naming Names* (New York: Viking, 1980); David Oshinsky, *A Conspiracy So Immense* (New York: Free Press, 1983); Michael P. Rogin, *The Intellectuals and McCarthy: The Radical Specter* (Cambridge: MIT Press, 1969); Richard H. Rovere, *Senator Joe McCarthy* (New York: Harcourt Brace Jovanovich, 1959); Allen Weinstein, *Perjury: The Hills-Chambers Case,* (New York: Knopf, 1978); Stanley I. Kutler, foreword to Whitfield, *Culture,* p. vii.

3. Joel Kovel, *Red Hunting in the Promised Land: Anticommunism and the Making of America* (New York: Basic Books, 1994), pp. 137–138.

4. Interview with Midge Decter, in Alexander Bloom, *Prodigal Sons: The New York Intellectuals and Their World* (New York: Oxford University Press, 1986), p. 311; Mary McCarthy, "The Groves of Academe," *TNY,* March 3, 1951, pp. 28–32.

5. Letters to *TNY:* Constance Morenus (Washington D.C.), May 5, 1951; Peter Brand Harman (New York, N.Y.), September 12, 1947. Box 952, Records of *TNY,* at the New York Public Library Rare Books, Manuscript Division, New York.

6. Thomas Kunkel, *Genius in Disguise* (New York: Random House, 1995), pp.

404–405. For a further discussion of dossiers on *New Yorker* writers, see Herbert Mitgang, *Dangerous Dossiers* (New York: Donald I. Fine, 1988).

7. Bernard DeVoto, "The Easy Chair: Due Notice to the F.B.I.," *Harper's Magazine*, 199, no. 1193, October 1949, pp. 65–68.

8. [E. B. White],"Notes and Comment," April 3, 1948, p. 21, and August 14, 1948, p. 17; Hannah Arendt in Whitfield, *Culture,* p. 14.

9. [E. B. White], "Notes and Comment," February 14, 1948, p. 17. See also Edmund Wilson, "Books: American Political Prisoners," *TNY,* May 13, 1950, pp. 125–127. In a review of two books written by political prisoners in the United States, Wilson claimed that they contained "information which may prove helpful in a coming era when a good many of us may have to go to jail." See also Francis Grey Patton, "A Friend of the Court," *TNY,* February 17, 1951, pp. 32–38, about a local southern judge who is trying to have a citizen arrested for circulating the Stockholm Peace Petition. "The country," Patton said, "is soon going to be Salem on a grand scale" (p. 38).

10. John P. Roche, *The Quest for the Dream: The Development of Civil Rights and Human Relations in Modern America* (New York Macmillan, 1963). Whitfield, *Culture,* pp. 10, 28–32. Whitfield cites remarks by Phyllis Schafly: she had won a Republican congressional primary in Illinois in 1952, campaigning with the warning that "only a Republican victory this year will end the striped-pants diplomacy of the New Deal, including the vertical stripes worn by Dean Acheson and the horizontal stripes now worn in jail by his good friend, Alger Hiss."

11. Alan Dunn, cartoon, August 30, 1947, p. 17. See also: Whitney Darrow, Jr., cartoon, November 27, 1948, p. 28. A department store Santa Claus holds a little boy on his knee and inquires: "Are you now, or have you ever been, a naughty boy?" See also "TOTT: Crisis," December 20, 1947, p. 20. This casual piece concerned "something else to charge up to communism"—a Santa Claus beard crisis. Because of the unavailability of yak hair, which cannot be imported from Communist China, Santas had to wear mohair or woolen beards, "which can't be combed, are easily soiled, and lose their curl in a flurry of rain or snow."

12. [E. B. White], "Notes and Comment," May 29, 1948, p. 15. See also his "Notes and Comment" of July 17, 1948, p. 17. This piece concerned a man who was barred from the elite Bailey's Beach in Newport, Rhode Island, because he was "suspected of being a Communist."

13. [E. B. White], "Notes and Comment," September 18, 1948, p. 21.

14. Letters to *TNY:* Peter Brand Harman (New York, N.Y.), September 12, 1947; Fred Graeser (Oakland, Calif.), May 2, 1953; Margaret Countryman (Mrs. T. M. Countryman) (Albert Lea, Minn.), February 26, 1954; Margaret E. Lighty (Mrs. Kent Lighty) (New York, N.Y.), April 27, 1953.

15. E. B. White, "Afternoon of an American Boy," *TNY,* November 29, 1947, pp. 38, 40.

16. White, "Noontime of an Advertising Man," *TNY,* June 25, 1949, pp. 25–26; Albert Hubbell, "Subversion in Columbus Circle," *TNY,* May 13, 1950, pp. 77–81; James Thurber, "A Glass of Fashion," *TNY,* December 27, 1947, pp. 20–21; C. H. Michaels, "The Deviationist Macaroon," *TNY,* September 2, 1950, pp. 50–56; E. J. Kahn, Jr., "Reflections on a Subversive Past," *TNY,* May 29, 1948, pp. 27–28.

17. E. J. Kahn, Jr., "The Wayward Press: The Greenwich Tea Party," *TNY,* April 15, 1950, pp. 109–124.

18. In his recent biography of Remington, Gary May comments that because the Lang piece was based almost solely on interviews with Remington and his lawyers, it revealed only that part of Remington's life that he was willing to expose. Remington had, in fact, been involved in radical politics at Dartmouth, had participated in the YCL, and had some association with some Soviet spies. While Lang's "Profile" ends in 1948, leaving Remington a broken but exonerated man, May's book follows the story to its horrific end. Indicted for perjury in 1950, Remington ended his days in Lewisberg Prison, beaten to death by a trio of inmates whose ringleader, a violent petty criminal with an IQ of 61, had a burning hatred of Communists. Gary May, *Un-American Activities: The Trials of William Remington* (New York: Oxford University Press, 1994), pp. vii–viii, 134–135.

19. Daniel Lang, "A Reporter at Large: The Days of Suspicion," *TNY,* May 21, 1949, pp. 37, 44.

20. Lang, "Suspicion," p. 40.

21. [E. B. White], "Notes and Comment," February 26, 1949, p. 19.

22. [E. B. White], "Notes and Comment," June 12, 1948, p. 17; "TOTT: Reward," October 16, 1948, p. 27; "TOTT: United Nations,"January 8, 1949, p. 22; "TOTT: Land of Oz," June 25, 1949, p. 17.

23. Frank Sullivan, "These Are the Trials That Try Men's Souls," *TNY,* July 2, 1949, pp. 20–22.

24. Lillian Ross, "Onward and Upward with the Arts: Come in, Lassie!" *TNY,* February 21, 1948, pp. 32–36, rpt. in March 21, 1994, p. 176.

25. Ibid., pp. 181, 178, 177.

26. [E. B. White], "Notes and Comment," December 6, 1947, pp. 34–35. See also his "Notes and Comment," December 13, 1947, p. 25, and April 14, 1951, p. 23; S. J. Perelman, "Don't Bring Me Oscars (When It's Shosies I Need)," *TNY,* March 13, 1948, pp. 29–30. In this satirical piece about an imaginary documentary film, Perelman poked fun at Hollywood's fear of "subversive" material. He claimed to have agonized over a choice of logo for his film company on just these grounds: "After toying with the idea of combining the emblems of J. Arthur Rank and M-G-M, to show a slave striking a lion, I rejected it as socialistic and devised one that portrayed a three-toed sloth pendant from a branch, over the motto 'Multum in Parvo.'"

27. [White], "Notes and Comment," August 6, 1949, p. 13; letter from Peter Brand Harman (New York, N.Y.), to *TNY*, September 12, 1947.
28. [E. B. White], "Notes and Comment," February 26, 1949, p. 19. A. J. Liebling, in his *New Yorker* column "The Wayward Press," systematically assailed journalists for their complicity in the anti-Communist investigations. See A. J. Liebling, "The Wayward Press: Re-De-Secretization," October 23, 1948, pp. 82, 85; "The Wayward Press: Peg and Sock," November 18, 1950, pp. 104–115; "The Wayward Press: Peg Gives up on U.S.A.," November 20, 1948, pp. 67–75; "The Wayward Press: Cassandra on Lake Michigan," January 14, 1950, pp. 68–74; "The Wayward Press: Aspirins for Atoms, Down With Babushkas!" January 7, 1950, pp. 52–56; and his "Books: The Whole Story," November 13, 1948, pp. 134–145. This is a review of the transcripts of the *Hearings before the Committee on Un-American Activities,* described by Liebling as one of "the important books of our generation." See also William Atwood, "Those Red Blonde Spy Queen Blues," *TNY,* August 28, 1948, pp. 58–61; Mary McCarthy, "The Groves of Academe," *TNY,* March 3, 1951, pp. 28–32.

4   SLOUCHING TOWARD ANTI-COMMUNISM

1. [E. B. White], "Notes and Comment," January 17, 1948, pp. 17–18.
2. White's world government pieces are collected in E. B. White, *The Wild Flag* (Boston: Houghton Mifflin, 1946).
3. See "TOTT: Milestone," March 8, 1947, pp. 28–29; "Notes and Comment," September 20, 1947, p. 19.
4. [E. B. White], "Notes and Comment," April 3, 1948, p. 21.
5. [E. B. White], "Notes and Comment," July 10, 1948, p. 11.
6. [E. B. White], "Notes and Comment," May 29, 1948, p. 15. See also A. J. Liebling, "We Adopt the Party Line," *TNY,* October 11, 1947, pp. 68–76. Liebling criticized the U.S. government's "endorsement" of the "most imbecilic feature of Soviet foreign policy," the restriction of the foreign press. To "come in and browse" is an American practice that is "not only traditional but sound," he argued, but "our reply to the iron curtain is to be another iron curtain."
7. See "Notes and Comment," April 26, 1947, p. 19.
8. Godfrey Hodgson, *America in Our Time* (Garden City: Doubleday, 1976), pp. 67–98; *The God That Failed,* ed. by Richard Crossman (New York, Harper & Row, 1950); Joel Kovel, *Red Hunting in the Promised Land: Anticommunism and the Making of America* (New York: Basic Books, 1994), p. 161. For discussions of the political transformations of postwar intellectuals, see Moses Rischin, "When the New York Savants Go Marching in," *Reviews in American History,* June 1989, p. 294; Alexander Bloom, *Prodigal Sons: The New York Intellectuals and Their World* (New York: Oxford University Press, 1986); Alan Wald, *The New York Intellectuals: The Rise and Decline of the Anti-Stalinist Left from the 1930s to the*

1980s (Chapel Hill: University of North Carolina Press, 1987); Terry Cooney, *The Rise of the New York Intellectuals: Partisan Review and Its Circle* (Madison: University of Wisconsin Press, 1986); Stephan A. Longstaff, "The New York Intellectuals: A Study of Particularism and Universalism in American High Culture" (Ph.D. diss. University of California, Berkeley, 1978); Richard Pells, *The Liberal Mind in a Conservative Age: American Intellectuals in the 1940s and 1950s* (Middletown, Conn.: Wesleyan University Press, 1989); Daniel Aaron, *Writers on the Left* (New York: Octagon Books, 1974); John P. Diggens, *Up from Communism: Conservative Odysseys in American Intellectual History* (New York: Harper & Row, 1975); William L. O'Neill, *A Better World: The Great Schism, Stalinism, and the American Intellectuals* (New York: Free Press, 1986).

9. Phillip Rahv, "Our Country and Our Culture," *Partisan Review,* 19 (May–June 1952), pp. 304–310. Stephen Whitfield, *The Culture of the Cold War* (Baltimore: Johns Hopkins University Press, 1991), p. 53; Hodgson, *America in Our Time,* pp. 117–118, 124.

10. James Chace, "America Knows Best: Review of *Promised Land, Crusader State,* by Walter McDougall," in *Los Angeles Times* Book Review section, May 4, 1997, p. 9.

11. Kovel, *Red Hunting,* p. 9.

12. For other *New Yorker* pieces that contain stereotyped portrayals of Russians and Cold War language, see Lillian Anshen Seidel, "The Inquisition," April 12, 1952, pp. 28–34; Joseph Wechsberg, "The Gray Young Republic," May 19, 1951, pp. 82–95; [E. B. White,] "Notes and Comment," March 15, 1952, p. 21.

13. Whitfield, *Culture,* p. 54. For a discussion of the attack on totalitarianism and the notion of "red fascism," see Les K. Adler and Thomas G. Paterson, "Red Fascism: The Merger of Nazi Germany and Soviet Russia in the American Image of Totalitarianism, 1930s–1950s," *American Historical Review,* 75 (April, 1970), pp. 1046–1064; Stephen J. Whitfield, "'Totalitarianism' in Eclipse: The Recent Fate of an Idea," in *Images and Ideas in American Culture: Essays in Memory of Phillip Rahv,* ed. by Arthur Edelstein (Hanover, N.H.: Brandeis University Press, 1979).

14. Genet, "Letter from Rome," *TNY,* May 1, 1948, pp. 84–89; Andy Logan, "A Reporter at Large: More Where They Want to Be," *TNY,* July 17, 1948, pp. 48–52; Joseph Wechsberg, "A Reporter in Vienna: Cameron, Lewis, Laborde, and Gorodnistove," *TNY,* March 16, 1948, pp. 61–73; Andy Logan, "A Reporter at Large: Letter from Vienna," *TNY,* November 20, 1948, pp. 76–82; Tracy Phillips, "A Reporter at Large: A Stopover in Minsk," *TNY,* June 7, 1947, pp. 92–105.

15. Genet, "Letter from Paris," *TNY,* June 30, 1951, pp. 42–43, June 14, 1952, p. 94, and May 7, 1949, pp. 96–102; see also her "Letter" of December 17, 1949, pp. 80–83; Mollie Panter-Downes, "Letter from London," *TNY,* February 24, 1951, pp. 69–73.

16. Joseph Wechsberg, "A Reporter at Large: Howling with the Wolves," *TNY,* September 23, 1950, pp. 35, 36, 48. See also Wechsberg, "Letter from Prague,"

August 6, 1949, pp. 44–50; Wechsberg, "Reporter at Large: Orchids in Siberia," September 24, 1949, pp. 58–72. This is an account of an old school chum of Wechsberg's who spent much of the war in a Russian forced-labor camp.

17. "Notes and Comment," January 19, 1946, p. 15; [E. B. White], "Notes and Comment," January 12, 1946, pp. 17–18; Jessamyn West, "Birds," *TNY*, September 20, 1947, p. 84.

18. [E. B. White], "Notes and Comment," December 14, 1946, p. 33. For a sampling of *New Yorker* commentary on the United Nations see [E. B. White], "Notes and Comment," January 12, 1946, pp. 17–18, January 19, 1946, p. 13, July 20, 1946, p. 13, and November 2, 1946, pp. 23–24; E. B. White, "Turtle Bay Diary," February 22, 1947, pp. 70–76 and March 1, 1947, pp. 76–80; "TOTT: Outsider," February 1, 1947, p. 20; [E. B. White], "Notes and Comment," August 10, 1946, p. 11, and June 1, 1946, pp. 17–18; "TOTT: No Empty Chairs," May 3, 1947, pp. 25–26; Geoffrey T. Hellman, "Profiles: From Within to Without," April 26, 1947, pp. 31–45 (a profile of architect Le Corbusier, the best-known member of the board of consultants set up to design the United Nations); Genet, "Letter from Paris," November 27, 1947, pp. 123–127; Phillip Hamburger, "Profiles: The Idea Is Everything," October 11, 1947, pp. 39–49 (a profile of Trygve Lie, the Secretary-General of the U.N.).

19. [E. B. White], "Notes and Comment," October 21, 1950, p. 23.

20. Phillip Hamburger, "Letter from Lake Success," *TNY*, July 29, 1950, p. 44; [E. B. White], "Notes and Comment," October 21, 1950, p. 23; Richard Rovere, "Letter from Lake Success," *TNY*, February 10, 1951, p. 44.

21. [E. B. White], "Notes and Comment," April 28, 1951, pp. 19–20.

22. [E. B. White], "Notes and Comment," May 19, 1951, p. 27, and October 21, 1950, p. 23.

23. [E. B. White],"Notes and Comment," October 21, 1950, p. 23; Hodgson, *America in Our Time*, p. 120. Rovere, "Letter from Lake Success," pp. 77–85.

24. Rovere, "Letter from Lake Success," p. 77; Rovere, "Letter from Lake Success—II," December 30, 1950, p. 54. See also Rovere, "Letter from Washington," January 27, 1951, pp. 64–70.

25. [E. B. White],"Notes and Comment," April 28, 1951, p. 19; Rovere, "Letter from Washington," May 19, 1951, pp. 68–76, and April 21, 1951, pp. 108, 109. See also Genet, "Letter from Paris," April 21, 1951, pp. 66–70, and May 5, 1951, pp. 57–64; E. J. Kahn, Jr., "Letter from Korea," *TNY*, April 21, 1951, pp. 122–125. Kahn wrote that the soldiers at the front are far more concerned about making it through another day than they are about MacArthur's firing, which they seem to accept merely as a "simple" and rather "remote, fact." For narrative accounts of the MacArthur firing see Richard H. Rovere and Arthur Schlesinger, Jr., *The General and the President* (New York: Farrar, Straus and Giroux, 1951); William Manchester, *The Glory and the Dream: A Narrative History of America, 1932–1972* (Boston: Little, Brown, 1974.)

26. [E. B. White], "Notes and Comment," May 12, 1951, p. 27; See also "TOTT: Wonderful Figure," June 16, 1951, pp. 24–25.

27. For examples of *TNY* reporting during the Korean War see E. J. Kahn, Jr., "A Reporter in Korea: No One but the Glosters," May 26, 1951, pp. 60–71; his "Letter from Korea," June 16, 1951, pp. 76–82; and "Letter from Korea: Little General," June 2, 1951, pp. 61–68; See also "Letter from Korea," June 9, 1951, pp. 84–88, June 23, 1951, pp. 56–60, June 30, 1951, pp. 60–66, and April 21, 1951, p. 123.

28. Christopher Rand, "Letter from Korea," *TNY*, March 17, 1951, pp. 107, 111, 115, 116. Bordering the final paragraph of Rand's piece that ends with the line: "Distance lends more than enchantment to the view out here," is an advertisement for Hormel Onion Soup featuring the following caption: "'Enchanting!' avers Mrs. Arthur Murray—executive director of Arthur Murray Dance Studios and wife of the famous dance master."

29. Midge Decter, in Alexander Bloom, *Prodigal Sons*, p. 311.

30. Foster Parents' Plan for War Children, Inc.(ad), *TNY*, December 16, 1950, p. 139; May 26, 1951, p. 107.

5   *THE NEW YORKER* IN BLACK AND WHITE

1. St. Clair McKelway, "On the Rocks," *TNY*, May 17, 1952, p. 28.

2. Ibid., p. 30. See also Phyllis McGinley, "Tiger, Tiger," *TNY*, January 19, 1946, p. 22.

3. Gary Gerstle, "The Working Class Goes to War," in *The War in American Culture*, ed. by Lewis A. Erenberg and Susan E. Hirsch (Chicago: University of Chicago Press, 1996), pp. 113–114. In his closely argued piece, "Ethnicity and Reform: Minorities and the Ambience of the Depression Years," Richard Weiss places the roots of this change in consciousness in the New Deal years, when tolerance toward Jews and Eastern Europeans grew in a reaction to the racism of totalitarian Germany. Weiss argues that anthropologists' introduction of the "culture" concept into the intellectual community also played a part in this change. *Journal of American History*, 66 (December 1979), pp. 566–585.

4. Gunnar Myrdal, *An American Dilemma* (New York: Harper & Brothers, 1944); Anthony Lewis, *Portrait of a Decade: The Second American Revolution* (New York: Random House, 1964), pp. 3–4; see also Kenneth J. Stampp, *The Peculiar Institution* (New York: Alfred A. Knopf, 1956); Melville J. Herskovits, *The Myth of the Negro Past* (New York: Harper & Brothers, 1941).

5. Lewis, *Portrait of a Decade*, p. 4. See also Thomas F. Gossett, *Race: The History of an Idea in America* (New York: Schocken Books, 1963).

6. Thomas Kunkel, *Genius in Disguise* (New York: Random House, 1995), pp. 268–269, 272.

7. Rea Irvin, cover paintings of March 31, 1934, November 21, 1936, and Decem-

ber 12, 1936; Perry Barlow, cover painting, January 18, 1941; John Updike, Introduction to *The Complete Book of Covers from The New Yorker* (New York: Alfred A. Knopf, 1989), p. vii.

8. Black Americans re-emerge in the magazine in the early sixties. See in particular James Baldwin, "Letter from a Region in My Mind," *TNY*, November 17, 1962, pp. 59–60.

9. E. J. Kahn, Jr., "Profiles: The Frontal Attack," *TNY*, September 4, 1948, pp. 28–38, and September 11, 1948, pp. 38–54. See also "Notes and Comment"(Paul Robeson), September 24, 1949, p. 23. A small body of writing in the postwar magazine did address the role played by structural poverty in the emiseration of black people, prefiguring Daniel Patrick Moynihan's *The Negro Family: The Case for National Action* published a decade later. The magazine ran several pieces about black heroin addicts, although in Berton Roueche's essay the fact that all of the addicts in the piece were black was treated as coincidental. Hyman Goldberg's study of truants linked truancy, race, and poverty (a black mother explained to a truant officer that her son had to stay home from school because it was snowing and his only pair of shoes had holes in them). Berton Roueche, "Annals of Medicine: A Pinch of Dust," June 23, 1951, pp. 35–42; Eugene Kinkead, "A Reporter at Large: Sixteen," *TNY*, November 10, 1951, pp. 44–63; Hyman Goldberg, "A Reporter at Large: Preferably Not Beaten," April 24, 1948, pp. 74–84.

10. Clifford Geertz,"Uses of Diversity," *Michigan Quarterly Review*, 25 (1986), pp. 105–123; See also Richard Rorty,"On Ethnocentrism: A Reply to Clifford Geertz," *Michigan Quarterly Review*, 25 (1986), p. 526; David Hollinger, "How Wide the Circle of We: American Intellectuals and the Problem of Ethos since World War One," *American Historical Review* (April 1993), pp. 318–319.

11. See Robert Lewis Taylor, "That Was the War: Rangoso, Rex," *TNY*, May 4, 1946, pp. 32–42.; "TOTT: Nyabongo's Project," January 26, 1952, pp. 17–18. Nyabongo was an East African Prince with an Oxford Ph.D. who was writing a book about the language of flowers; "TOTT: Ugh, Ugh," June 12, 1948, pp. 18–19 (interview with Chief Crazy Bull); "TOTT: Living," June 28, 1952, pp. 19–20 (interview with Miss Universe candidate from India, whose husband was the "chief government architect of West Bengal").

12. Daniel Alain, cartoon, January 28, 1950, p. 27; Charles Addams, cartoon, May 3, 1947, p. 28; Charles Addams, cartoon, October, 12, 1946, p. 39.

13. Otto Sogolow, cartoon, May 10, 1947, p. 23; Syd Hoff, cartoon, June 28, 1952, p. 31.

14. Chon Day, cartoon, December 21, 1946, p. 24; Whitney Darrow, Jr., cartoon, February 22, 1947, p. 30; Claude Smith, cartoon, March 15, 1947, p. 32. For another *TNY* item in which women's hair styles and primitive culture are linked, see "TOTT:Thar She Blows!" which described an exhibit at the Museum of Natural History called "From the Neck Up," in which "dazzling headgear

from John-Fredericks, the Fiji Islands, the Congo, Lilly Dache, and Greenland" were displayed side by side. December 13, 1947, pp. 26–27.

15. Charles Addams, cartoon, October 11, 1947, p. 38; Robert Day, cartoon, September 17, 1949, p. 28; Charles Addams, cartoon, May 13, 1950, p. 24.

16. Dwight Macdonald, "Laugh and Lie Down," *Partisan Review*, 4, December 1937, pp.48–49; Henri Bergson, *Laughter: An Essay on the Meaning of the Comic*, translated by Cloudesley Brereton (New York: Macmillan, 1911).

17. John Lardner, "That Was Pugilism: The White Hopes—I," *TNY*, June 25, 1949, pp. 56–57.

18. John Lardner, "That Was Pugilism: Battling Siki," *TNY*, November 19, 1949, pp. 112, 113.

19. Lardner, "Siki," pp. 112, 114, 118.

20. Ibid., pp. 112, 113.

21. See also "TOTT: Joe's Place," September 14, 1946, pp. 22–23. This was a casual piece about Joe Louis's new restaurant in Harlem.

22. A. J. Liebling, "Letter from Helsinki," August 23, 1952, p. 64. See also A. J. Liebling, "Letter from the Olympics," August 9, 1952, p. 39. On the finals of the relays, he wrote: "The American men, with a team that included two Negroes, won the four-hundred-meter relay in fast time, and Jamaica, with four Negroes, won the sixteen-hundred-meter relay from the United States in one of the finest races I have ever seen." This idea of racial inclusiveness as a metaphor for postwar American exceptionalism can also be found in *TNY* writing about the Nuremberg trials. In one piece Andy Logan remarked on the presence of "proud, alert and colored" American guards in the courtroom; "Letter from Germany," *TNY*, May 8, 1948, p. 98.

23. A. J. Liebling, "A Reporter at Large: A Hundred and Eighteen Pounds," *TNY*, February 9, 1952, p. 62.

24. See Dwight Macdonald, book review of Michael Harrington's *The Other America*, *TNY*, January 19, 1963, p. 83. An interesting gap in the magazine's interest in the "color line" was the lack of attention it gave to Jackie Robinson's April 1947 debut at Ebbetts Field. While *Newsweek, Time, Life, The New Republic*, and even *The Reader's Digest* covered Robinson's career in some detail, publishing no fewer than 25 articles about him between 1947 and 1949, between April of 1947 and May of 1953 *TNY* did not publish a single piece about him. In the 1950 "Profile" of Branch Rickey, the Dodgers general manager, which credited the legendary manager with bringing Robinson to the team and thus breaking the color line in baseball, Robinson himself was barely mentioned. See Robert Rice, "Profile: Thoughts on Baseball (Branch Rickey)," *TNY*, May 27, 1950, pp. 32, 36; June 3, 1950, pp. 30–34; "Rookie," *The New Republic*, May 19, 1947, p. 10; J. Brubaker, "Small Beginnings," *The New Republic*, June 9, 1947, p. 38; "Buttoned Lip," *Newsweek*, April 21, 1947, p. 88; "Baseball: Batting at Robinson," *Newsweek*, May 19, 1947, p. 88; "Safe at

First?" *Time,* April 21, 1947, p. 55; "Portrait," *Life,* April 21, 1947, p. 100, April 28, 1947, p. 37.
25. Richard O. Boyer, "Bop," *TNY,* July 3, 1948, pp. 28–37.
26. "TOTT: Scoop," May 25, 1946, p. 18.
27. Frances Gray Patton, "A Nice Name," *TNY,* February 26, 1949, p. 24. See also Patton, "Let It Rest," March 8, 1952, pp. 33–38, and "A Piece of Luck," April 1, 1950, pp. 30–33.
28. Patton, "Name," pp. 24, 26.
29. Ibid., pp. 27–28.
30. Ibid., pp. 24, 26, 30.
31. Ibid., p. 24, 30.
32. John O'Hara, "Ellie," *TNY,* October 19, 1946, pp. 29–30.
33. J. D. Salinger, "Uncle Wiggily in Connecticut," *TNY,* March 20, 1948, p. 36.
34. Jean Stafford, "Pax Vobiscum," *TNY,* July 23, 1949, pp. 21, 22, 23.
35. Ibid., pp. 23–24.

6   THE ROMANCE OF THE OTHER

1. Leslie Fiedler argued that American literature used the Indian to represent that part of the white self that had been destroyed by the rapaciousness of capitalism and the worship of science. See Fiedler, *The Return of the Vanishing American* (New York: Stein and Day, 1968).
2. Jackson Lears, *Fables of Abundance: A Cultural History of Advertising in America* (New York: Basic Books, 1994) p. 252; William Whyte, *The Organization Man* (New York: Simon and Schuster, 1956), p. 310; David Riesman, *The Lonely Crowd* (New Haven: Yale University Press, 1953); Lewis Mumford, *The City in History* (New York: Harcourt, Brace, 1961), p. 486; Ada Louise Huxtable, "Clusters Instead of 'Slurbs,'" *New York Times Magazine* (February 9, 1964), pp. 10, 37. See also Jackson Lears, "A Matter of Taste," in *Recasting America,* ed. by Lary May (Chicago: University of Chicago Press, 1989), pp. 44–46.
3. For other expressions of the nagging self-doubt experienced by Americans in the postwar period, see C. Wright Mills, *The Power Elite* (New York: Oxford University Press, 1956); Clement Greenberg, "The Plight of Our Culture," *Commentary,* 15 (June 1953).
4. Jean Stafford, "Pax Vobiscum," *TNY,* July 23, 1949, p. 24.
5. Robert Berkhoffer, *The White Man's Indian* (New York: Vintage Books, 1979), pp. 76–85. The transformation of the Noble Savage into the Child of Nature owed much to the French and American revolutions. With the emergence of a new social order, the hypothetical state of nature inhabited by a rational, enlightened noble savage lost much of its utility. By the nineteenth century the Indian had been transformed into an intuitive child of nature.
6. Berkhoffer, *White Man's Indian,* p. 71. There are notable exceptions to the

portrayal of Indians as savage brutes—in particular the works of James Fenimore Cooper (although his bad Indians far outnumber his good ones) and Henry Wadsworth Longfellow's *The Song of Hiawatha*, 1855. See also Lewis Henry Morgan's *League of the Ho-de-no-sau-nee, Iroquois*, 1851; James Nelson Barker, *The Indian Princess*, 1808; and Washington Irving, *Sketchbook*, 1819. For examples of the work of early anthropologists see Ruth Benedict, *Patterns of Culture* (Boston: Houghton Mifflin, 1934); Margaret Mead, *Coming of Age in Samoa* (New York: William Morrow, 1928); For a description of the development of the Boasian school see George W. Stocking, Jr., ed., *The Shaping of American Anthropology, 1883–1911: A Franz Boas Reader* (New York: Basic Books, 1974.) pp. 1–20.

7. Ralph E. Friar and Natasha A. Friar, *The Only Good Indian . . . The Hollywood Gospel* (New York: Drama Book Specialists, 1972). For the impact anthropology had on the depiction of Native Americans and dark-skinned others, see Richard Weiss, "Culture and the Quest for National Integration during the Crisis of the Great Depression," pp. 15–18, Ms, 1997. In the postwar period scholarly writing about Native Americans, like scholarly writing about African Americans, began to undergo a radical revision. See Henry Nash Smith, *Virgin Land: The American West as Symbol and Myth* (Cambridge: Harvard University Press, 1950); Roy Harvey Pearce, *Savages of America: A Study of the Indian and the Idea of Civilization* (Baltimore: Johns Hopkins University Press, 1953).

8. Edmund Wilson, "A Reporter at Large: Shalako—I," *TNY*, April 4, 1949, pp. 78–91; "Shalako—II," April 16, 1949, pp. 92–106. An indictment of white consumer culture was a frequent subtext in the magazine's cartoons and cover art concerning Indians. See Julian De Miskey, cover painting, August 16, 1947.

9. Wilson, "Shalako—II," p. 104.

10. Ibid., pp. 106, 104–105.

11. [E. B. White], "Notes and Comment," May 12, 1951, p. 23.

12. Robert Day, cartoons, June 29, 1946, p. 27, and June 15, 1946, p. 17.

13. "TOTT: Talking Leaves," April 14, 1951, pp. 23–24.

14. Jean Stafford, "A Summer Day," *TNY*, September 11, 1948, p. 29.

15. Ibid., p. 32.

16. Ibid., pp. 33–35. See also Mary Carter-Roberts, "Flash Flood," *TNY*, May 24, 1952, pp. 94–97.

17. Charles Addams, cartoon, May 8, 1948, p. 27.

18. Charles Addams, cartoons, November 28, 1950, p. 29, and January 24, 1948, p. 23.

19. Winthrop Jordan, *White over Black: American Attitudes toward the Negro, 1550–1812* (Chapel Hill: University of North Carolina Press, 1968), pp. 89–91. See also George Fredrickson, *The Black Image in the White Mind* (Middletown, Conn.: Wesleyan University Press, 1971), pp. 52–55.

20. Brendan Gill, *Here at The New Yorker* (New York: Carroll & Graf, 1987), p. 313. Joseph Mitchell, "Mohawks in High Steel," *TNY*, September 17, 1949, pp. 38–

40; reprinted in *Up in the Old Hotel* (New York: Pantheon, 1992). Pagination from reprint, pp. 275, 281.

21. Mitchell, "Steel," pp. 284, 282.
22. Ibid., pp. 286–287.
23. Alice Marriot, "Beowulf in South Dakota," *TNY*, August 2, 1952, pp. 46, 47. See also her "Father-in-Law Taboo," *TNY*, September 13, 1952, pp. 94–101.
24. Marriot, "Beowulf," p. 51.
25. Native American ability to negotiate entrepreneurial capitalism was a frequent motif in *TNY* cartoons. See Lundy, cartoon, February 9, 1952, p. 62: a Navajo uses an air compressor to spray paint an Indian pot; Robert Day, cartoon, February 23, 1952, p. 34: a Hopi sells umbrellas to tourists as they arrive at a rain dance.
26. David Halberstam, *The Fifties* (New York: Random House, 1993), pp. 116–202; Richard Yates, *Revolutionary Road* (Westport, Conn.: Greenwood Press, 1961); Mumford, *The City in History*, p. 486; Huxtable, "'Slurbs,'" p. 10, p. 37; Lears, *Abundance*, p. 253.
27. Victoria Lincoln, "Comfort," *TNY*, July 20, 1946, pp. 19, 20.
28. Lincoln, "Comfort," p. 20. To be sure, Latin American men were not only portrayed in terms of their transformative power vis-a-vis white women. *TNY* also published many cartoons about sleeping Mexicans. See Garrett Price, cartoon, September 29, 1951, p. 37.
29. Victoria Lincoln, "In the Reeds by the River," *TNY*, September 28, 1946, pp. 29, 27.
30. Ibid., p. 31.
31. Jessamyn West, "Love, Death, and the Ladies' Drill Team," *TNY*, September 22, 1951, pp. 34, 33.
32. Ibid., pp. 34, 35–36.
33. Robert Clurman, "Mr. Mookerjhee," *TNY*, July 9, 1949, p. 47. See also Albert Halper, "The Wallet," *TNY*, February 3, 1951, pp. 48–61; Mona Gardner, "The Eternity of the Matter," *TNY*, August 16, 1952, pp. 28–33.
34. Clurman, "Mookerjhee," pp. 48, 49–50.
35. Berkhoffer, *Indian*, p. 77.
36. James A. Maxwell, "Arab Editor," *TNY*, September 21, 1946, pp. 28, 29.
37. Ibid., p. 29.
38. Ibid., p. 30.

7 MANAGING WITH SERVANTS

1. Gunnar Myrdal, *An American Dilemma* (New York: Harper and Row, 1944), pp. 3–12, pp. 24–25.
2. "TOTT: Cue," October 5, 1946, p. 30.
3. Richard Brodhead, *Cultures of Letters: Scenes of Reading and Writing in Nineteenth-Century America* (Chicago: University of Chicago Press, 1993), p. 10;

"TOTT: In Time," December 27, 1952, p. 12; "TOTT: Thoughtful," March 25, 1950, p. 24.

4. "TOTT: Deadlocked," October 3, 1948, p. 19.

5. "TOTT: Aristocratic," July 7, 1946, p. 14.

6. "TOTT: Open Sesame," January 28, 1950, pp. 20–21; "TOTT: In Time," December 27, 1952, pp. 12–13.

7. Peter De Vries, "Pygmalion," *TNY*, March 22, 1952, pp. 28, 29.

8. Peter De Vries, "They Also Sit," *TNY*, March 20, 1948, pp. 98, 100. See also Louise Field Cooper, "Triangle," *TNY*, February 23, 1952, pp. 33–36.

9. "TOTT: Custom of the Country," September 3, 1949, p. 21.

10. "TOTT: Equestrienne," May 7, 1949, p. 27.

11. Elizabeth McConaughy, "Rudi," *TNY*, December 11, 1948, pp. 67, 69.

12. The powerful bond between live-in domestics and the children they care for was certainly the subtext of the two *TNY* covers discussed in the preface. See Edna Eicke, cover painting, October 28, 1950; Perry Barlow, cover painting, November 24, 1951.

13. Ludovic Kennedy, "Grace Arrowhead," *TNY*, September 9, 1950, p. 92. See also N. M. Graham, "Journey to Dringhouses," *TNY*, April 16, 1949, pp. 30–33.

14. Kennedy, "Grace Arrowhead," pp. 92–93, 95–97.

15. See also Mollie Panter-Downes, "Intimations of Mortality," *TNY*, August 23, 1952, pp. 19–21.

16. Peter Taylor, "What You Hear from 'Em?" *TNY*, February 10, 1951, pp. 31, 38.

17. Ibid., p. 31.

18. See also John Cheever, "The Common Day," *TNY*, August 2, 1947, pp. 19–20.

19. Tom Wolfe, "Lost in the Whichy Thicket: *The New Yorker*—II," *New York Herald Tribune,* April 18, 1965, p. 20.

20. Elaine Tyler May, *Homeward Bound: American Families in the Cold War Era* (New York: Basic Books, 1988), pp. 169–174. See also Betty Friedan, *The Feminine Mystique* (New York: Dell, 1963).

21. Frances Gray Patton, "The Falling Leaves," *TNY*, November 22, 1947, p. 37.

22. Ibid., pp. 41, 42.

23. Peter Taylor, "Middle Age," *TNY*, November 6, 1948, pp. 29, 30.

24. For an example of a story about African-American domestics told from inside their experience, see Peter Taylor, "Bad Dreams," *TNY*, May 19, 1951, pp. 32–42.

25. Peter Taylor, "A Wife of Nashville," *TNY*, December 3, 1949, pp. 43, 46, 49, 55, 58.

26. Ibid., pp. 65–66.

6   THE WAR BETWEEN MEN AND WOMEN

1. Claude Smith, cartoon, April 23, 1949, p. 26; Dwight Macdonald, "Profiles: The Foolish Things of the World—I," *TNY*, October 4, 1952, pp. 37–62.

2. Elaine Tyler May, "Explosive Issues: Sex, Women and the Bomb," in *Recasting American: Culture and Politics in the Age of Cold War*, ed. by Lary May (Chicago: University of Chicago Press, 1989), pp. 154–170; Jackson Lears, *No Place of Grace: Antimodernism and the Transformation of American Culture, 1880–1920* (New York: Pantheon Books, 1981), p. 98; For statistics on the demographic trends in family life, see U.S. Department of Commerce, Bureau of the Census, *Historical Statistics of the United States, Colonial Times to 1970* (Washington, D.C.: Government Printing Office, 1975), pt. 1, pp. 49, 54, 55, 64. For the historical implications of these demographic trends, see Andrew Cherlin, *Marriage, Divorce, Remarriage* (Cambridge: Harvard University Press, 1981). See also Sara Evans, *Personal Politics* (New York: Vintage Books, 1979), p. 5.

3. Mary McCarthy, "Up the Ladder from *Charm* to *Vogue*," in *On the Contrary: Articles of Belief, 1946–1961* (New York: Farrar, Straus, and Giroux, 1961), pp. 172–192. Subscription figures are from Audit Bureau of Circulations, *Publisher's Statement, 1925–1960* (Chicago: ABC); *Character of Readers* (of *The New Yorker*) (New York: F-R Publishing Corp., 1946 and 1949); Tom Wolfe, "Lost in the Whichy Thicket: *The New Yorker*—II," *New York Herald Tribune*, April 18, 1965, pp. 20, 22, 24. As for the tonier general-interest magazines like *Atlantic, Harper's*, and the *Saturday Review*, when they did weigh in on the subject of domestic life, they tended to underwrite notions of momism—monster moms ruling the roost and eroding national rigor.

4. Letters to Helen Hokinson reprinted in Dale Kramer, *Ross and The New Yorker* (Garden City: Doubleday, 1951), pp. 133, 283; Helen Hokinson's obituary, *TNY*, November 11, 1949, p. 160. See also Brendan Gill, *Here at The New Yorker* (New York: Carroll & Graf, 1987), p. 213.

5. Helen Hokinson, cartoons, May 17, 1947, p. 25, September 13, 1947, p. 46, and March 26, 1949, pp. 22–23.

6. Helen Hokinson, cover paintings, May 4, 1946, November 12, 1949, June 10, 1950, June 22, 1946, April 17, 1948, August 6, 1949, February 8, 1947, June 23, 1951, February 8, 1947, June 23, 1951, and August 19, 1950.

7. Peter Arno, cartoons, December 25, 1948, p. 26, March 29, 1947, p. 30, and August 20, 1949, p. 29.

8. Richard Taylor, cartoon, October 19, 1946, p. 31; Mischa Richter, cartoon, November 11, 1948, p. 25; Robert Day, cartoon, August 2, 1947, p. 18; Whitney Darrow, Jr., cartoon, October 4, 1952, p. 36. See also Richard Taylor, cartoon, February 22, 1947, p. 29; Whitney Darrow, cartoon, April 5, 1947, p. 25. In a cartoon that reverses the usual gender roles, Arno depicts a wealthy elderly woman gazing lustfully at two handsome young baseball players at Yankee Stadium as the team manager says to her: "Sometimes we sell them, lady, but only to other teams." Peter Arno, cartoon, September 6, 1947, p. 31.

9. Thomas Kunkel, *Genius in Disguise* (New York: Random House, 1995), pp. 353, 358.

10. Gill, *Here*, p.29, James Thurber, *My Years with Ross* (Boston: Little Brown, 1957); Kunkel, *Genius*, pp. 170–171, 59; Jane Grant, *Ross, The New Yorker, and Me* (New York: Reynal, 1968); Kunkel, *Genius*, p. 75.

11. For an interesting example of the liberated, adventure-seeking woman in the late 1920s and 1930s, see Susan Ware, *Still Missing: Life and Times of Amelia Earhart*(New York: Norton, 1993).

12. For examples of *New Yorker* "Profiles" in which women professionalize traditional women's work, see Angelica Gibbs, "Down the Leash" (about Blanche Saunders, dog obedience trainer), November 24, 1951, pp. 42–64; Eugene Kinkead, "Physician in the Flower Beds" (about Cynthia Westcott, plant pathologist), July 26, 1952, pp. 26–43; Angelica Gibbs, "Recurrent and Irreducible" (about Jessica Garretson Cosgrave, educator, founder of Finch Junior College), April 13, 1946, pp. 35–51; John Bainbridge, "Striking a Blow for Grandma" (about Margaret Rudkin, President, Pepperidge Farms, Inc.), May 22, 1948, pp. 38–51; Angelica Gibbs, "With Palette Knife and Skillet" (about Diane Wilson Lucas, owner of a cooking school) May 28, 1949, pp. 34–53.
   A 1956 *Fortune* study of female executives found that all the women surveyed claimed to place home and family ahead of business. In this survey, Mrs. Frances Corey, the first woman Senior Vice-President of Macy's, argued that in business women were "equal-but-special." Her contribution, she claimed, was specifically feminine. "My reaction is much more emotional—and emotion is a necessary commodity. There are places where I can't fill the bill as well as a man and I don't try." Katherine Hamill, "Women as Bosses," *Fortune*, 53, no. 6 (June 1956) pp. 219, 106–107.

13. E. J. Kahn, Jr., "Profiles: The Years Alone—I," *TNY*, June 12, 1948, pp. 30–43; Phillip Hamburger, "Television: Mrs. Roosevelt's Tea Party," *TNY*, February 25, 1950, pp. 94–95.

14. E. J. Kahn, Jr., "Profiles: The Years Alone—I," *TNY*, June 12, 1948, p. 30; Macdonald, "The Foolish Things of the World—I," pp. 37–62; II, October 11, 1952, pp. 37–58. Each year the magazine published about 50 "Profiles." In the decade between 1935 and 1945, 33 of these concerned women. Between 1945 and 1953, 20 of the magazine's "Profiles" were about women.

15. While Ross carelessly called homosexuals "fairies" or "pansies," his biographer and other historians of the magazine have pointed out that he was surrounded by dozens of gay friends and staff members and was, for his time, "rather sophisticated in his outlook on the subject." Certainly, the issue of homosexuality did not come between Ross and the magazine's Paris correspondent Janet Flanner (Genet), whose homosexuality was widely known. See Gill, *Here*, p. 29; Kunkel, *Genius*, pp. 271–272.

16. Kunkel, *Genius*, pp. 271–272; Janet Flanner, "Profile: A Woman in the House," *TNY*, May 8, 1948, p. 34.

17. Berton Roueche, "A Cup of Lemon Verbena," *TNY*, October 23, 1948, pp. 93, 94.

18. For an academic model of this kind of feminism, see Mirra Komarovsky, *Blue Collar Marriage* (New York: Random House, 1962), pp. 49, 57. Discussing discontent among housewives, Komarovsky notes that "educated, middle-class housewives" may be discontent with their lot, but that she found "little evidence of status frustrations among working class wives"; "Such untroubled acceptance of housewifery stems from the lack of exposure to certain values."

19. Angelica Gibbs, "Profiles: One Sweet Little Business," July 31, 1948, pp. 26–29, 33. Evans, *Personal Politics,* pp. 13–14; May, *Homeward Bound;* May, "Explosive Issues," pp.154–155. See also Andy Logan, "Profiles: Grips and Taxes—I," February 3, 1951, pp. 36–54; II, February 10, 1951, pp. 39–53; "TOTT: Club Meeting," April 23, 1949, pp. 20–21.

20. Lillian Ross, "A Reporter at Large: Symbol of All We Possess," October 22, 1949, pp. 33, 35, 48.

21. See also Walter Bernstein, "A Reporter at Large: Mingle," June 24, 1950, pp. 60–71. This is a piece about a popular phenomenon—the combination of mixer dance and self-help lecture. Bernstein depicts sad-eyed girls with bad skin trying to look inconspicuous as Dr. Banks, the hearty speaker, implores them to "mingle."

22. Wilma Shore, "The Moon Belongs to Everyone," *TNY,* September 3, 1949, p. 29. See also Wilma Shore, "Lock, Stock, and Barrel," *TNY,* July 15, 1950, pp. 23–25.

23. Aldous Huxley, quoted in Anatole Broyard, *Kafka Was the Rage: A Greenwich Village Memoir* (New York: Carol Southern Books, 1993), p. viii.

24. Whitney Darrow, Jr. cartoon, August 5, 1950, p. 32; F. B. Modell, cartoon, October 8, 1949, p. 35; Alan Dunn, cartoon, October 4, 1951, p. 29; Charles Addams, cartoon, January 28, 1950, p. 29.

25. May, *Homeward Bound,* pp. 74, 96, 116. Also see Phillip Wylie, *Generation of Vipers* (New York: Rinehart, 1942). For examples of "momism" see Rachel Rubin, "Whose Apronstrings?" *American Home,* 31 (May 1944), p. 28; Amran Scheinfeld, "Are American Moms a Menace?" *Ladies Home Journal,* November 1945, pp. 36, 38, 140; Edward A Strecker, "What Is Wrong with American Mothers?" *Saturday Evening Post,* 24 October 1946, p. 14; Wainwright Evans, "Are Good Mothers Unfaithful Wives?" *Better Homes and Gardens,* July, 1941, pp. 23, 66, 67. For an discussion of the "momism" of an earlier period—the matrophobia of the 1920s, see Ann Douglas, *Terrible Honesty: Mongrel Manhattan in the 1920s* (New York: Farrar, Straus and Giroux, 1995), especially chap. 6, "The Dark Legend of Matricide," pp. 217–253.

26. Carl Rose, cartoon, August 11, 1951, p. 33; Frank Modell, cartoon, September 23, 1950, p. 36; Frank Modell, cartoon, January 27, 1951, p. 31; Dana Fradon, cartoon, September 27, 1952, p. 25; Anatol Kovarsky, cartoon, July 8, 1950, p. 31; Richard Decker, cartoon, June 19, 1948, p. 24; Frank Modell, cartoon, December 18, 1948, p. 35. See also Sally Benson, "Seeing Eye," *TNY,* September 27, 1947, pp. 28, 30.

27. F. B. Modell, cartoon, November 10, 1951, p. 30; Chon Day, cartoon, January 21, 1950, p. 26.

28. Chon Day, cartoon, January 7, 1950, p. 34; Bernard Wiseman, cartoon, January 27, 1951, p. 20; Charles Addams, cartoon, May 24, 1947, p. 23; Barney Tobey, cartoon, November 11, 1951, p. 37; Leslie Stark, cartoon, December 22, 1951, p. 22.

29. Kunkel, *Genius*, p. 327; James Reid Parker, "Westchester Igloo," *TNY*, January 5, 1952, pp. 27–29.

30. Charles Addams, cartoons, July 15, 1950, p. 26, July 12, 1947, p. 26, and January 19, 1952, p. 31; Sam Cobean, cartoon, December 4, 1948, p. 35; Angostura Bitters ad, *TNY*, April 22, 1950, p. 44; Carl Rose, cartoon, July 21, 1951, p. 19. See also Charles Addams, cartoon, August 19, 1950, p. 31; Garrett Price, cartoon, November 11, 1950, p. 42; Charles Addams, cartoons, November 17, 1951, p. 33, April 2, 1949, p. 27, May 14, 1949, p. 27, and September 9, 1950, p. 25.

31. Daniel Alain, cartoon, July 5, 1947, p. 16; Whitney Darrow, cartoon, September 28, 1946, p. 33; Mischa Richter, cartoon, February 2, 1952, p. 48. Also see Whitney Darrow, cartoon, November 18, 1950, p. 55; James Reid Parker, "The Finishing Touch," March 30, 1946, pp. 30–33; Nettie Kline, "A Regrettable Incident," January 26, 1946, pp. 74–75. See also Chon Day, cartoon, December 6, 1947, p. 42.

32. Helen Hokinson, cartoon, April 23, 1947, p. 76; Richard Decker, cartoon, January 10, 1948, p. 31; Carl Rose, cartoon, September 16, 1950, p. 101; Mischa Richter, cartoon, June 21, 1952, p. 88; Whitney Darrow, cartoon, April 14, 1951, p. 25; Barbara Ehrenreich, *The Hearts of Men: American Dreams and the Flight from Commitment* (New York: Anchor Books, 1983), pp. 38–39.

33. Clifford E. Clark, "Ranch House Suburbia," in *Recasting America*, pp. 171–191; Lewis Mumford, *The City in History* (New York: Harcourt, Brace, 1961), p. 486. Jackson Lears, "A Matter of Taste," in *Recasting America*, p. 47. For accounts of the development of the suburban housing boom, see Clifford E. Clark, Jr., *The American Family Home* (Chapel Hill: University of North Carolina Press, 1986), esp. chaps. 7, 8; Paul A. Carter, *Another Part of the Fifties* (New York: Columbia University Press, 1983); Joseph B. Mason, *History of Housing in the U.S. 1930–1980* (Houston: Gulf, 1982), pp. 46–61; Harry Henderson, "The Mass-Produced Suburbs. How People Live in America's Newest Towns," *Harper's*, 30 (November 1953): p. 26; Herbert Gans, *The Levittowners* (New York: Pantheon, 1967), pp. 16–17; David Halberstam, *The Fifties* (New York: Fawcett Columbine, 1993), pp. 134–37, 139–42, 146. Among postwar social critics concerned with the vacuity of American culture are David Riesman, *The Lonely Crowd: A Study of the Changing American Character* (New Haven: Yale University Press, 1953); C. Wright Mills, *The Power Elite* (New York: Oxford University Press, 1956); Dwight Macdonald, *Against the American Grain* (New York: Random

House, 1952); William Whyte, *The Organization Man* (New York: Simon & Schuster, 1956).

34. David Langdon, cartoon, April 12, 1952, p. 25.

35. Ehrenreich, *Hearts*, pp. 29–30, 40; Phillip Wylie, "The Abdicating Male," *Playboy*, November 1956, p. 29; Robert Lindner, "Must You Conform?" (New York: Rinehart, 1955); George B. Leonard, Jr., "The American Male: Why Is He Afraid to Be Different?" *Look*, February 18, 1958, p. 95; J. Robert Moskin, "The American Male: Why Do Women Dominate Him?" *Look*, February 4, 1958, p. 77. Also see Richard Yates's 1961 novel, *Revolutionary Road* (Westport, Conn.: Greenwood Press, 1961), which is considered by many critics to be the *War and Peace* of postwar suburban domestic angst.

36. Ehrenreich, *Hearts*, pp. 32–35; Riesman, *Lonely Crowd*; Whyte, *Organization Man*.

37. Ehrenreich, *Hearts*, pp. 32–35.

38. Yates, *Revolutionary Road*, pp. 59–60; Ehrenreich, *Hearts*, p. 40.

39. Nathaniel Benchley, "The Castaways," *TNY*, April 14, 1951, pp. 30, 35–37. After the war increasing numbers of *TNY* staffers and contributors left New York City, many settling in western Connecticut and Bronxville, New York.

40. Peter De Vries, "Household Words," *TNY*, May 20, 1950, pp. 84–87. See also Peter De Vries, "Where There's Fire," *TNY*, August 19, 1950, p. 23; Robert Hutchinson, "Suburban Wife's Song," *TNY*, September 23, 1950, p. 32; Phyllis McGinley, "Letter from a Country Inn," *TNY*, August 3, 1946, p. 30.

41. May, *Homeward Bound*, pp. 169–174. See also Betty Friedan, *The Feminine Mystique* (New York, Dell, 1963); Kenneth Jackson, *The Crabgrass Frontier* (New York, Oxford University Press, 1985); May, "Explosive Issues," pp. 154–170; Phyllis McGinley, "Occupation: Housewife," in "Sonnets from Westchester," *TNY*, April 4, 1946, p. 34.

42. Decla Dunning, "Wait for the Dial Tone," *TNY*, May 28, 1949, pp. 56, 58.

43. Esther Evarts, "Just Depressed," *TNY*, May 7, 1949, pp. 69, 71, 74.

44. Ibid., p. 72.

45. Sam Cobean was the artist most associated with the magazine's fantasy balloon genre. Sam Cobean, cartoons, August 26, 1950, p. 24, February 5, 1949, p. 24, and September 30, 1950, p. 21; Anatol Kovarsky, cartoon, November 11, 1948, p. 55; Frank Modell, cartoon, May 15, 1948, p. 115. Also see Sam Cobean, cartoons, January 21, 1950, p. 27, April 23, 1949, pp. 32–33, November 2, 1946, pp. 30–31, March 18, 1950, p. 38, February 24, 1951, p. 36, and July 8, 1950, p. 23.

46. Updike, Introduction, *The Complete Book of Covers*, pp. vi–vii; Constantin Alajalov, cover painting, February 9, 1952; Perry Barlow, cover painting, January 26, 1952; Garrett Price, cover painting, June 21, 1952; Leonard Dove, cover painting, May 24, 1952; Mary Petty, cover painting, May 3, 1952; Leonard Dove, cover painting, March 22, 1952. The number of women (excluding little

girls) on the magazine's covers declined precipitously after the war. In 1939, for example, 37 of 51 covers included women. In 1941 only twenty-five women were included on covers, and many of them were part of large groups of people. In 1951 there were 20. In 1952 there were only 13.

47. Kunkel, *Genius*, p. 367. Circulation figures from Audit Bureau of Circulations from December 31st of each year. I have combined subscription and newsstand sales. At the beginning of the war, the magazine's circulation was about 150,000. The great leap in *TNY* circulation occurred between 1945 and 1947 and then leveled out. It began to climb again in 1949. ABC's study of *TNY* circulation by population groups indicates that large numbers of subscribers lived in communities containing fewer than ten thousand people. The percentages of *TNY* readers by gender is from the magazine's own marketing department reports based on a random sampling of subscribers.

48. Tom Wolfe, "Lost in the Whichy Thicket: *The New Yorker*—II," *New York Herald Tribune*, April 18, 1965, pp. 20, 22, 24.

49. "TOTT: Lady Trustee," May 21, 1949, p. 24.

9 GOODS AND GOODNESS

1. Joseph Wood Krutch, "The Profession of a New Yorker," *Saturday Review of Literature*, January 30, 1954, p. 16; Ann Douglas, *Terrible Honesty: Mongrel Manhattan in the 1920s* (New York: Farrar, Straus and Giroux, 1995), p. 23. See also Robert Ripley, *Believe It or Not!* (New York: Simon & Schuster, 1929).

2. Carl Rose, cartoon, August 16, 1947, p. 37; King's Ransom ad, August 16, 1947, p. 45.

3. Douglas, *Honesty*, p. 23; See also Marion Meade, *Dorothy Parker: What Fresh Hell Is This?* (New York: Villard Books, 1988); Scott Elledge, *E. B. White: A Biography* (New York: W. W. Norton, 1985), p. 132; E. J. Kahn, Jr., *About the New Yorker and Me* (New York: Penguin Books, 1988), p. 242.

4. Brendan Gill, *Here at The New Yorker* (New York: Caroll & Graf, 1987), pp. 299, 115; See also John Cheever, *Journals* (New York: Knopf, 1991); Susan Cheever, *Home before Dark: A Biographical Memoir of John Cheever* (Boston: Houghton Mifflin, 1984); Thomas Kunkel, *Genius in Disguise* (New York: Random House, 1985).

5. John Cheever, "Sutton Place Story," *TNY*, June 29, 1946, p. 19. See also "TOTT: Realist," January 19, 1948, p. 19.

6. "Character of Readers," published by *The New Yorker* , 1949, 1954, 1956; "Unsigned review of 'The Lost Weekend' in "Goings on about Town," *TNY*, November 6, 1948, p. 18.

7. Barbara Ehrenreich, *The Hearts of Men: American Dreams and the Flight from Commitment* (New York: Anchor Books, 1983), pp. 31, 36–37.

8. Garrett Price, cartoon, August 2, 1947, p. 29; Saul Steinberg, cartoon, June 1,

1946, p. 36; Sam Cobean, cartoon, November 22, 1947, pp. 38–39; Peter Arno, cartoon, April 22, 1950, p. 37.

9. Raymond Sokolov, *Wayward Reporter: The Life of A. J. Liebling* (New York: Harper & Row, 1980), pp. 16, 41, 142. Between 1930 and 1945 the magazine published 18 pieces concerning wrestlers, boxers, saloon keepers, chorus girls, etc. Between 1945 and 1971, only four pieces in this genre appeared.

10. Thomas B. Gilmore points out that many of the most incisive literary studies of alcoholism appeared just before or around the time of repeal, including Dorothy Parker's "Big Blonde" (1929), in *The Complete Stories of Dorothy Parker* (New York: Penguin, 1995); F. Scott Fitzgerald's "Babylon Revisited" (1931), in *The Portable F. Scott Fitzgerald* (New York: The Viking Press, 1945); Eugene O'Neill's *The Iceman Cometh* (New York: Random House: 1939). Thomas B. Gilmore, *Equivocal Spirits: Alcoholism and Drinking in Twentieth-Century Literature* (Chapel Hill: University of North Carolina Press, 1987) pp. 16–17. See also Tom Dardis, *The Thirsty Muse: Alcohol and the American Writer* (New York: Ticknor & Fields, 1989).

11. Jackson Lears, "A Matter of Taste," in *Recasting America: Culture and Politics in the Age of Cold War,* ed. by Lary May (Chicago, University of Chicago Press, 1989), pp. 39–40.

12. Barbara Ehrenreich, *Fear of Falling* (New York: HarperCollins, 1990), pp. 75–77, 84–85.

13. James Thurber, "Six for the Road," *TNY,* December 18, 1948, pp. 25–26. The story faces a full-page cartoon of a small boy approaching a drunken Santa who is lying in a doorway swigging from a pint bottle. The child, unaware of Santa's impaired state, is saying: "and roller skates, and a magic set, and a train with real smoke, and a . . ." Whitney Darrow, cartoon, December 18, 1948, p. 24.

14. Thurber, "Six," pp. 25–26; Benchley, "Deck the Halls," pp. 17–24.

15. Gill, *Here,* p. 309; John McNulty, "Bartender Here Takes Deep Dislike to 'Deep in the Heart of Texas,'" *TNY,* May 2, 1942, p. 15; "A Man like Grady, You Got to Know Him First," *TNY,* September 26, 1942, p. 20.

16. John McNulty, "This Lady Was a Bostonian They Call Them," *TNY,* March 28, 1942, p. 19.

17. John McNulty, "Third Avenue Medicine," *TNY,* Dec. 13, 1947, pp. 30–31; "People Don't Seem to Think Things Out Straight in This Gin Mill," Feb. 26, 1944, p. 20; "Bartender Here," p. 15; "Man Here Keeps Getting Arrested All the Time," June 22, 1942, p. 15.

18. John McNulty, "Eleven Dollars a Day," *TNY,* February 3, 1951, p. 34; "Slightly Crocked," *TNY,* September 7, 1946, p. 27.

19. John O'Hara, "Everything's Satisfactory," *TNY,* March 23, 1946, pp. 25–26.

20. John O'Hara, "Drawing Room B," *TNY,* April 19, 1946, pp. 25–28.

21. John O'Hara, "The Dry Murders," *TNY,* October 18, 1947, pp. 33–34

22. [E. B. White], "Notes and Comment," November 16, 1946, p. 23. The affinity of

New Yorker readers for elite goods and the enormous buying power of the magazine's subscribers is well substantiated. A 1948 *New Yorker* promotional kit for advertisers bears the headline: "*The New Yorker*, The National Magazine that moves goods." For an analysis of the economic status of the magazine's readers, see "Character of Readers," *New Yorker* Magazine, Inc., 1949. For a detailed description of the success of a specific ad campaign in this period, see Stephen Fox, *The Mirror Makers: A History of American Advertising and Its Creators* (New York: Morrow, 1984), pp. 230–232. Here Fox discusses "The Man in the Hathaway Shirt" campaign, which ran exclusively in *The New Yorker* between 1951 and 1955.

23. Thomas Kunkel, *Genius in Disguise* (New York: Random House, 1995), pp. 134–135, 198.

24. Kunkel, *Genius*, p. 198.

25. In her business history of *The New Yorker*, Gigi Mahon explains that many contributors had no idea what the business side ("State" to editorial's "Church") actually did. One writer she interviewed explained that many people in editorial "thought that the business guys just pasted labels on the magazine and sent it out." Gigi Mahon, *The Last Days of The New Yorker* (New York: McGraw Hill, 1988), p. 40; Kunkel, *Genius*, pp. 212–214.

26. Roland Marchand, *Advertising the American Dream* (Berkeley: University of California Press, 1985), xvii–xviii; Michael Schudson, *Advertising, The Uneasy Persuasion: Its Dubious Impact on American Society* (New York, 1984), 214–218.

27. For statistics on *TNY* advertising lineage during this period, see *Printers' Ink* (New York: Decker Communications, 1945–1953); Association of National Advertisers, *Magazine Circulation and Rate Trends, 1940–1959* (New York, 1960).

28. '21' Brands ad, December 21, 1946, p. 37; Drambuie ad, November 13, 1948, p. 119; Tribuno ad, September 14, 1948, p. 92; Vat 69 ad, November 30, 1946, p. 135.

29. Pierre Bourdieu, *Distinction: A Social Critique of the Judgement of Taste* (Cambridge: Harvard University Press, 1984), pp. 71–72; James T. Patterson, *Grand Expectations* (New York: Oxford University Press, 1996), p. 70.

30. Benedictine ad, May 15, 1948, p. 101; Cheery Heering ad, November 2, 1946, p. 63; Lanson ad, November 9, 1946, p. 57; Melrose Rye Whiskey ad, November 30, 1946, p. 144; Haig and Haig ad, November 20, 1948, p. 157; Remy Martin ad, February 15, 1947, p. 75.

31. Many *New Yorker* liquor ads, for example, played upon the United Nations logo or emphasized a one-world theme in their promotions. See Johnny Walker ad, November 2, 1946, p. 84; Cinzano ad, November 2, 1946, p. 89; Vat 69 ads, November 2, 1946, p. 100, and November 30, 1946, p. 135; Haig & Haig ad, December 7, 1946, p. 116; Champagne Dry Monopole ad, December 14, 1946, p. 147.

32. [E. B. White], "Notes and Comment," March 22, 1947, p. 25. On this same point, see Schudson, *Advertising*, p. 224.

33. An examination of *TNY* advertising lineage figures for March of 1947 (the month in which White's satiric "Notes and Comment" appeared) reveals that the magazine had already sold 148,217 lines, a figure surpassed only by *The Saturday Evening Post, Life, Time,* and *Business Week.* See "National Weeklies Advertising Lineage for March, 1947," *Printer's Ink,* April 11, 1947, p. 142.

34. [E. B. White], "Notes and Comment," July 15, 1947, p. 15.

35. Ibid., January 19, 1946, p. 13.

36. Northrop Frye, *The Educated Imagination* (Indianapolis: University of Indiana Press, 1964), pp. 138–39; *The Modern Century* (Toronto: Oxford University Press, 1967), pp. 26–27. See also Schudson, *Advertising,* passim.

37. Charles Addams, cartoon, September 7, 1946, p. 23.

38. Richard Taylor, cartoon, April 12, 1947, pp. 26–27; See also Saul Steinberg, cartoon, September 20, 1947, p. 21.

39. Sam Cobean, cartoon, July 17, 1948, p. 19.

40. Ehrenreich, *Fear,* pp. 75–77, 84–85.

41. Ibid., pp. 14–15. Ehrenreich explains that these "class clues . . . help guarantee that a lawyer, for example, does not unwittingly fall into the company of some lower status person, such as an off-duty plumber or postal worker"; Louis Menand, "A Friend Writes," *The New Republic,* February 26, 1990, p. 33; Bourdieu, *Distinction,* pp. 77, 91, 31.

COnCLUSIOn

1. Richard Pells, *The Liberal Mind in a Conservative Age: American Intellectuals in the 1940s and 1950s* (Middletown, Conn.: Wesleyan University Press, 1989), pp. 186–189; Cushing Strout, "Individuals Well Organized," in *The Development of an American Culture,* ed. by Stanley Coben and Lorman Ratner (New York: Prentice Hall, 1968), p. 219; C. Wright Mills, *The Power Elite* (New York: Oxford University Press, 1956); Dwight Macdonald, *Against the American Grain* (New York: Random House, 1956); William Whyte, *The Organization Man* (New York: Simon & Schuster, 1957); David Riesman, *The Lonely Crowd* (New Haven: Yale University Press, 1950).

2. Jackson Lears, "A Matter of Taste," in *Recasting America,* ed. by Lary May (Chicago: University of Chicago Press, 1989), p. 45.

3. F-R Publishing Corporation, "The New Yorker: Editorial Policy and Purpose" (New York, 1946), p.3; "Character of Readers," published by *The New Yorker* Magazine, 1949, 1954, 1956.

4. [E. B. White], "Notes and Comment," November 16, 1946, p. 23.

5. Promotional pamphlet, "It's not the size, it's the ferocity," *New Yorker* Publishing, 1948, p. 7.

6. Irving Howe, "The Treason of the Critics," *The New Republic,* June 12, 1989, p. 29; Christopher P. Wilson, "The Rhetoric of Consumption: Mass Market

Magazines and the Demise of the Gentle Reader, 1880–1920," in *The Culture of Consumption*, ed. by Richard Wrightman Fox and T. J. Jackson Lears (New York: Pantheon Books, 1983), p. 43.

7. Louise Owen, "Maximum of Bricks, Minimum of Straw," *TNY*, March 11, 1950, p. 28.

8. Eugene Kinkead, "Reporter at Large: The Study of Something New in History," October 26, 1957, pp. 114–130; pagination from Eugene Kinkead, *In Every War But One* (New York: W. W. Norton, 1959), pp. 17, 15, 10, 18, 150, 11–12.

9. Students for a Democratic Society, "The Port Huron Statement," 1960, reprinted in *Takin' It to the Streets: A Sixties Reader*, ed. by Alexander Bloom and Wini Breines (New York: Oxford University Press, 1995), pp. 61–74.

10. Godfrey Hodgson, *America in Our Time* (New York: Vintage Books, 1978) pp. 320–321.

ACKNOWLEDGMENTS

During the eight years I spent researching, writing, and revising this book, I often lapsed into daydreams about all the splendid things I would say to acknowledge the people who sustained me during this process. But now that the moment is upon me, I find that I am not quite equal to the task. These thank-yous seem like a small recompense for so much generous support.

I am deeply grateful to the Department of History at UCLA, which is where this project was born and where it found its first friends. My mentor and friend, Joyce Appleby, saved me from myself time after time. She often understood this project better than I did and found gentle ways to suggest that I remain curious about the past rather than judge it in the harsh light of present-mindedness. Bruce Schulman's constant encouragement, intellectual generosity, and unflagging friendship have bolstered me all along the way. The book would not have seen the light of day without his efforts. Mary Yeager has provided me with a rare combination of keen intellectual guidance and loving personal support. While she consistently offered honest and incisive criticism of my work, she also once baked me a birthday cake from scratch. Martha Banta's meticulous reading of my work and her canny understanding of the relationship between a text and its historical context have played an impor-

243

tant role in the progress of this project. The central idea for this book came to me in Paul Boyer's seminar about the cultural impact of the atom bomb. I thank him for his encouragement. Alex Saxton offered support and sustenance to me when this project was in its earliest, most daunting stages. He taught me by example that conscience and compassion are essential to the practice of history. Herman Ooms helped me to understand the richness of the world that lurked beneath the surface of the text. His counsel has proved invaluable. Richard Weiss has been both good friend and adviser as I headed into the later, lonelier stages of revision. I am in his debt. A special thanks to Patricia Moore for her comradeship and her intellectual and technical support. I also want to express my gratitude to Barbara Bernstein, Gary Nash, Ken Sokoloff, and Trudy Saxton.

Babette Lazurus, of *The New Yorker*'s Marketing Division, helped me with circulation and marketing survey information that has been invaluable. The staff of the Rare Books and Manuscripts Division of the New York Public Library, where the Records of *The New Yorker* Magazine Collection are housed, was infinitely courteous and helpful.

At Harvard University Press my editor, Joyce Seltzer, offered honest and sage guidance at each stage of the process of rewriting and editing. I learned quickly to trust her unvarnished and unerring editorial good sense. I will always be indebted to Cherie Weitzner Acierno, both for her initial enthusiasm about this project and her perceptive editorial and organizational suggestions. And finally, I want to express my gratitude to Anita Safran, an editor with a remarkable gift for transforming murkiness into clarity.

Many friends have provided emotional support and encouragement during the years I devoted to this project. Often they contributed the most to my work by helping me to put it aside—to go to a ball game, or watch a movie, or raft down a river. My thanks to Jennifer Schmidt, Harvey Marks, Danny Franceschi, the Bill Hills, John Lithgow, Renee Shafransky, Lynn Deegan, Barbara Wilson, Brook Tuthill, Randa Haines, Jim and Keven Bellows, Trixie Merkin, Terry Bisson, Judy Jensen, Wendy Keyes, the late Charlie Millhaupt, Malou Flato, John Taliaferro, Larry Laszlo,

Guy Martin, Sarah Crichton, Judy Crichton, Giles Kotcher, Gere Kava-naugh, Bill and Robin Lappen, Roberta Price, John Boyd, Vicki Laszlo, the late Ruth Conte, Anne Makepeace, Sandy Mendelson, Leila Acenas, Patricia Travis, Robert Walsh, Guy Paul, Natalie Moody, the late Howard Gilman, Sherri Sonnett, Ann Buck, Tom Clark, Alice Kilian, Phil Swirbul, Dexter Gordon, Rex Arrasmith, Alan Warnick, Al Hall, and the women of Via De La Paz.

Finally there is the inner circle—the people who make up my family. I thank Thor Evensen for letting me be his *belle-mère*. My life-long friend, David Ansen, has been my rock through this sometimes difficult proc-ess. He is the one who remains. Most of all I owe an enormous debt of love and gratitude to my light, my daughter, Molly, who grew up with this project and is now a woman who finds it interesting. And last, I lovingly acknowledge my parents, who did not live to see this book completed, and who were charter members of the culture it seeks to illuminate.

INDEX

Acheson, Dean, 68
Addams, Charles, 86, 109, 169, 201–202
Advertising, 4, 193–203, 208–209
African Americans, 77–100; and domestic service, 128, 137–146, 147–148; and humor, 126; and Indians, 109, 110; and poverty, 227n9. *See also* Race
Alain, Daniel, 169–170
Alcohol, alcoholism, 181–193, 195, 198–203
American exceptionalism, 26, 63, 68, 228n22
Angell, Roger: "Some Pigs in Sailor Suits," 29
Anti-Communism, 41–42, 44–45, 46, 53, 54, 58, 62–66, 72. *See also* Communism; Soviet Union
Arno, Peter, 154–155, 186, 233n8
Atomic age. *See* Nuclear age
Audience. *See* Readership

Benchley, Nathaniel: "The Castaways," 174; "Deck the Halls," 185, 188
Bikini Atoll, 28–30, 106–107
Bliven, Bruce, 20
Bok, Edward, 4
Boyer, Richard O.: "Bop," 91

Cartoons: and alcohol, 183, 186; and ethnicity, 106–107; and gender wars, 168–171, 177–178; and House Un-American Activities Committee, 221n11; and "Men of Distinction" promotion, 201–203; and race, 83, 84–86; and women, 152–155, 164–165, 166–167. *See also* Humor
Caughnawaga people, 111–112, 113
Chambers, Jay, 50
Cheever, John: "Sutton Place Story," 184
Child, children, 184
Class, 124–148; and alcohol, 189, 193, 203; and feminism, 160; and readership, 13; and women, 163
Clurman, Robert: "Mr. Mookerjhee," 119–121
Cobean, Sam, 178, 202
Coming-of-age story, 134–137, 148
Communism, 150, 152, 161, 165. *See also* Anti-Communism; Soviet Union
Consumerism, 4, 182–183, 194–196, 198–199, 202, 203–204. *See also* Materialism
Crawford, Cheryl, 159
Culture, 13, 14

Day, Dorothy, 158
Day, Robert, 155
Democracy, 58–59
Dengel, Veronica, 160–161
DeVoto, Bernard, 44–45
De Vries, Peter: "Household Words," 174–175; "Pygmalion," 129–130; "They Also Sit," 131–132, 144
Dunning, Decla: "Wait for the Dial Tone," 175–176

Education, 151
Egalitarianism, 125, 129
Ehrenreich, Barbara, 172–173
Ethnicity, 101–123; and "other," 136, 148. *See also* Race
Evart, Esther: "Just Depressed," 176–177

Family: and gender roles, 150–151, 152, 157, 158; Mrs. Dengel on, 161; and postwar anxiety, 8–9; and race, 138; and suburbs, 172. *See also* Marriage; Men; Women
F.B.I., 44, 47
Feminism, 156–157, 160, 164. *See also* Women
Flanner, Janet, 65–66, 159
Frye, Northrop, 201
Fuchs, Karl, 62

Gibbs, Angela: "One Sweet Little Business," 160–161
Gillespie, Dizzy, 91
Gold digger, 154–155
Goods. *See* Consumerism; Materialism
Grant, Jane, 156

Hamburger, Philip, 69, 70, 157
Harper's, 44
Hellman, Geoffrey T.: "Reporter at Large," 31
Hersey, John: "Hiroshima," 36
Hiss, Alger, 46–47, 62
Hokinson, Helen, 152–154, 155, 170
Hollywood, 54–56
Home, 8, 164, 165, 171–172

Hoover, J. Edgar, 44
House Un-American Activities Committee: and DeVoto, 44, 47–48, 49–50; hostility toward, 40–41, 43; mockery of, 54, 221n11; and politics, 42; and style, 53; and White, 44, 55–57. *See also* Anti-Communism; Communism; Politics
Hubbell, Albert, 50–51
Humor, 78–79, 84–87, 126, 130–131, 152–155, 164–165. *See also* Cartoons

Identity, 5, 14
Indians, 103–106, 107–108, 229nn1,5,6

Jackson, Charles: "The Lost Weekend," 187
Johnson, Jack, 87–88, 89

Kahn, E. J., Jr., 184; "The Greenwich Tea Party," 51; "Letter from Korea," 225n25; "Reflections on a Subversive Past," 51; "The Years Alone," 157, 158
Kennedy, Ludovic: "Grace Arrowhead," 134–137
Kincaid, Eugene: "The Study of Something New in History," 210
Korean War, 58, 63, 64, 66–71, 74, 75, 210
Kroll, Ernst: "In a Georgetown Garden," 27
Krutch, Joseph, 181

Lang, Daniel, 31–36, 51–53; "The Atomic City," 33–34; "Blackjack and Flashes," 34–35; "A Fine Moral Point," 33
Lardner, Ring: "Battling Siki," 88–89; "The White Hopes," 87–88
Laurence, William, 27
Liberalism: and anti-Communism, 62–66, 72; and class, 125–126; and democracy, 58–59; and nuclear age, 32; and politics, 18–19; postwar, xi–xii, 75; and race, 79, 99–100; and Roosevelt, 40; and social justice, 207; and White, 59, 64
Liebling, A. J.: "One Hundred and Eighteen Pounds," 90–91; "We Adopt the Party Line," 223n6
Lincoln, Victoria: "Comfort," 114–115; "In the Reeds by the River," 115–116

Lippmann, Walter, xii
Logan, Andy, 65–66
Lord Calvert's, 198–199, 201–203
Louis, Joe, 87–88, 90

MacArthur, Douglas, 72–73, 225n25
Macdonald, Dwight, 19, 21, 86–87; "The Foolish Things of the World," 158
Magazines, 3–5, 6, 20, 151
Marriage: and Addams, 169; and postwar anxiety, 150, 151; and Shore, 163; and women, 158, 159, 165. *See also* Family; Men; Women
Marriot, Alice: "Beowulf in South Dakota," 112–113
Materialism, 102–103, 119, 120, 170–171, 175. *See also* Consumerism
Maxwell, James: "Arab Editor," 121–122
McCarthy, Mary, 37–38; "The Groves of Academe," 42–43
McCarthyism, 41–42. *See also* Anti-Communism; Communism; House Un-American Activities Committee
McConaughy, Elizabeth: "Rudi," 133–134
McGinley, Phyllis: "Operation Housewife," 175
McKelway, St. Clair: "On the Rocks," 78–79
McNulty, John, 183, 187; "Eleven Dollars a Day," 191; "Slightly Crocked," 191; "Third Avenue Medicine," 190–191; "This Lady Was a Bostonian They Call Them," 190
Men: and Arno, 154, 155; and family, 151; and Hokinson, 153; and suburbs, 172; and women, 159; and women's domination, 164, 165–167, 171, 173–175. *See also* Family; Marriage; Women
"Men of Distinction" promotion, 198–199, 201–203
Mexican-Anglo relations, 116–118
Michaels, C. H., 51
Miss America Pageant, 161–163
Mitchell, Joseph: "Mohawks in High Steel," 110–112, 113

Momism, 165, 166, 173, 233n3. *See also* Women
Morality, 30–31, 32, 34, 38–39
Mundt-Nixon Bill, 53–54
Myrdal, Gunnar, 80

Native American. *See* Indian
New Republic, The, 20
New York, 9–10
New Yorker, The: as community, 2; covers, 81–82, 237n46; "Fateful Night," 26; "Gags Away," 26; image of, 11, 21–23, 37, 38–39, 41–42, 44, 46, 82, 206–208, 209; influence of, x–xii, 3, 7, 9, 10, 14–16, 21–22; and nuclear age, 21; and race, 81; role of, 14–16; "Talking Leaves," 107; "That Was Pugilism," 87–89; and women, 156–157, 178–179; and World War II, 21–22
Noble Savage, 104, 113, 121, 229n5
North, 96–99
Nuclear age, 19–21, 22, 23–39, 62, 151

O'Hara, John, 192–193; "Drawing Room B," 192; "Ellie," 95; "Everything's Satisfactory," 191–192
Owen, Louise: "The Williamsons," 209

Parker, James Reid: "Westchester Igloo," 167–168
Patton, Frances Gray, 92–93; "The Falling Leaves," 140–146; "A Nice Name," 93–95
Pegler, Westbrook, 44
Perelman, S. J.: "Don't Bring Me Oscars (When It's Shosies I Need)," 222n26
Periodical. *See* Magazines
Politics, 18–19, 58–60, 74–75. *See also* House Un-American Activities Committee
"Port Huron Statement, The," 211
Poverty, 75, 227n9
Prejudice, 91–92. *See also* Ethnicity; Race

Race, 24, 77–100, 126, 139–140, 207, 226n3, 228nn22,24. *See also* Ethnicity

Rand, Christopher: "Letters from Korea," 74
Readership: and advertising, 196; and affluence, 210; and alcohol, 184, 185; and anti-Communism, 48; as community, 13–17; connection with, 1–2; and domestic servants, 128; growth in, 238n47; loyalty of, x; typical, 10–12; and urban population, 5–7; and women, 139, 151–152, 179
Remington, William W., 51–53, 222n18
Riesman, David, 173
Ripley, Robert, 182
Robinson, Jackie, 228n24
Roosevelt, Eleanor, 157–158, 159
Roosevelt, Franklin D., 40
Ross, Harold: and advertising, 194; and alcohol, 183; and anti-Communism, 44; character of, 2–3; and consumerism, 194; and homosexuality, 234n15; and nuclear age, 22; policy of, 22–23; and race, 81; and readership, 5–6; and White, 24; and women, 156; and World War II, 21, 22
Ross, Lillian: "Come in Lassie," 54–55; "Symbol of All We Possess," 161–163
Roueche, Berton: "A Cup of Lemon Verbena," 160
Rovere, Richard, 71–72, 73

Sachs, Alexander, 31
Salinger, J. D.: "Uncle Wiggily in Connecticut," 96
Science, 30–31, 32, 34
Segregation, 80–81
Sequoyah, 107
Servant, 124–148
Sexuality, 151, 158, 159, 234n15
Shalako, 104–106
Shapiro, Karl: "Homecoming," 27
Shawn, William, 23, 37, 44
Shore, William: "The Moon Belongs to Everyone," 163–164
Siki, 88–89
Society: and alcohol, 186–187; and humor, 86–87; universal, 83–85
South, 92–96, 126, 140

Soviet Union, 59, 60–62, 63, 64–66, 70–71, 75, 77. See also Anti-Communism; Communism
Sports, 87–91
Stafford, Jean: "Pax Vobiscum," 97–99; "A Summer's Day," 108
Status: and advertising, 195–197; and alcohol, 202, 203–204; and domestic service, 125, 130–131, 132, 133, 134, 147; and egalitarianism, 206; and goods, 182
Stereotype, 81–83, 85, 113
Stimson, Henry L.: "The Decision to Drop the Bomb," 36–37
Suburbs, 9, 172, 173–177
Sullivan, Frank: "The Cliché Expert Testifies on the Atom," 28; "These Are the Trials That Try Men's Souls," 54
Surrogacy, 138

Taylor, Peter: "Middle Age," 142–144; "What You Hear from 'Em?", 137–139; "A Wife of Nashville," 144–146
Thomas, J. Parnell, 49–50
Thurber, James, 22; "A Glass of Fashion," 51; "Six for the Road," 188–189
Tilley, Eustace, 1
Tradition, 197–198
Truman, Harry, 72, 73

United Nations: hopes for, 59; and Korean War, 66–71, 72; and United States, 67, 68, 69, 71, 72; and White, 25, 60, 66–67, 68, 69, 70, 72
United States: and affluence, 7–9, 205–206, 210–211; and culture, 102–103, 113–114, 116, 122–123; and economy, 7–8; and education, 12–13; and family, 8–9; and homes, 8; and Korean War, 210; postwar role of, 58–61; and race, 79, 80–81, 226n3, 228n22; and social inequity, 75–76, 77; and suburbs, 9; and United Nations, 67, 68, 69, 71, 72
Universalism, 25
Updike, John, 82
Urban population, 5

Wallace, Henry, 62

Washington Post, The, 20

Wechsburg, Joseph: "Howling with the Wolves," 66

West, Jessamyn, 67; "Love, Death, and the Ladies' Drill Team," 116–118

White, E. B.: and advertising, 193–194; "Afternoon of an American Boy," 49–50; and alcohol, 184, 199, 200–201; and anti-Communism, 45, 47–48, 49–50, 53, 56–57; and Hollywood, 56; and Indians, 106; and Korean War, 68, 70–71; and Lang, 34; and liberalism, 59, 64; and MacArthur, 72–73; and Mundt-Nixon Bill, 53–54; and *The New Yorker,* 207; "Noontime of an Advertising Man," 50; and nuclear age, 29, 30, 31; and politics, 59; on postwar age, 23–26; and Soviet Union, 61–62, 70–71; style, 69, 71; and United Nations, 66–67, 68, 69, 70, 72

White, Katherine Angell, 23, 156

Whites: and domestic service, 126, 128, 140, 142, 147–148; and ethnic others, 103, 113; and Indians, 104, 105–106, 107

Whyte, William F.: *The Organization Man,* 173

Wilson, Edmund, 104–106

Wolfe, Tom, 139, 179

Women: and class, 235n18; and covers, 237n46; and domestic service, 139, 140, 147–148; and men, 149–180, 233nn3,8; and work, 234n12. *See also* Family; Marriage; Men

Work, and women, 151, 156, 157, 159

World War I, 5, 6, 7

World War II: and advertising, 197–198; and affluence, 7; and family, 150; and Macdonald, 19; and magazines, 6; and morality, 19, 103; and *The New Yorker,* 21–22; and race, 79; and Ross, 21, 22; and women, 155–156

Wylie, Philip: *Generation of Vipers,* 165

Zuni, 104–10